Chapter 46 Excitement

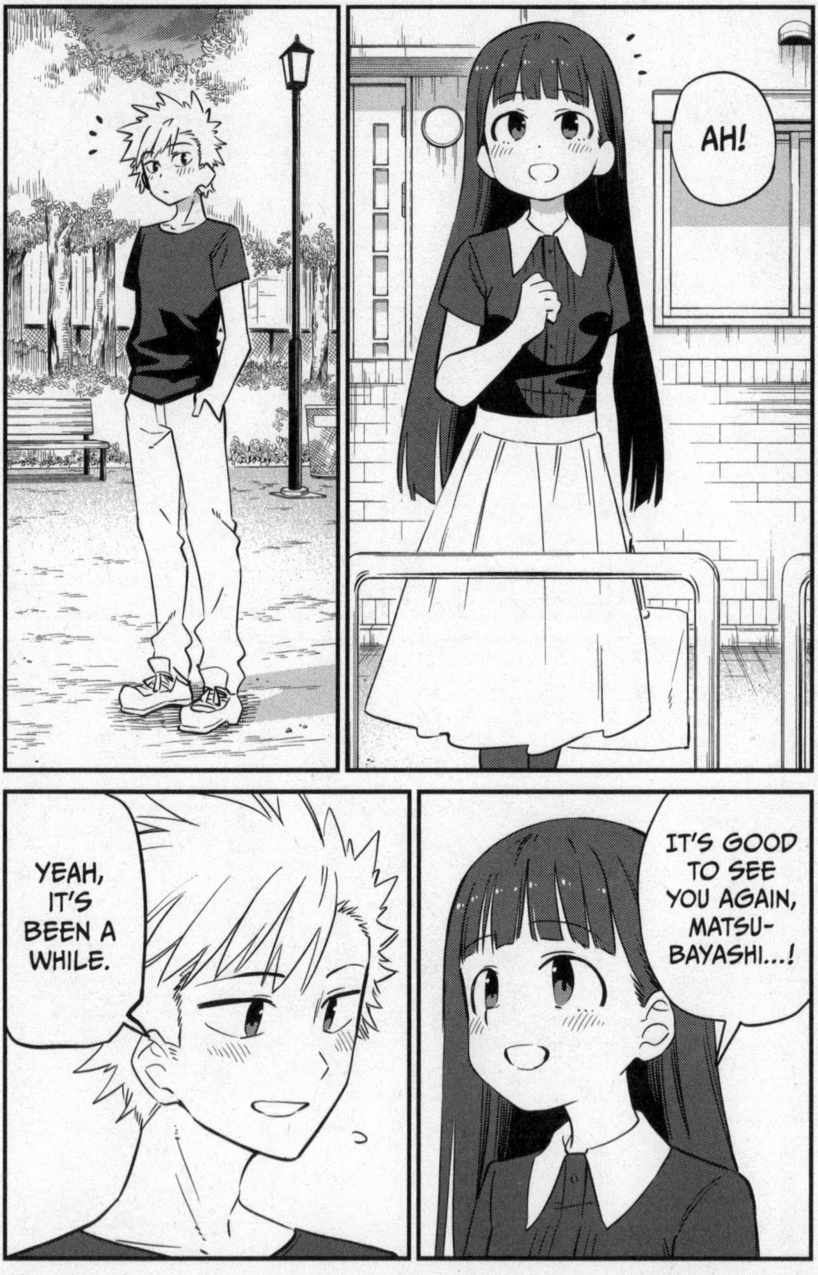
AH!
IT'S GOOD TO SEE YOU AGAIN, MATSU-BAYASHI...!
YEAH, IT'S BEEN A WHILE.

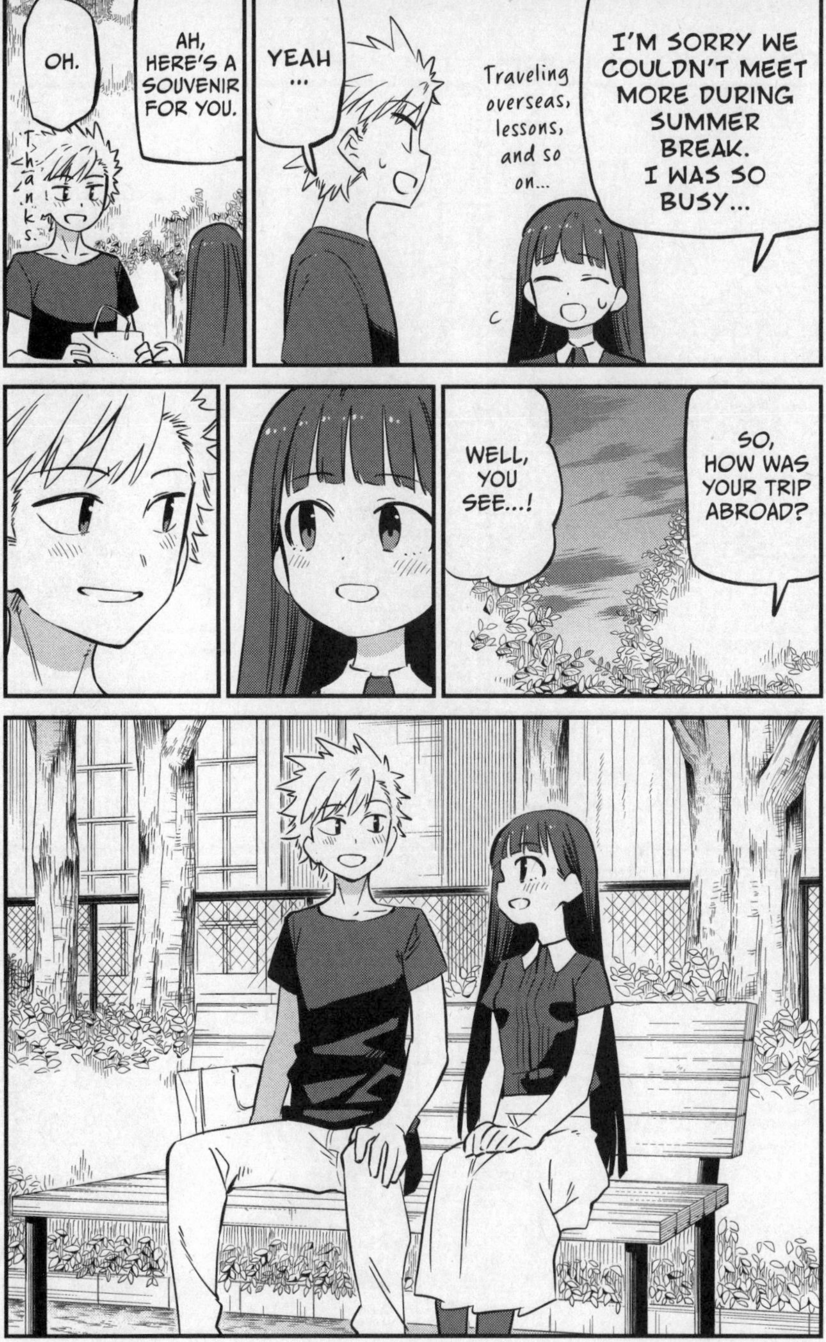

I'M SORRY WE COULDN'T MEET MORE DURING SUMMER BREAK. I WAS SO BUSY...
Traveling overseas, lessons, and so on...
YEAH ...
AH, HERE'S A SOUVENIR FOR YOU.
OH.
Thanks!
SO, HOW WAS YOUR TRIP ABROAD?
WELL, YOU SEE...!

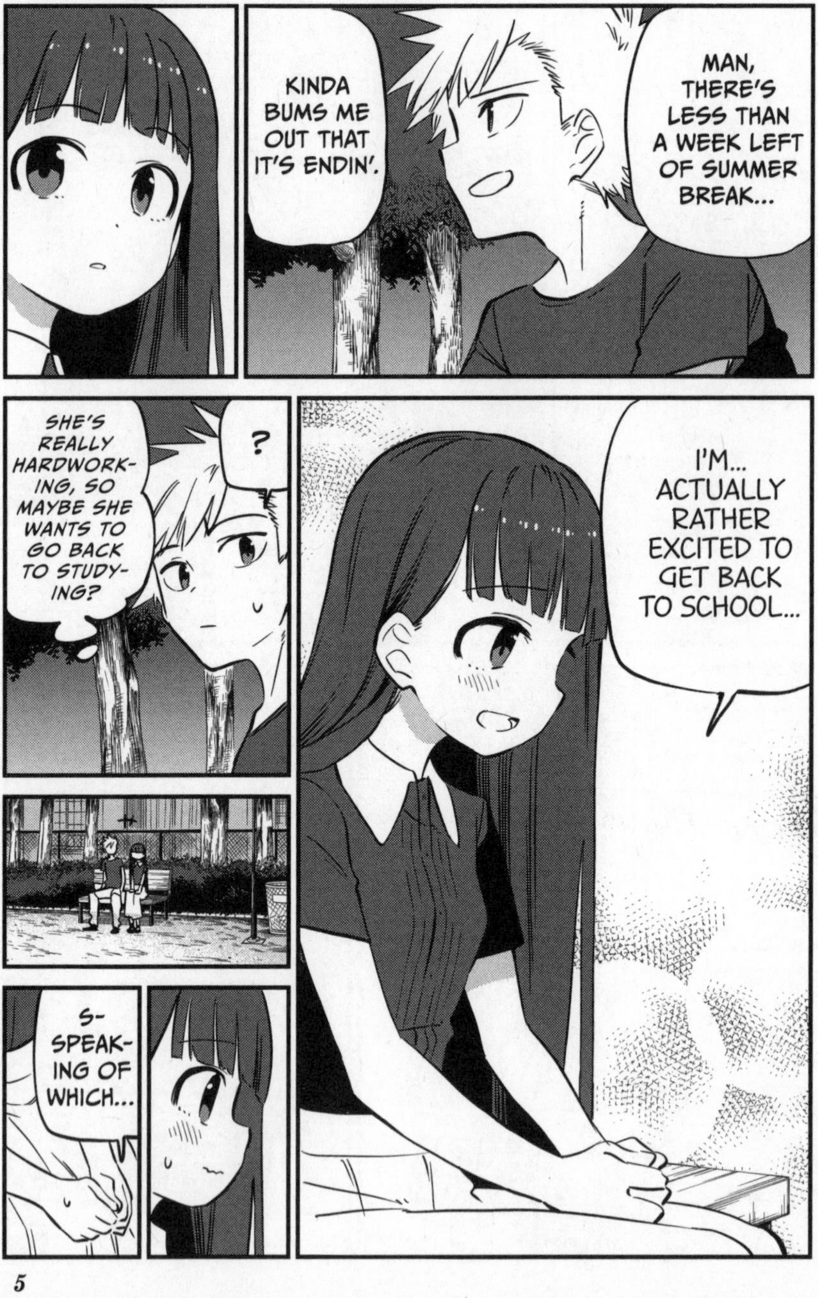
MAN, THERE'S LESS THAN A WEEK LEFT OF SUMMER BREAK...
KINDA BUMS ME OUT THAT IT'S ENDIN'.
I'M... ACTUALLY RATHER EXCITED TO GET BACK TO SCHOOL...
?
SHE'S REALLY HARDWORKING, SO MAYBE SHE WANTS TO GO BACK TO STUDYING?
S-SPEAKING OF WHICH...

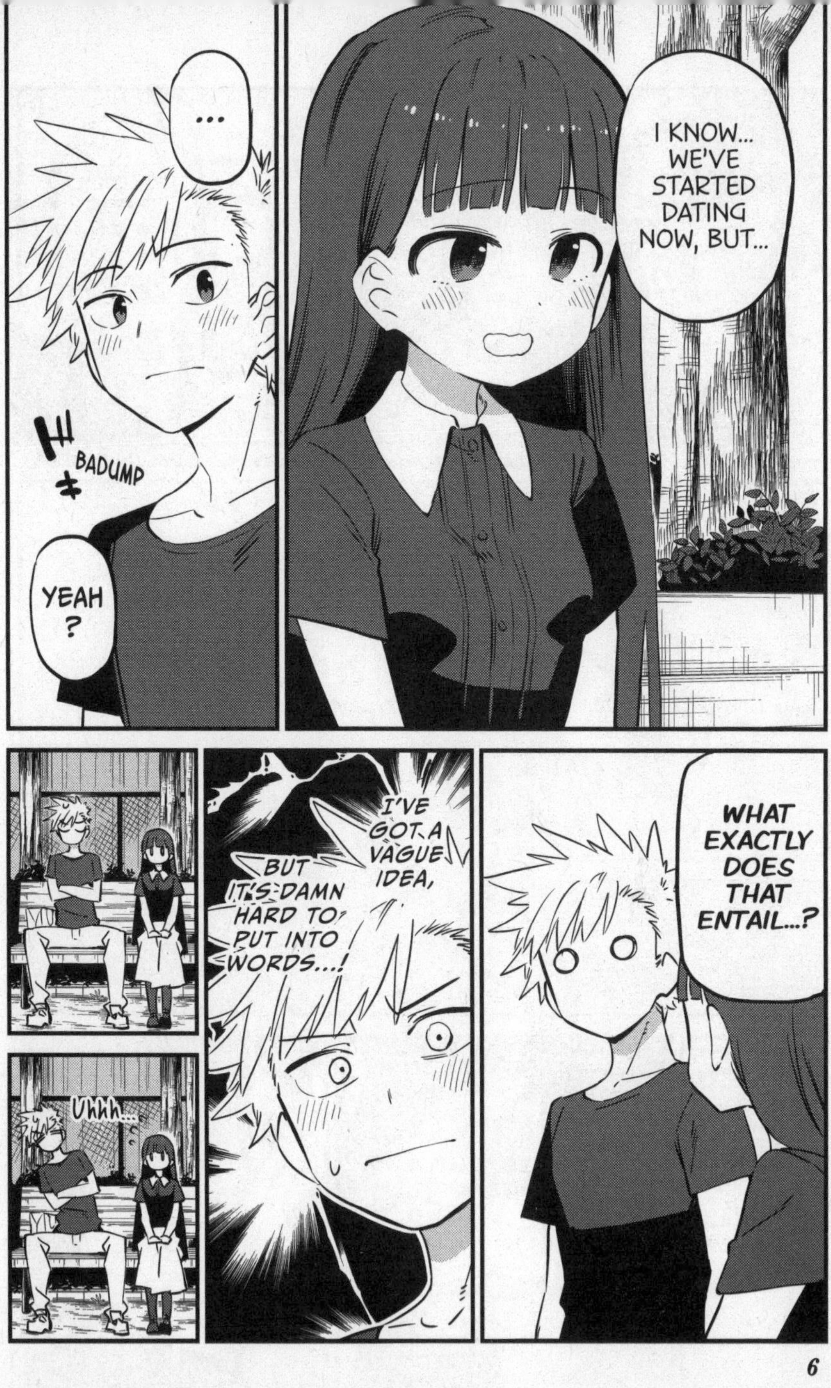
I KNOW... WE'VE STARTED DATING NOW, BUT...
...
BADUMP
YEAH?
WHAT EXACTLY DOES THAT ENTAIL...?
I'VE GOT A VAGUE IDEA,
BUT IT'S DAMN HARD TO PUT INTO WORDS...!
Uhhh...

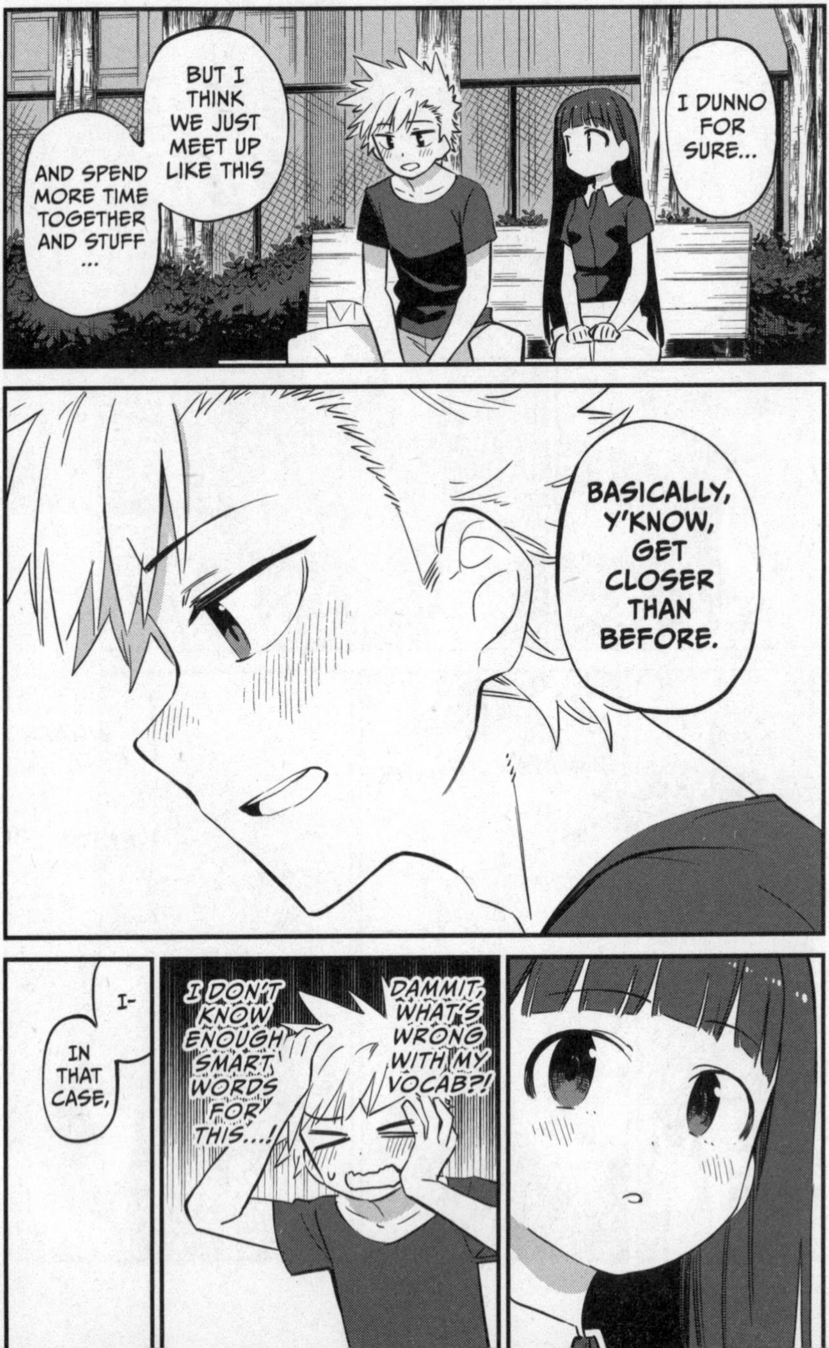
I DUNNO FOR SURE...
BUT I THINK WE JUST MEET UP LIKE THIS
AND SPEND MORE TIME TOGETHER AND STUFF ...
BASICALLY, Y'KNOW, GET CLOSER THAN BEFORE.
DAMMIT, WHAT'S WRONG WITH MY VOCAB?!
I DON'T KNOW ENOUGH SMART WORDS FOR THIS...!
I-
IN THAT CASE,

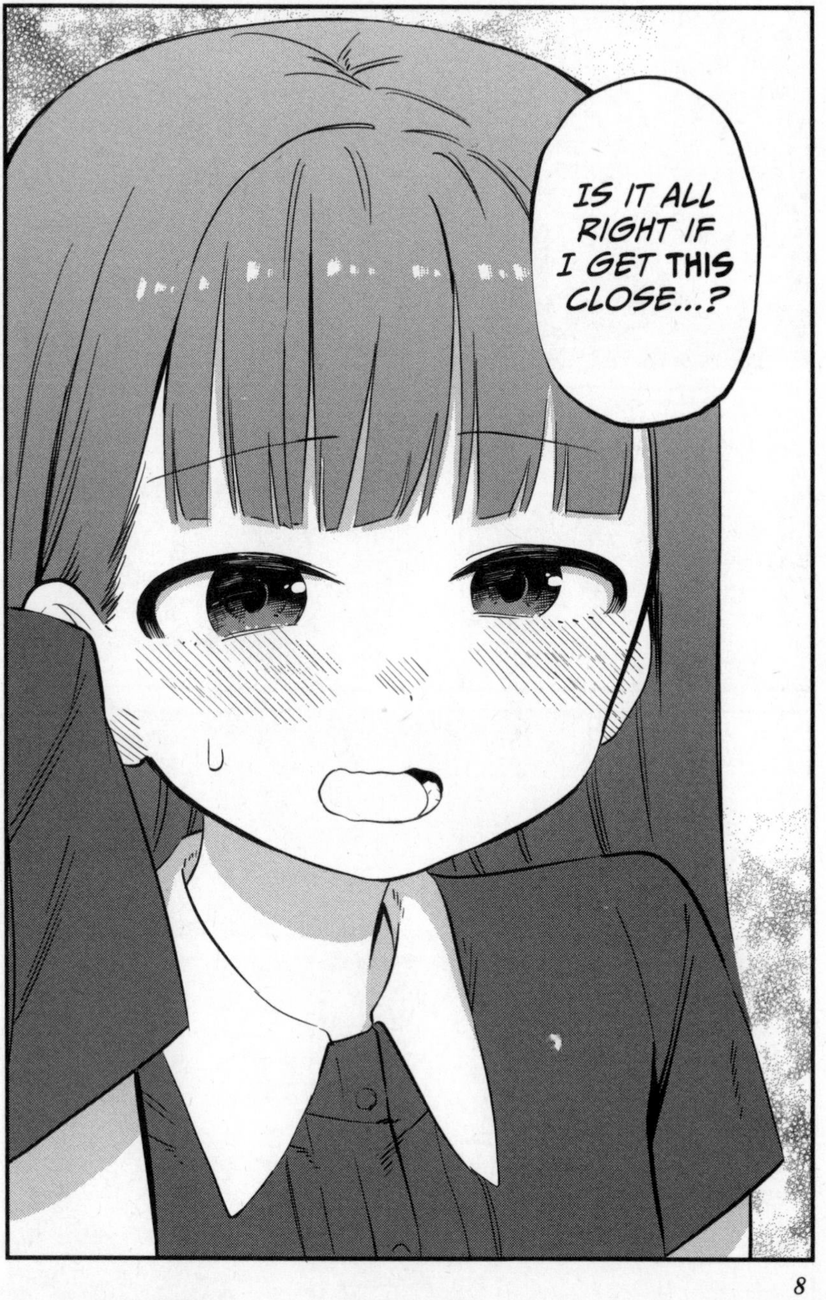
IS IT ALL RIGHT IF I GET THIS CLOSE...?

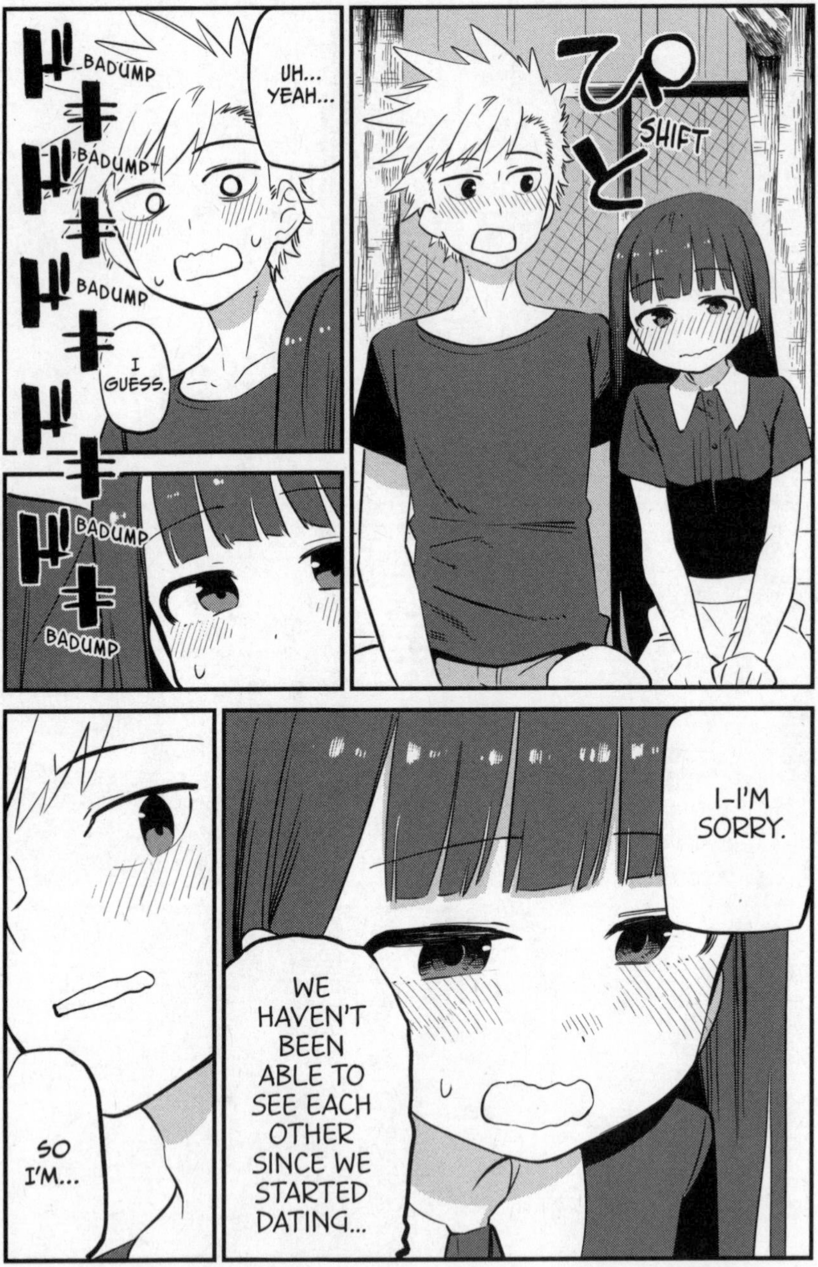
ぴと
SHIFT
UH... YEAH...
ドキ
BADUMP
ドキ
BADUMP
ドキ
BADUMP
ドキ
I GUESS.
ドキ
BADUMP
ドキ
BADUMP
I-I'M SORRY.
WE HAVEN'T BEEN ABLE TO SEE EACH OTHER SINCE WE STARTED DATING...
SO I'M...

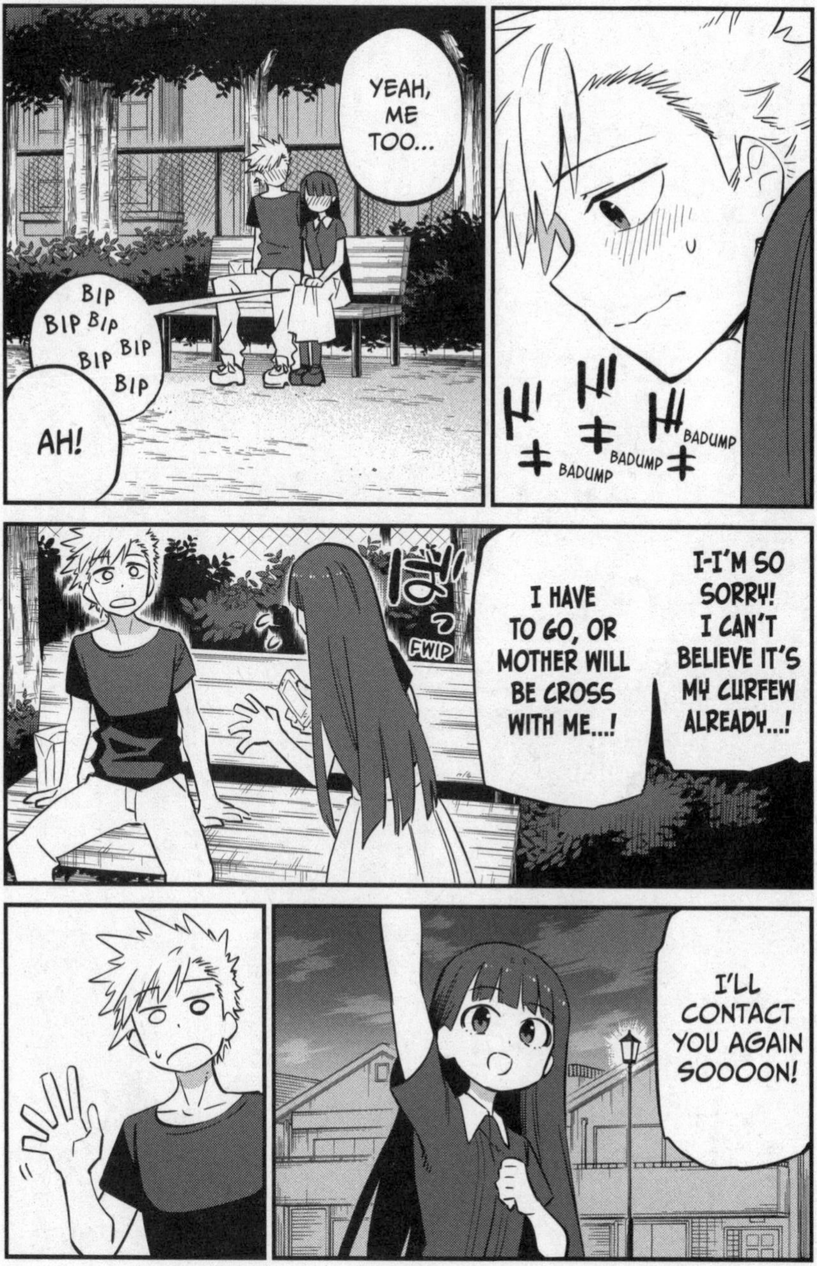
BADUMP
BADUMP
BADUMP
YEAH, ME TOO...
BIP BIP BIP BIP BIP BIP
AH!
I-I'M SO SORRY! I CAN'T BELIEVE IT'S MY CURFEW ALREADY...!
I HAVE TO GO, OR MOTHER WILL BE CROSS WITH ME...!
FWIP
I'LL CONTACT YOU AGAIN SOOOON!

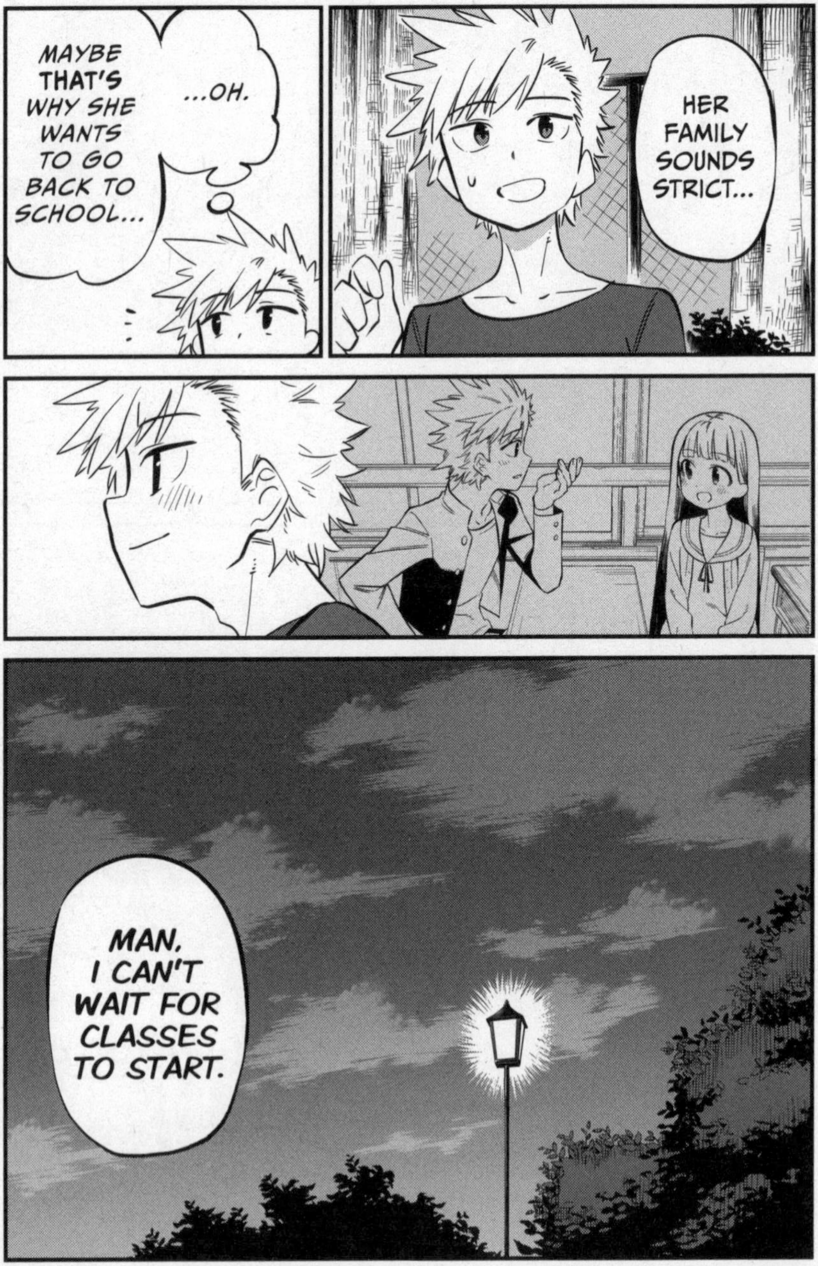
HER FAMILY SOUNDS STRICT...
...OH.
MAYBE THAT'S WHY SHE WANTS TO GO BACK TO SCHOOL...
MAN, I CAN'T WAIT FOR CLASSES TO START.

Chapter 47 Back from Break

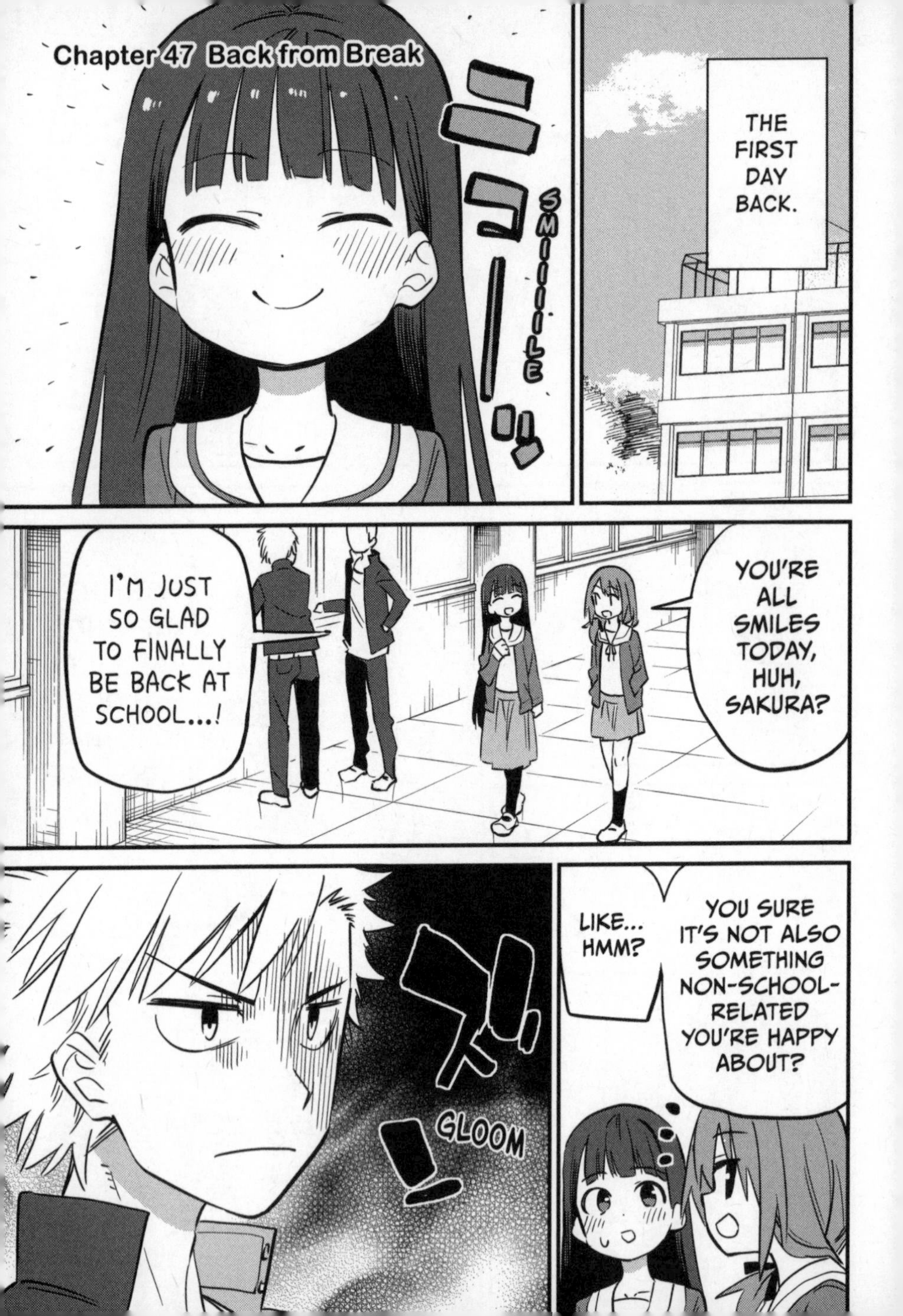
THE FIRST DAY BACK.
SMIIIIILE
YOU'RE ALL SMILES TODAY, HUH, SAKURA?
I'M JUST SO GLAD TO FINALLY BE BACK AT SCHOOL...!
YOU SURE IT'S NOT ALSO SOMETHING NON-SCHOOL-RELATED YOU'RE HAPPY ABOUT?
LIKE... HMM?
GLOOM

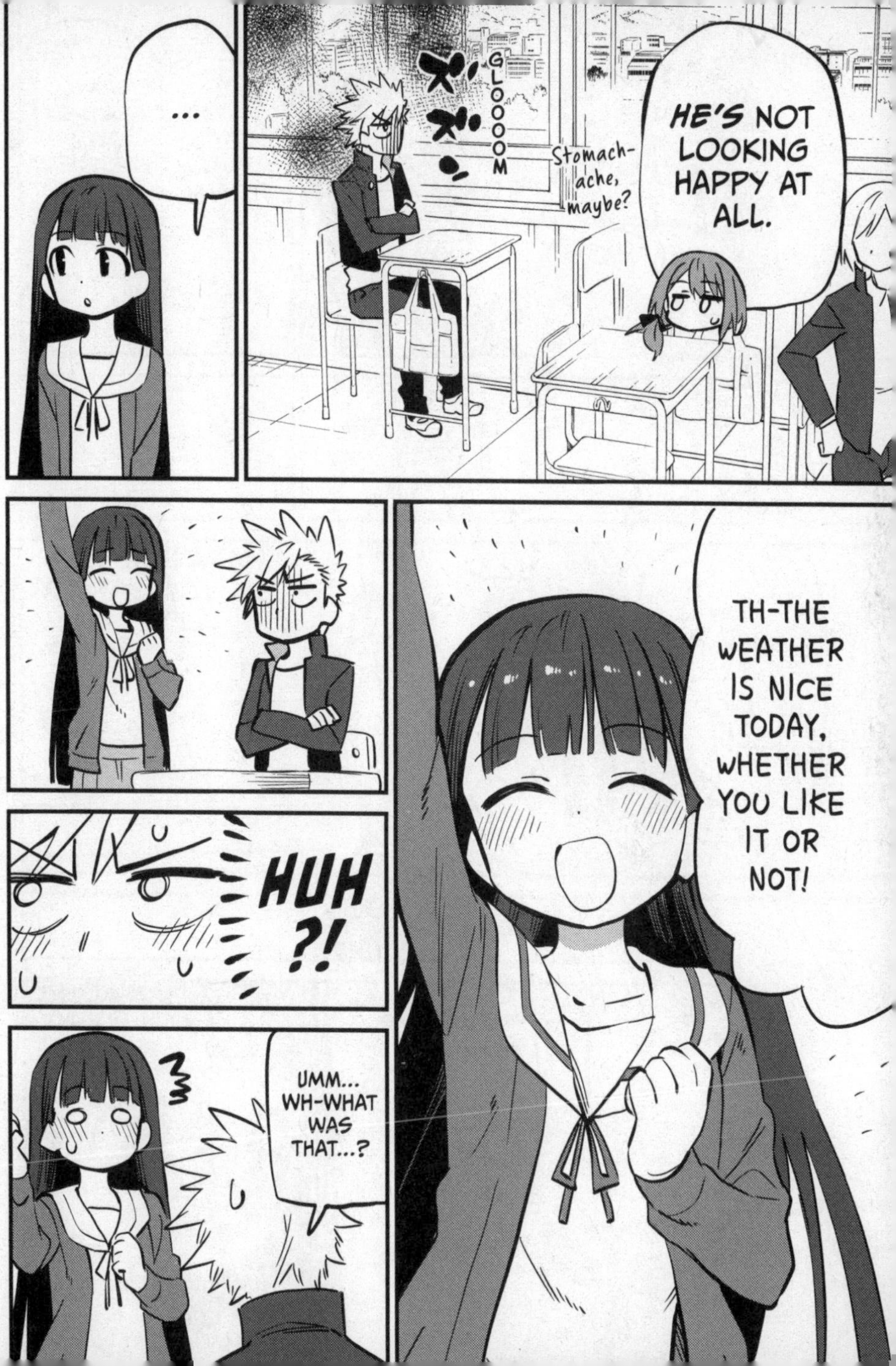
HE'S NOT LOOKING HAPPY AT ALL.
Stomach-ache, maybe?
GLOOOOOM
...
TH-THE WEATHER IS NICE TODAY, WHETHER YOU LIKE IT OR NOT!
HUH?!
UMM... WH-WHAT WAS THAT...?

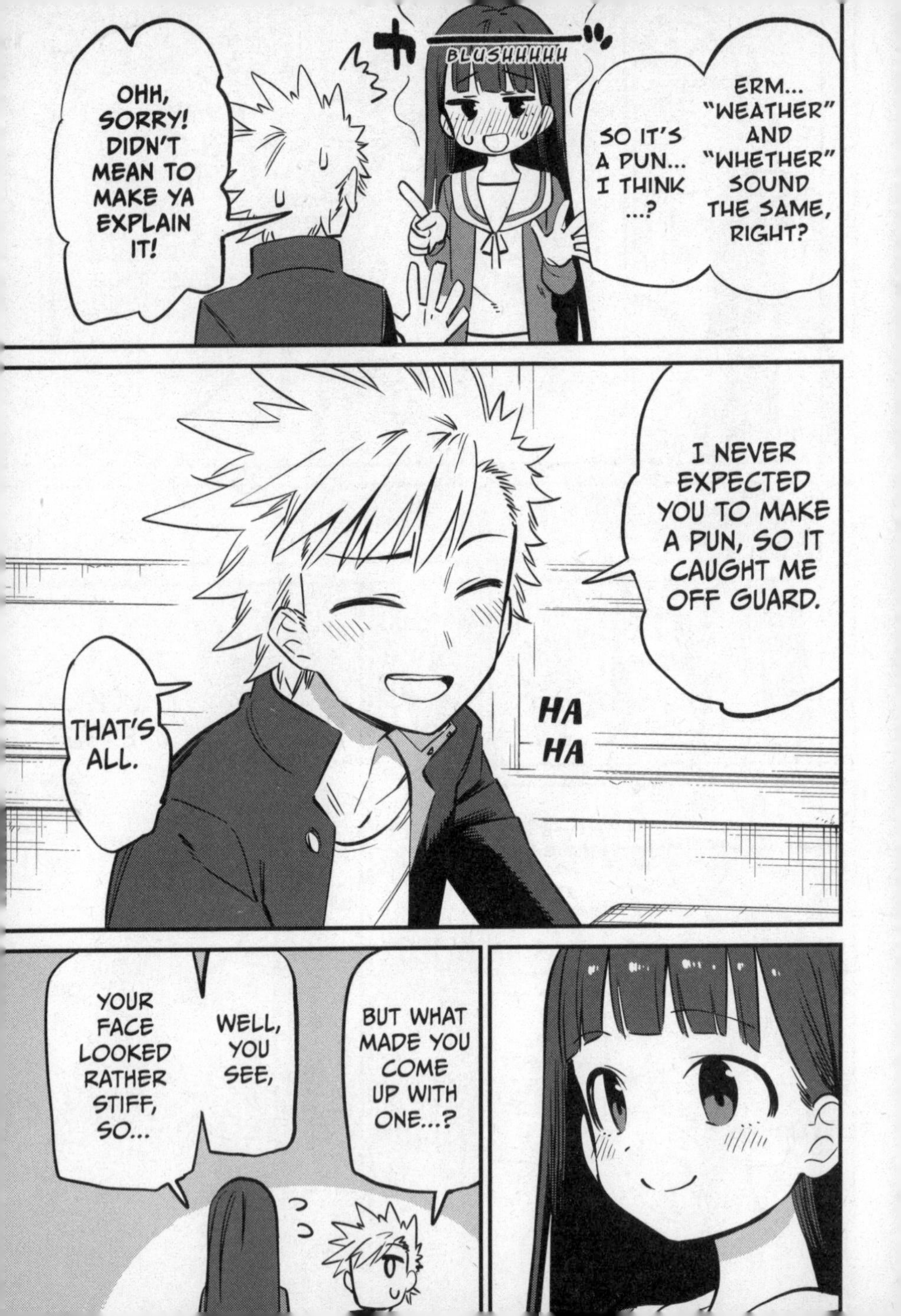
BLUSHHHHH
ERM... "WEATHER" AND "WHETHER" SOUND THE SAME, RIGHT?
SO IT'S A PUN... I THINK ...?
OHH, SORRY! DIDN'T MEAN TO MAKE YA EXPLAIN IT!
I NEVER EXPECTED YOU TO MAKE A PUN, SO IT CAUGHT ME OFF GUARD.
HA HA
THAT'S ALL.
BUT WHAT MADE YOU COME UP WITH ONE...?
WELL, YOU SEE,
YOUR FACE LOOKED RATHER STIFF, SO...

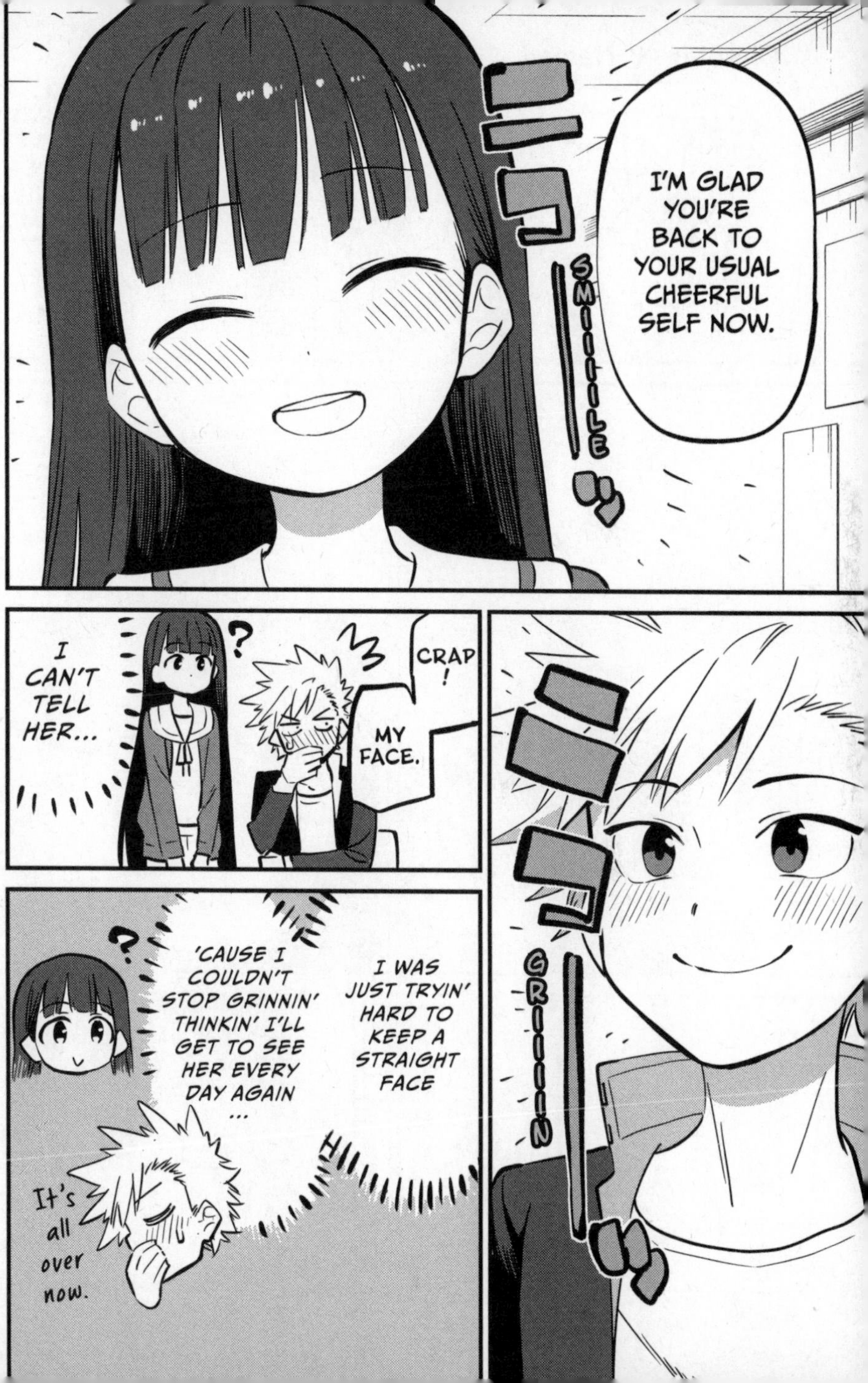
I'M GLAD YOU'RE BACK TO YOUR USUAL CHEERFUL SELF NOW.
SMIIIIILE
GRIIIIIN
CRAP! MY FACE.
I CAN'T TELL HER...
I WAS JUST TRYIN' HARD TO KEEP A STRAIGHT FACE
'CAUSE I COULDN'T STOP GRINNIN' THINKIN' I'LL GET TO SEE HER EVERY DAY AGAIN ...
It's all over now.

Chapter 48 Names

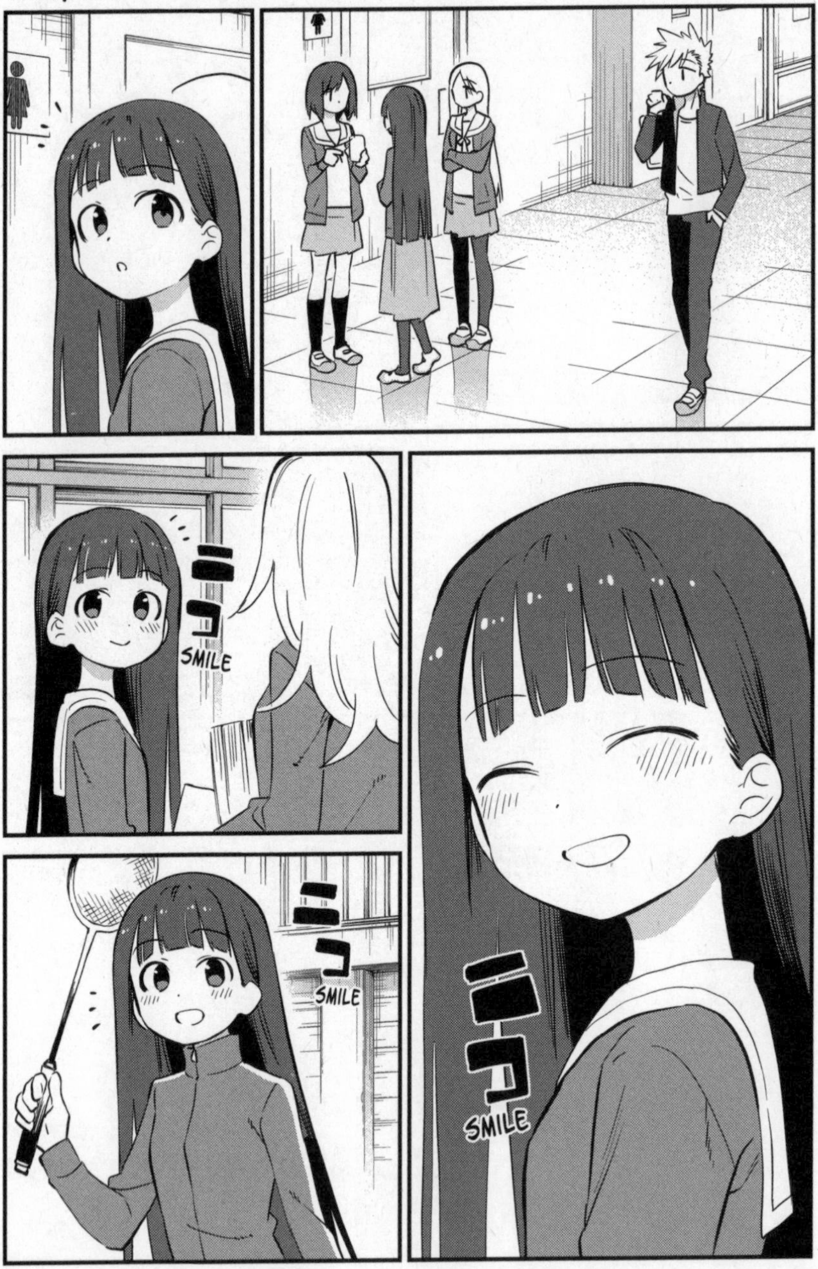
ニコ
SMILE
ニコ
SMILE
ニコ
SMILE

I'M SO DAMN HAPPY...
WE'RE KEEPING OUR RELATIONSHIP A SECRET, AND THOSE TWO ARE THE ONLY ONES WHO KNOW,
You got it~
SO WE CAN'T DO MUCH AT SCHOOL. BUT...
UNLIKE BEFORE, EVERY TIME OUR EYES MEET, S'LIKE...
IT'S LIKE WE'RE GETTING THROUGH TO EACH OTHER. IT'S NICE, ISN'T IT?

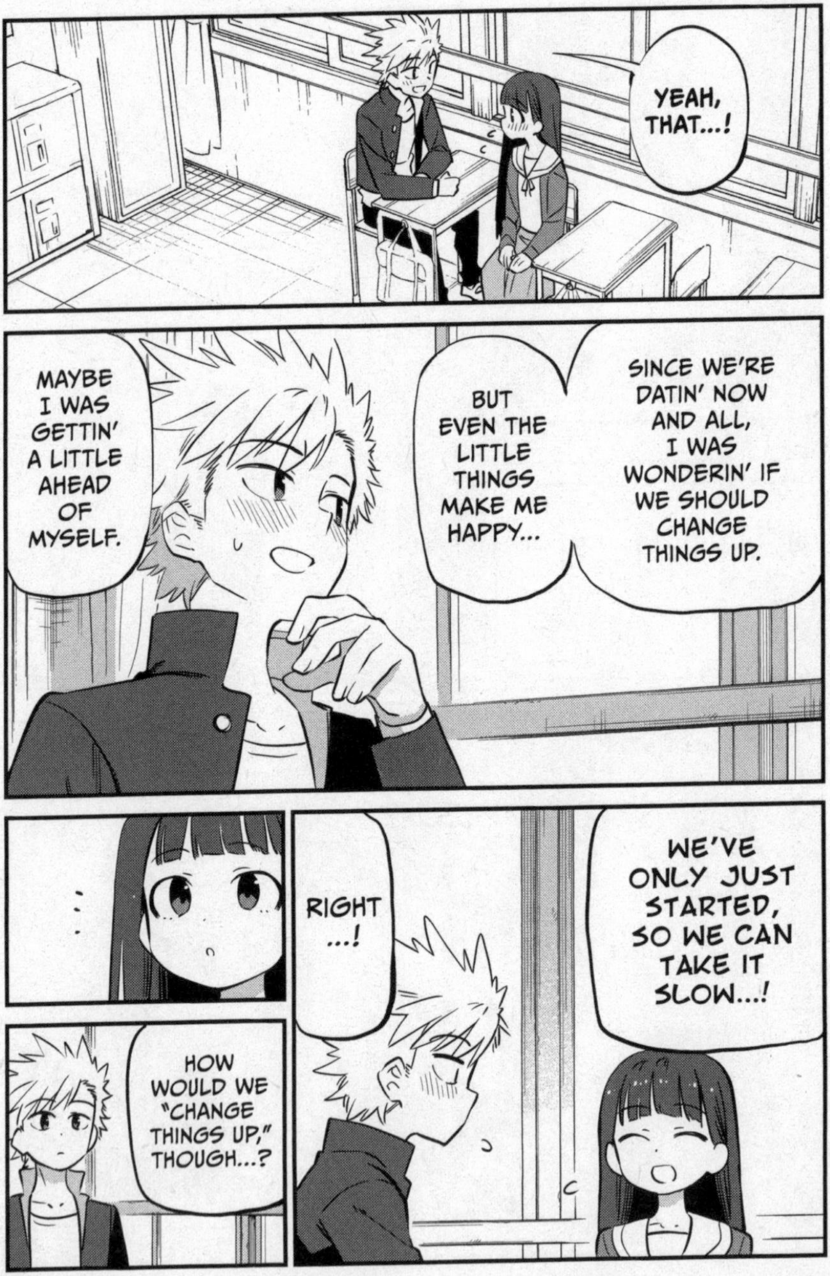
YEAH, THAT...!
SINCE WE'RE DATIN' NOW AND ALL, I WAS WONDERIN' IF WE SHOULD CHANGE THINGS UP.
BUT EVEN THE LITTLE THINGS MAKE ME HAPPY...
MAYBE I WAS GETTIN' A LITTLE AHEAD OF MYSELF.
WE'VE ONLY JUST STARTED, SO WE CAN TAKE IT SLOW...!
RIGHT ...!
HOW WOULD WE "CHANGE THINGS UP," THOUGH...?

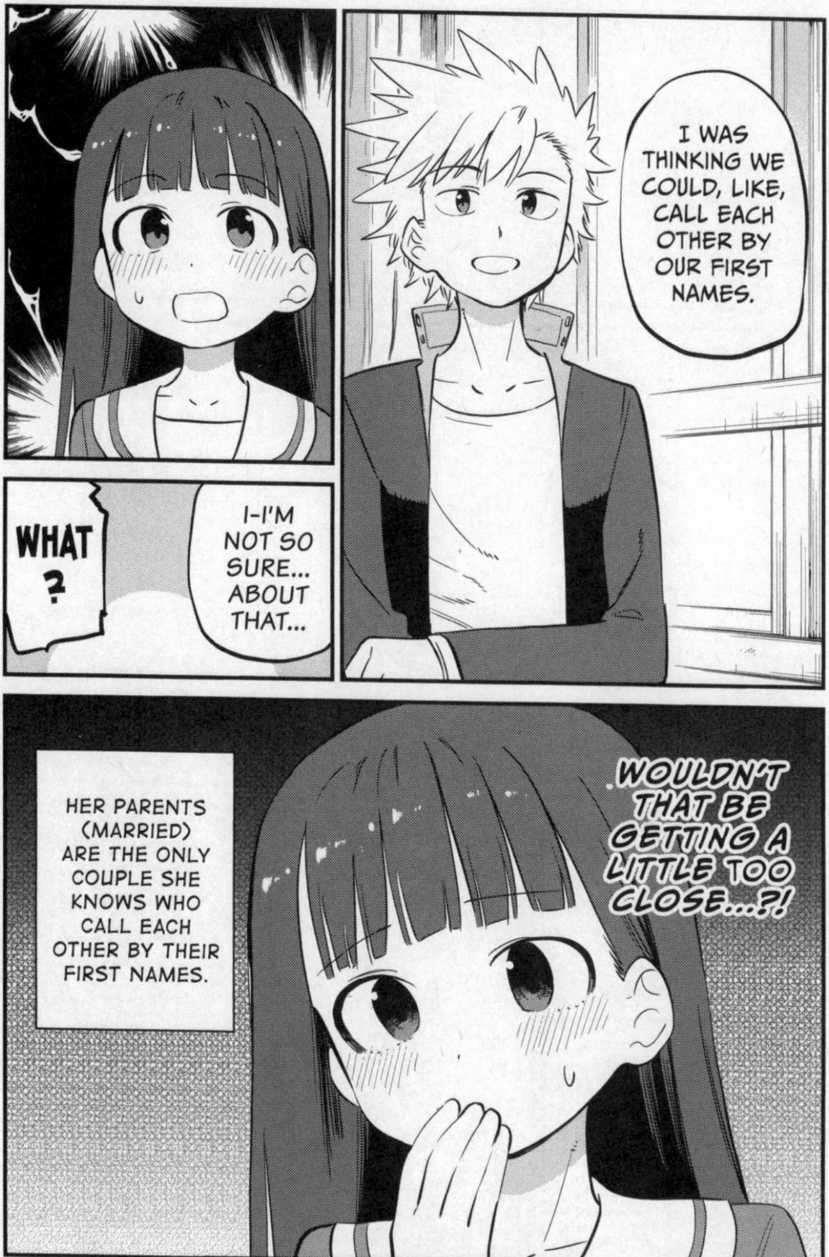
I WAS THINKING WE COULD, LIKE, CALL EACH OTHER BY OUR FIRST NAMES.
I-I'M NOT SO SURE... ABOUT THAT...
WHAT ?
WOULDN'T THAT BE GETTING A LITTLE TOO CLOSE...?!
HER PARENTS (MARRIED) ARE THE ONLY COUPLE SHE KNOWS WHO CALL EACH OTHER BY THEIR FIRST NAMES.

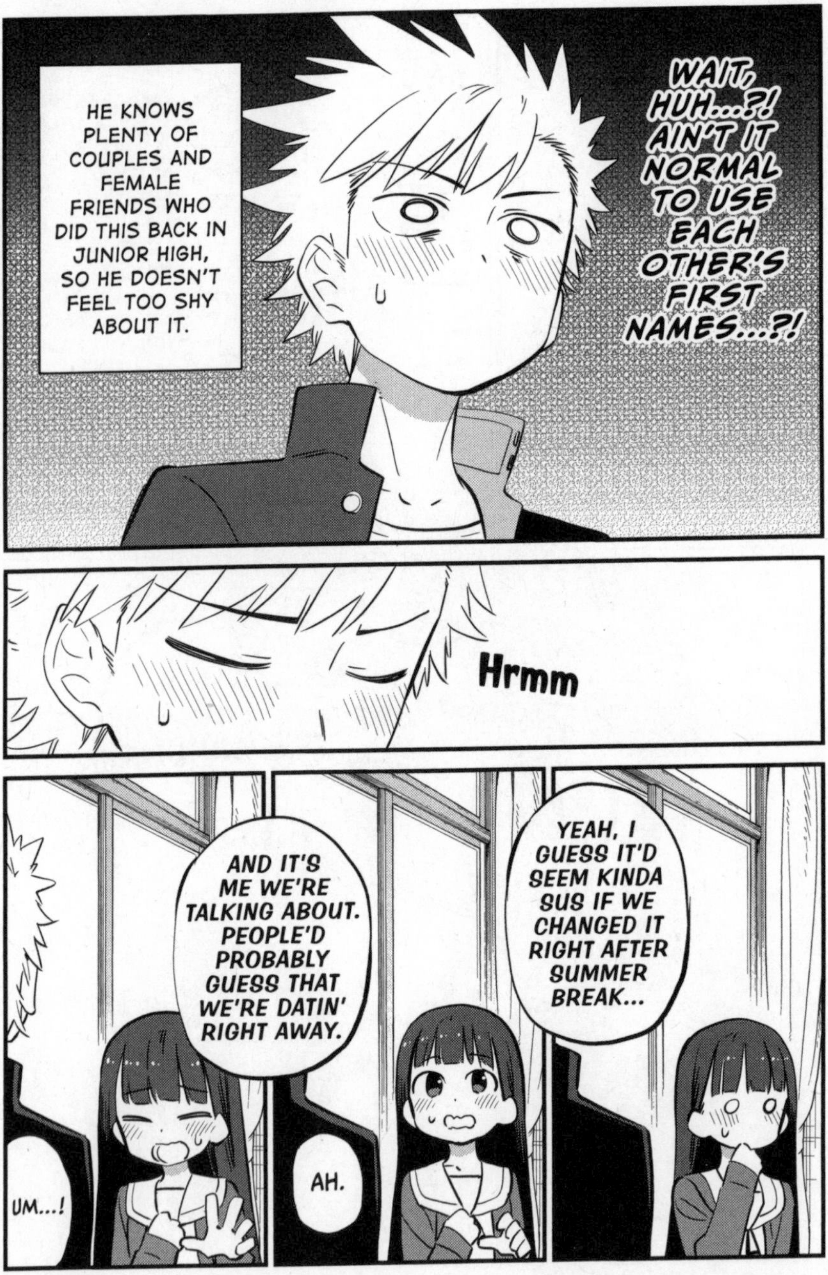
WAIT, HUH...?! AIN'T IT NORMAL TO USE EACH OTHER'S FIRST NAMES...?!
HE KNOWS PLENTY OF COUPLES AND FEMALE FRIENDS WHO DID THIS BACK IN JUNIOR HIGH, SO HE DOESN'T FEEL TOO SHY ABOUT IT.
Hrmm
YEAH, I GUESS IT'D SEEM KINDA SUS IF WE CHANGED IT RIGHT AFTER SUMMER BREAK...
AND IT'S ME WE'RE TALKING ABOUT. PEOPLE'D PROBABLY GUESS THAT WE'RE DATIN' RIGHT AWAY.
AH.
UM...!

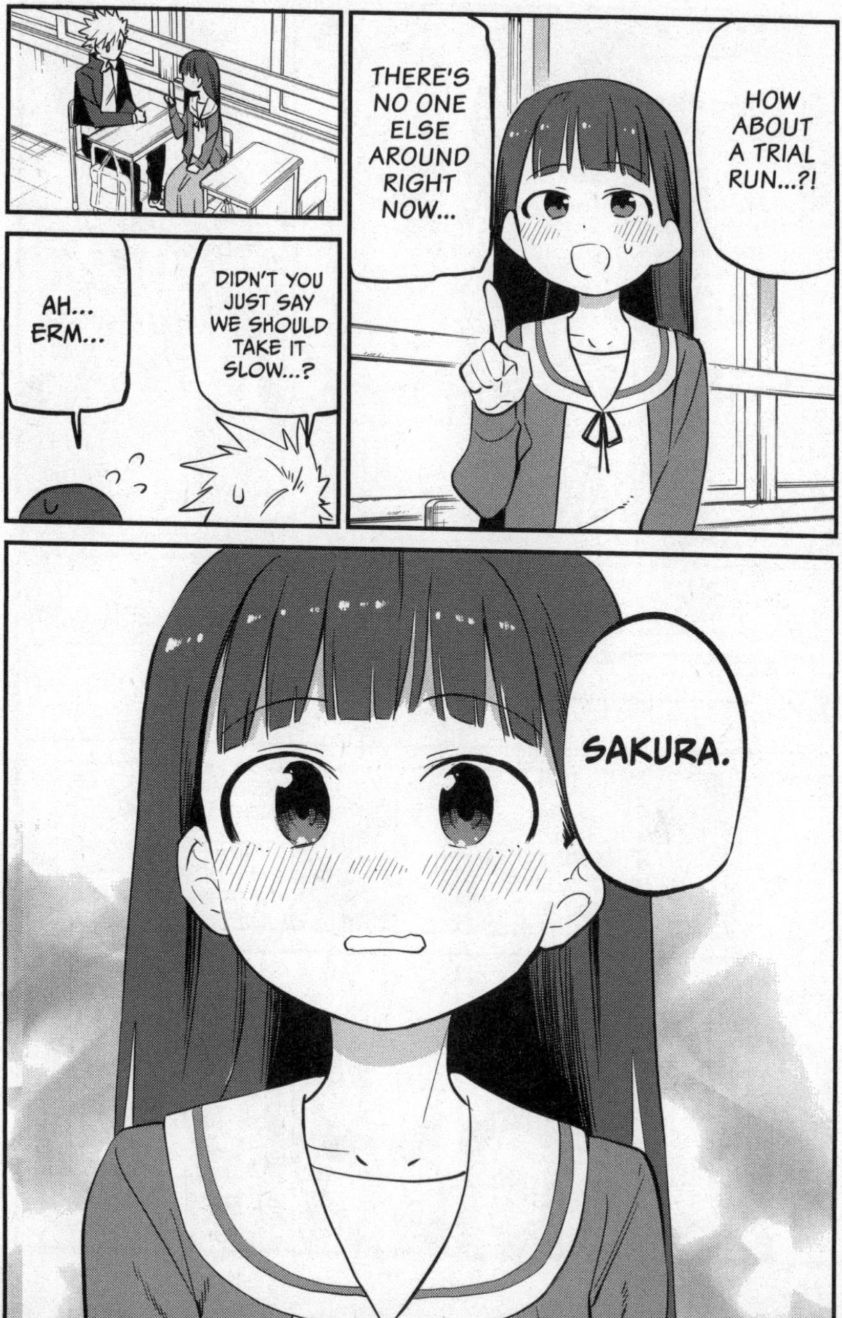
HOW ABOUT A TRIAL RUN...?!
THERE'S NO ONE ELSE AROUND RIGHT NOW...
DIDN'T YOU JUST SAY WE SHOULD TAKE IT SLOW...?
AH... ERM...
SAKURA.

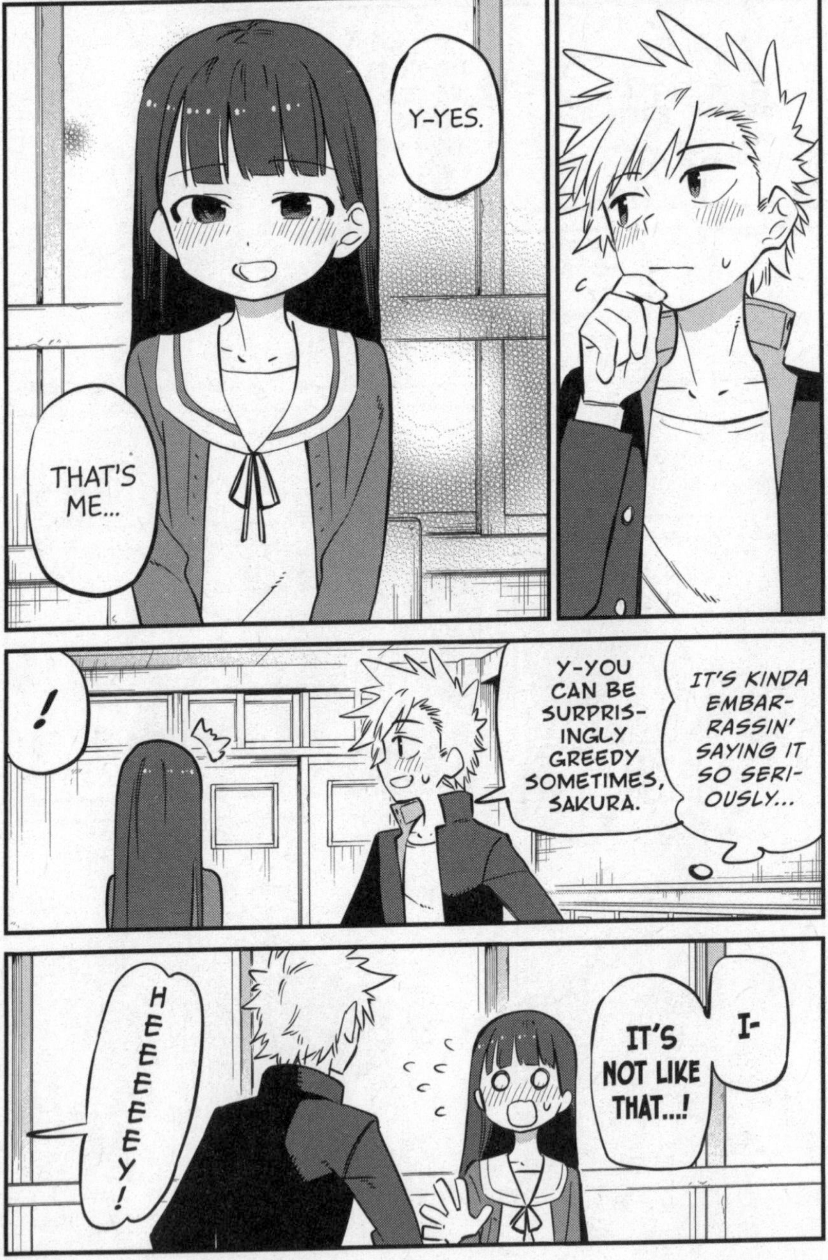
Y-YES.
THAT'S ME...
IT'S KINDA EMBARRASSIN' SAYING IT SO SERIOUSLY...
Y-YOU CAN BE SURPRISINGLY GREEDY SOMETIMES, SAKURA.
!
I-
IT'S NOT LIKE THAT...!
HEEEEEY!

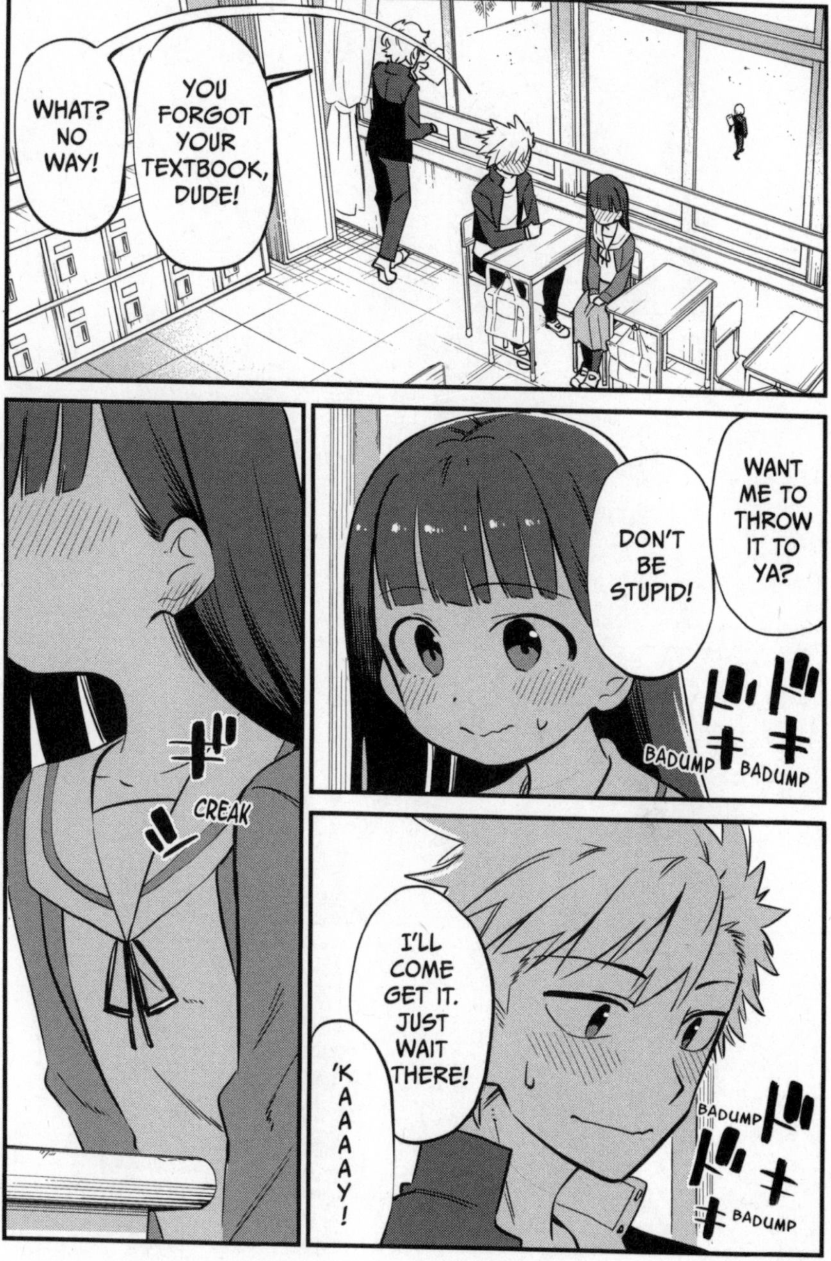
YOU FORGOT YOUR TEXTBOOK, DUDE!
WHAT? NO WAY!
WANT ME TO THROW IT TO YA?
DON'T BE STUPID!
BADUMP BADUMP
I'LL COME GET IT. JUST WAIT THERE!
'KAAAAAY!
BADUMP BADUMP
CREAK

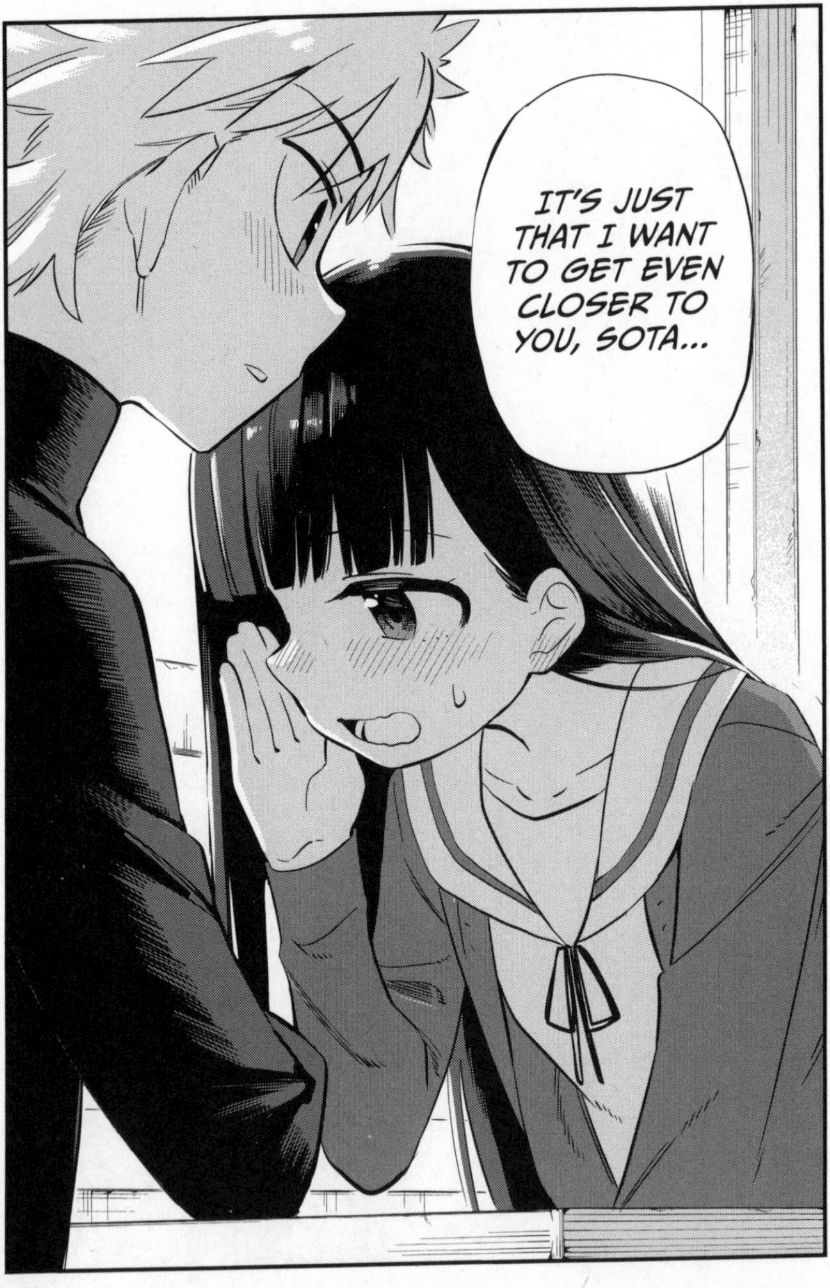
IT'S JUST THAT I WANT TO GET EVEN CLOSER TO YOU, SOTA...

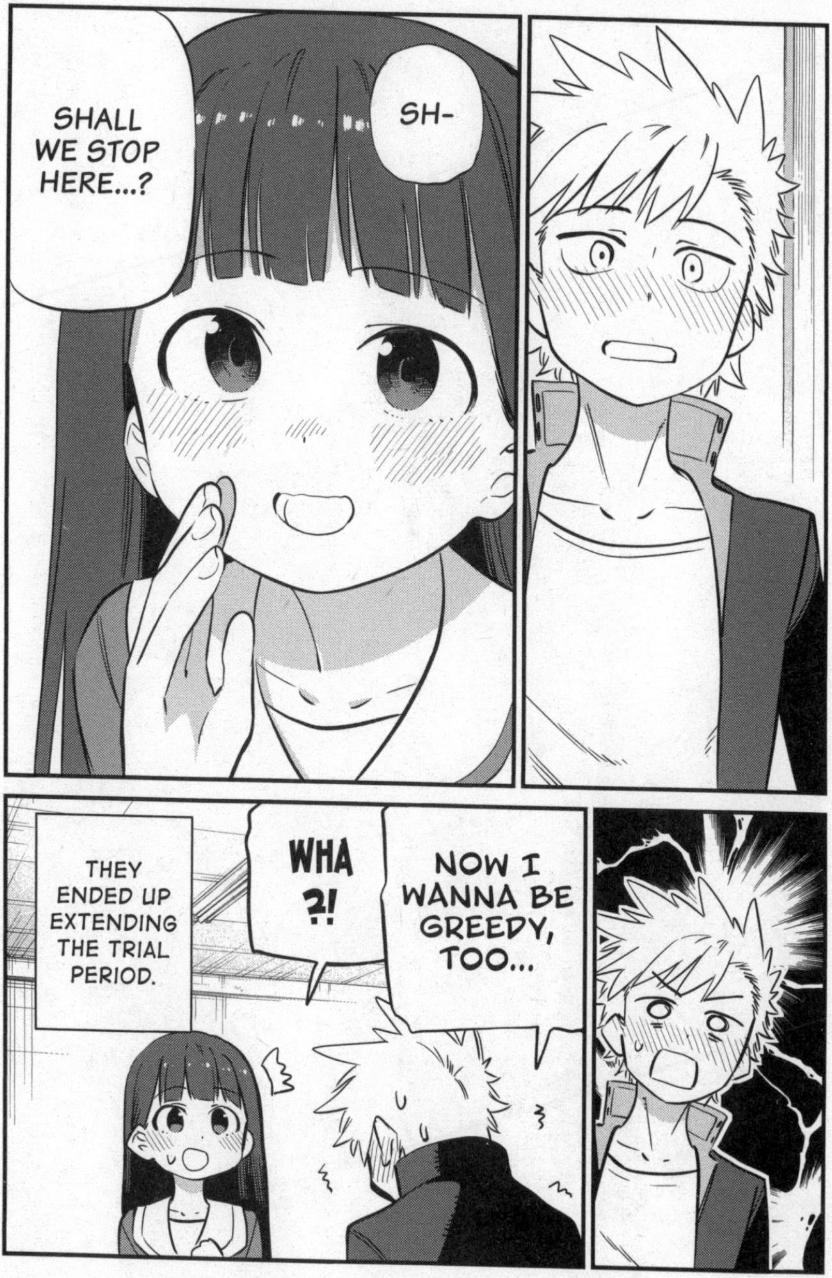
SH-
SHALL WE STOP HERE...?
NOW I WANNA BE GREEDY, TOO...
WHA ?!
THEY ENDED UP EXTENDING THE TRIAL PERIOD.

Chapter 49-Game

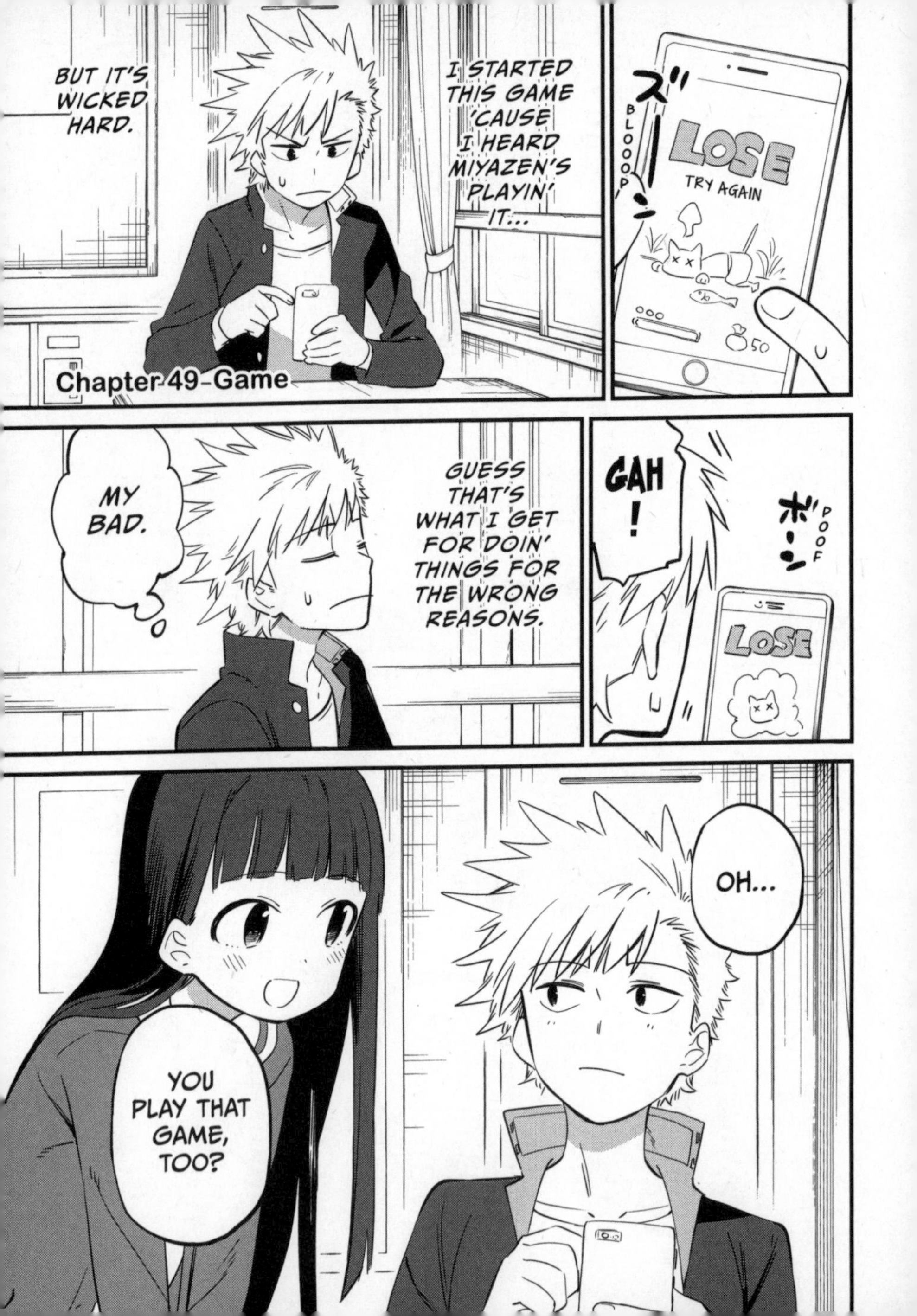
BLOOOOP!
LOSE
TRY AGAIN
50
I STARTED THIS GAME 'CAUSE I HEARD MIYAZEN'S PLAYIN' IT...
BUT IT'S WICKED HARD.
GAH!
POOF
LOSE
GUESS THAT'S WHAT I GET FOR DOIN' THINGS FOR THE WRONG REASONS.
MY BAD.
OH...
YOU PLAY THAT GAME, TOO?

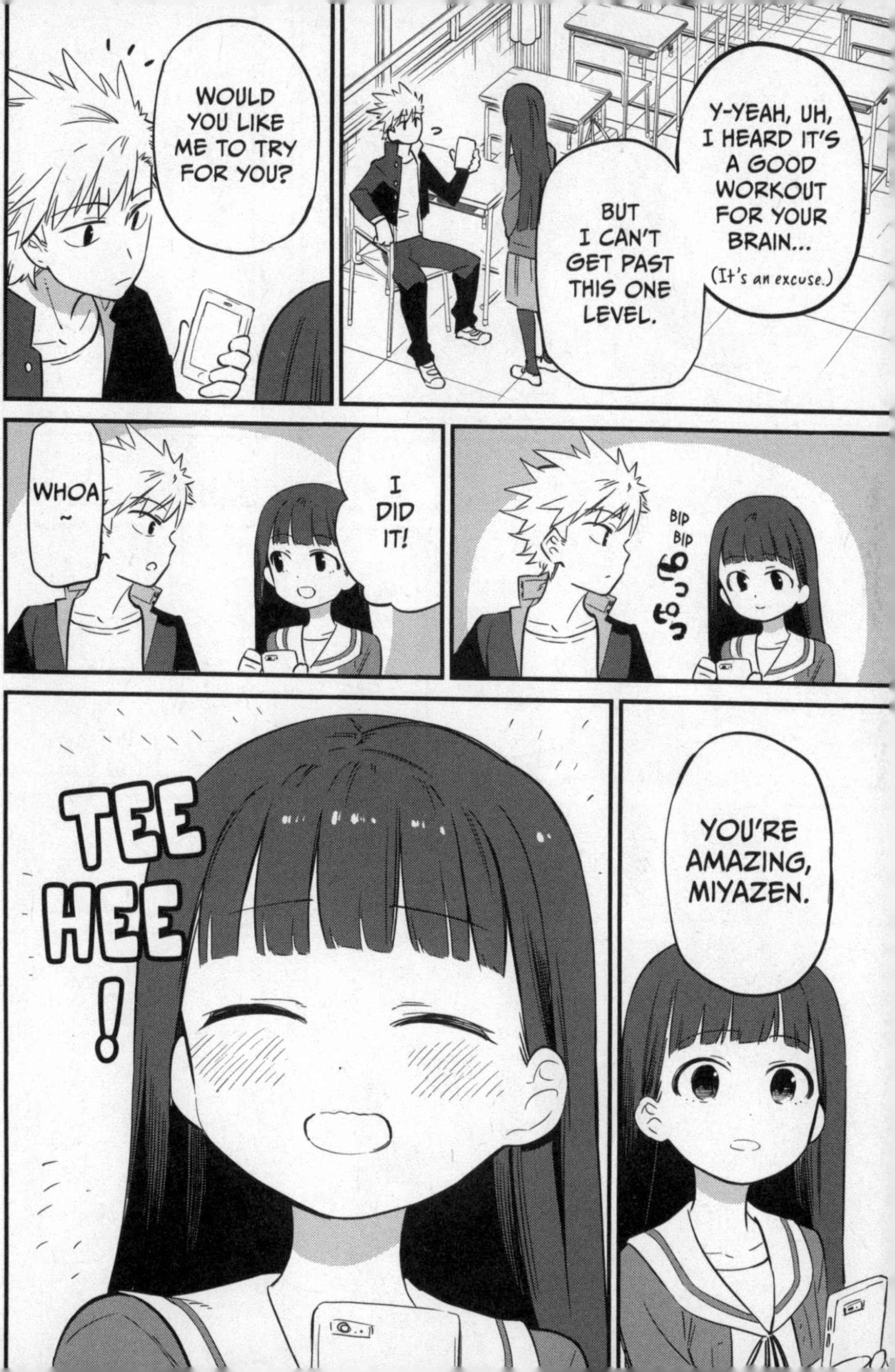
Y-YEAH, UH, I HEARD IT'S A GOOD WORKOUT FOR YOUR BRAIN...
(It's an excuse.)
BUT I CAN'T GET PAST THIS ONE LEVEL.
WOULD YOU LIKE ME TO TRY FOR YOU?
BIP BIP
I DID IT!
WHOA ~
YOU'RE AMAZING, MIYAZEN.
TEE HEE!

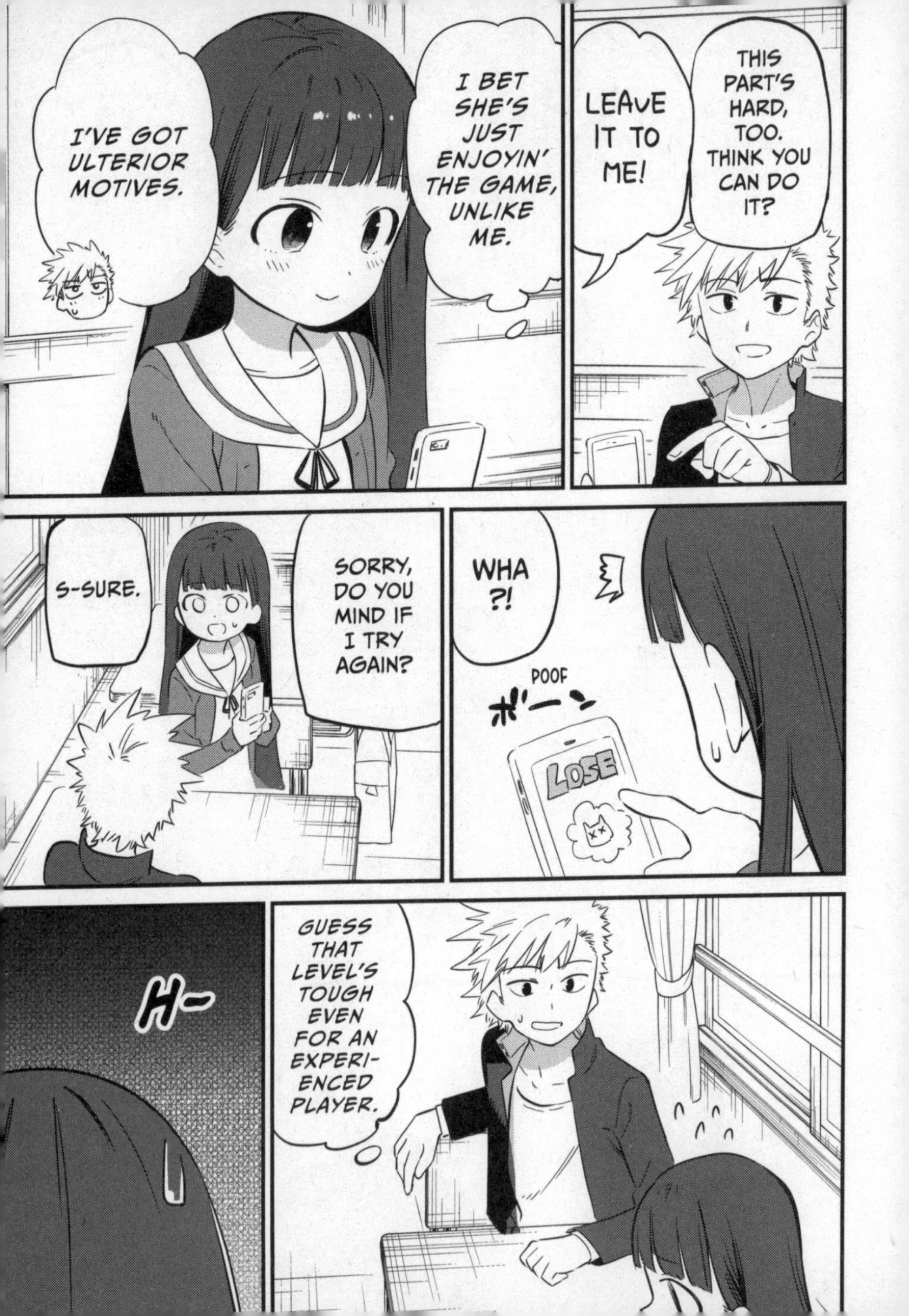
THIS PART'S HARD, TOO. THINK YOU CAN DO IT?
LEAVE IT TO ME!
I BET SHE'S JUST ENJOYIN' THE GAME, UNLIKE ME.
I'VE GOT ULTERIOR MOTIVES.
WHA ?!
POOF
LOSE
SORRY, DO YOU MIND IF I TRY AGAIN?
S-SURE.
GUESS THAT LEVEL'S TOUGH EVEN FOR AN EXPERI-ENCED PLAYER.
H-

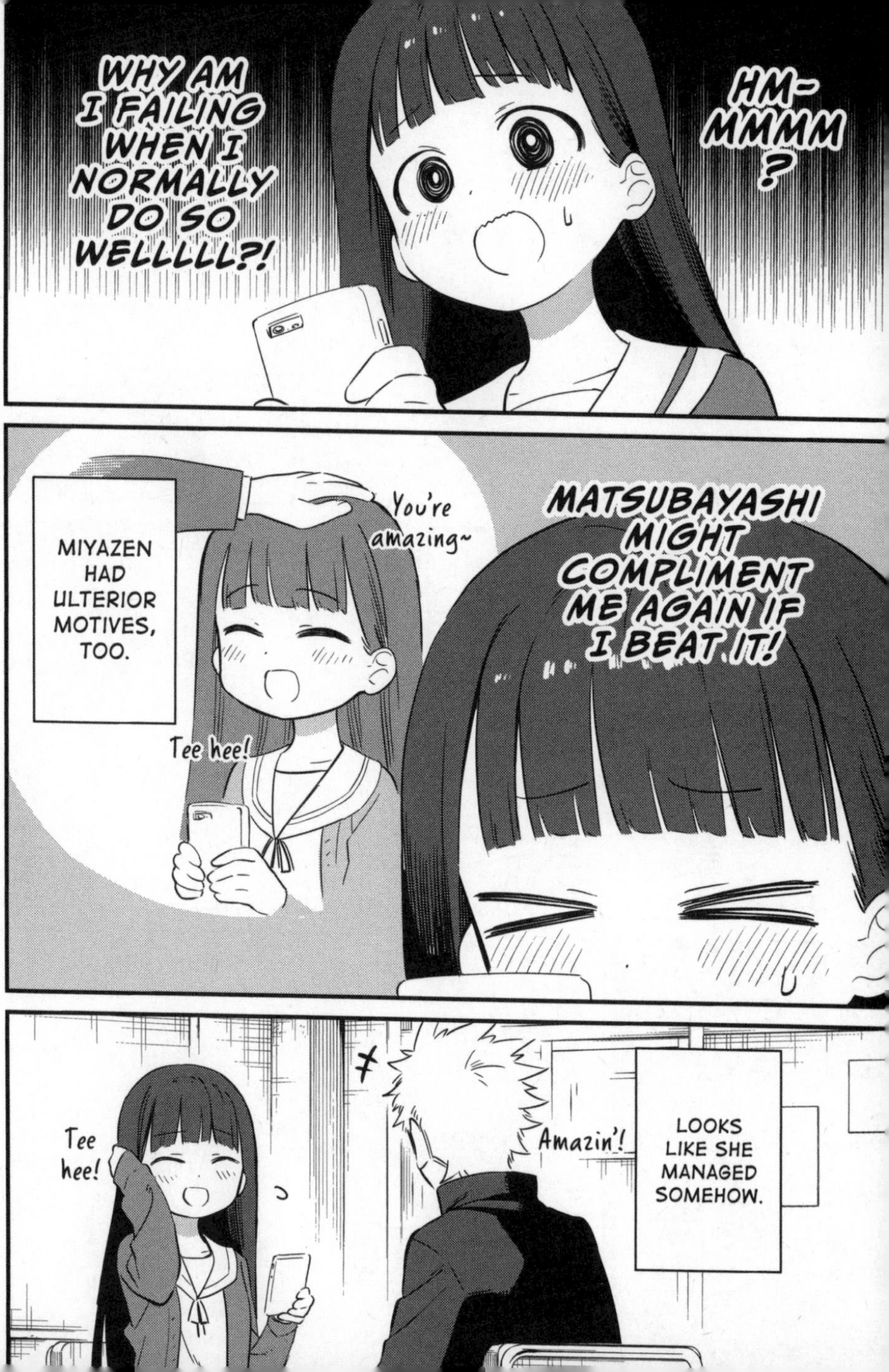
HM-MMMM?
WHY AM I FAILING WHEN I NORMALLY DO SO WELLLLL?!
MATSUBAYASHI MIGHT COMPLIMENT ME AGAIN IF I BEAT IT!
You're amazing~
MIYAZEN HAD ULTERIOR MOTIVES, TOO.
Tee hee!
LOOKS LIKE SHE MANAGED SOMEHOW.
Amazin'!
Tee hee!

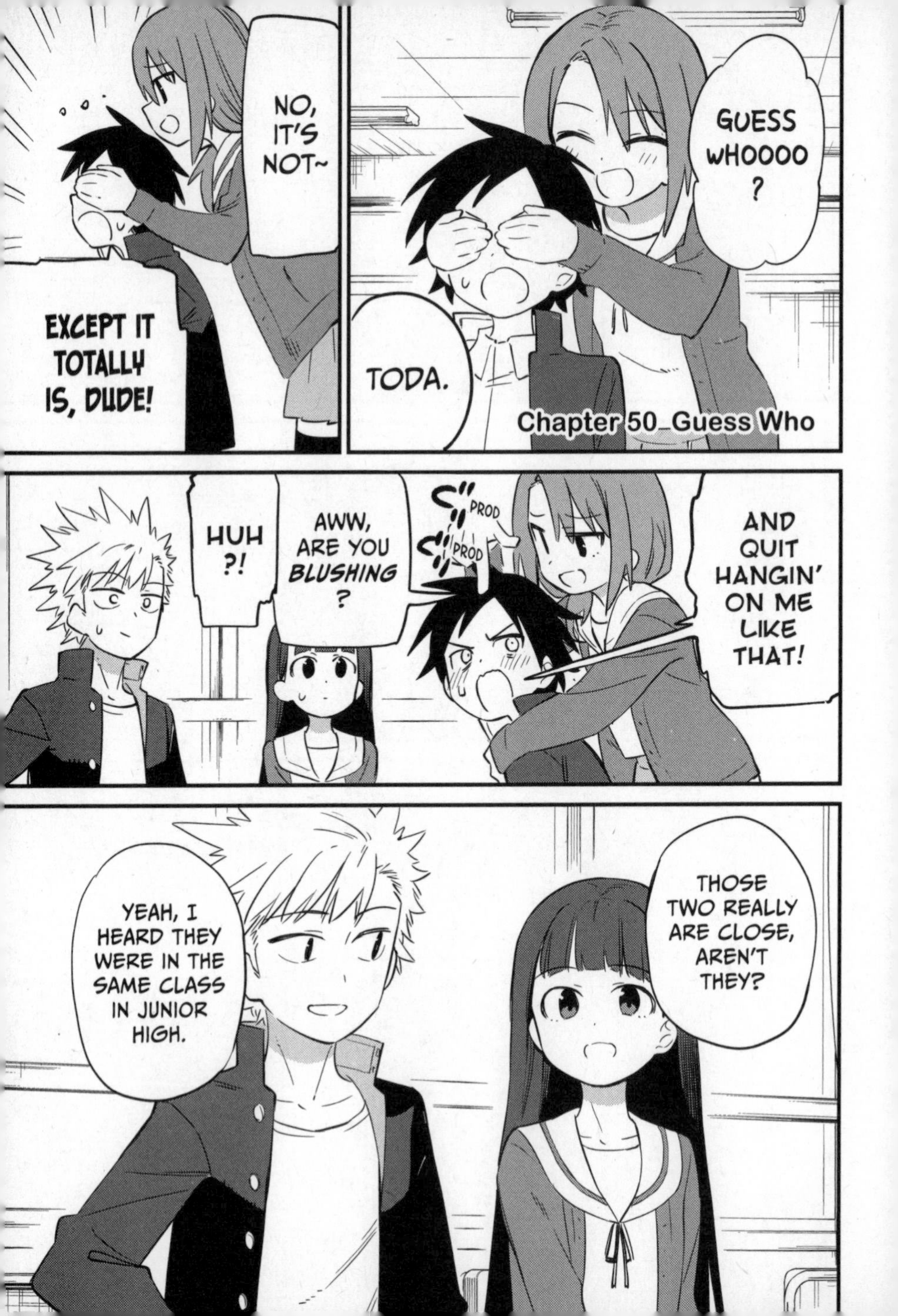
GUESS WHOOOO?
TODA.
Chapter 50_Guess Who
NO, IT'S NOT~
EXCEPT IT TOTALLY IS, DUDE!
AND QUIT HANGIN' ON ME LIKE THAT!
PROD
PROD
AWW, ARE YOU *BLUSHING*?
HUH?!
THOSE TWO REALLY ARE CLOSE, AREN'T THEY?
YEAH, I HEARD THEY WERE IN THE SAME CLASS IN JUNIOR HIGH.

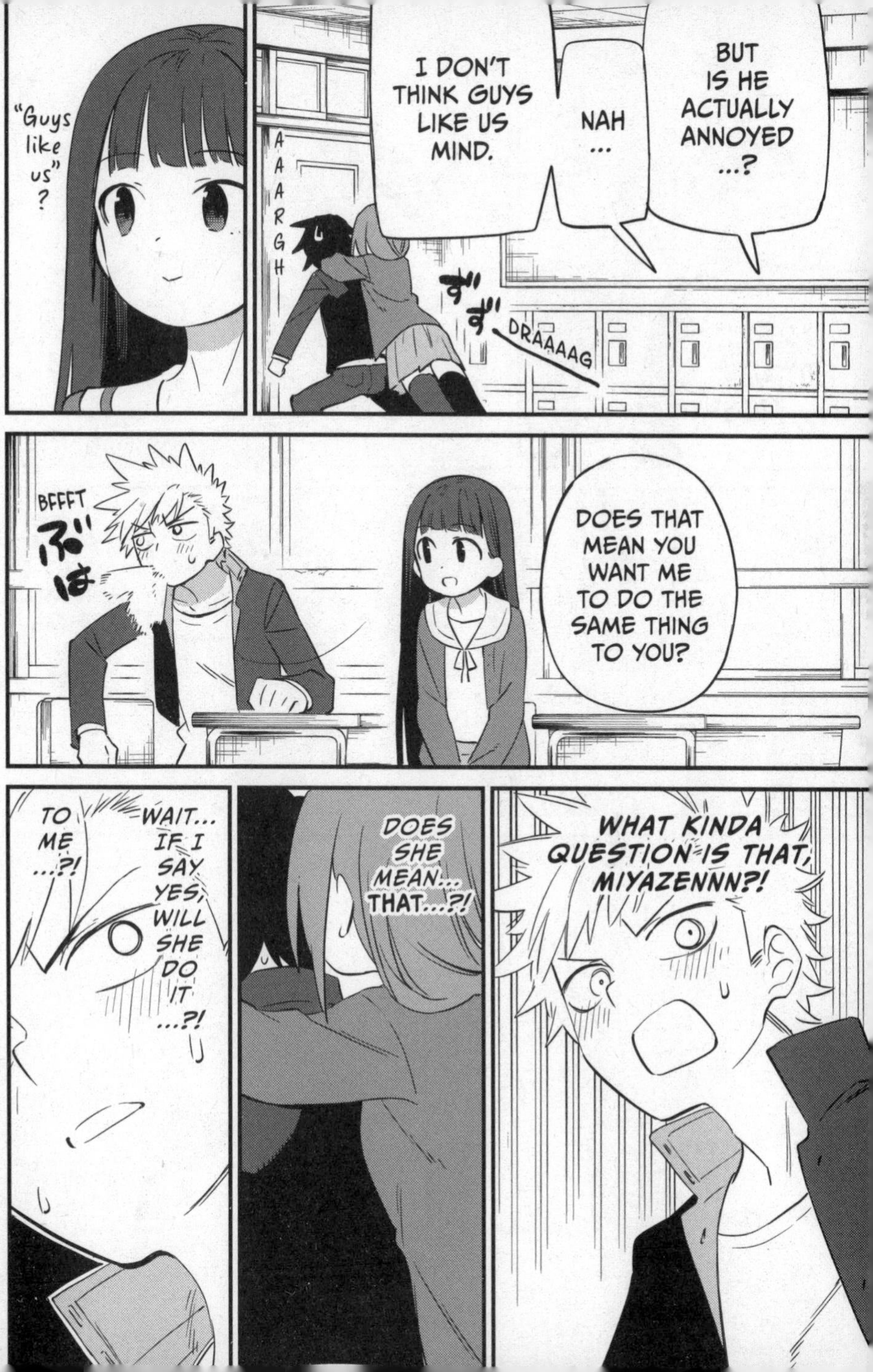
BUT IS HE ACTUALLY ANNOYED ...?
NAH ...
I DON'T THINK GUYS LIKE US MIND.
AAAARGH
ずず
DRAAAAG
"Guys like us"?
DOES THAT MEAN YOU WANT ME TO DO THE SAME THING TO YOU?
BFFFT
ぶは
WHAT KINDA QUESTION IS THAT, MIYAZENNN?!
DOES SHE MEAN... THAT...?!
WAIT... IF I SAY YES, WILL SHE DO IT ...?!
TO ME ...?!

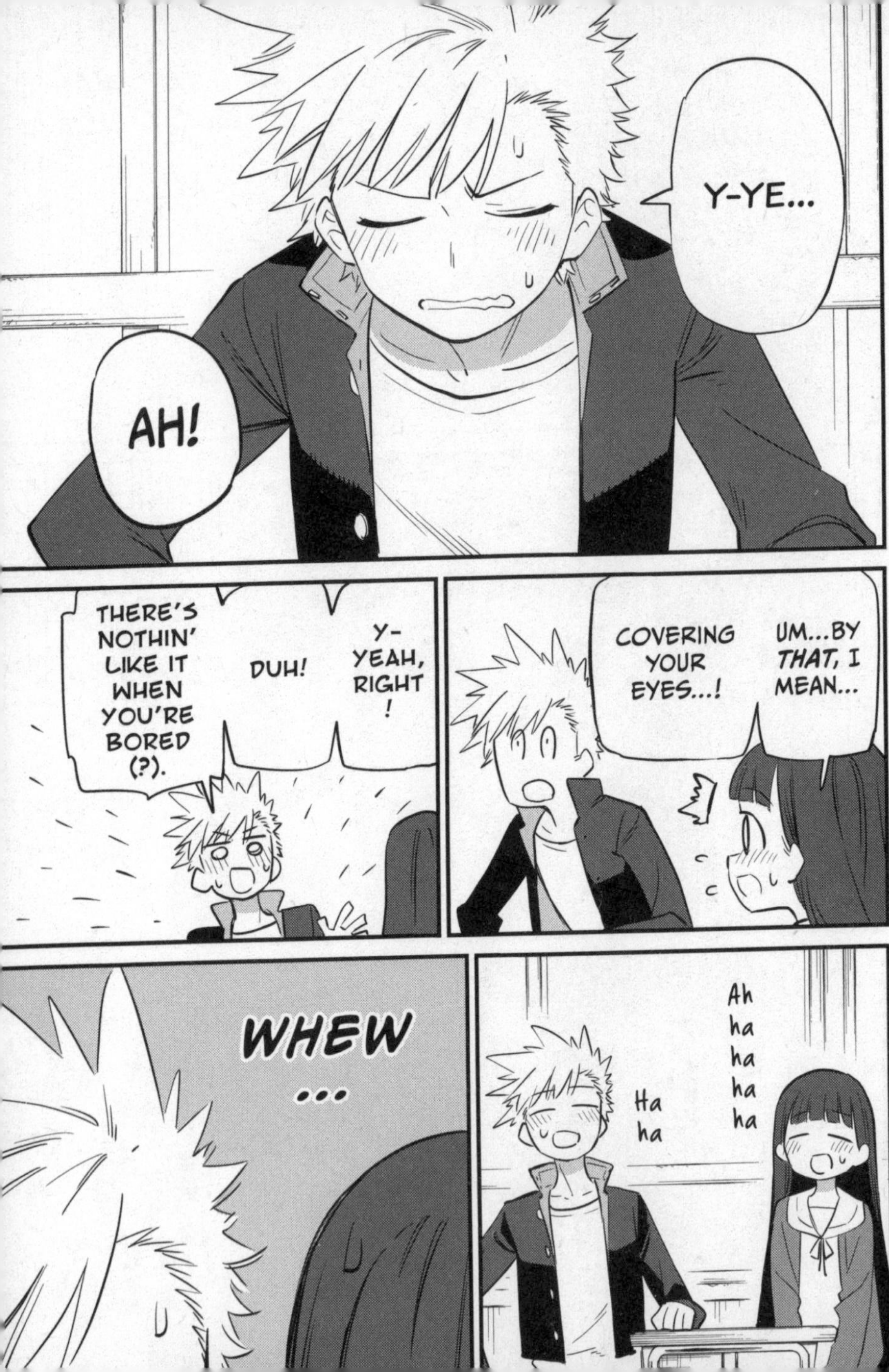
Y-YE...
AH!
UM...BY *THAT*, I MEAN...
COVERING YOUR EYES...!
Y-YEAH, RIGHT!
DUH!
THERE'S NOTHIN' LIKE IT WHEN YOU'RE BORED (?).
Ah ha ha ha ha
Ha ha
WHEW...

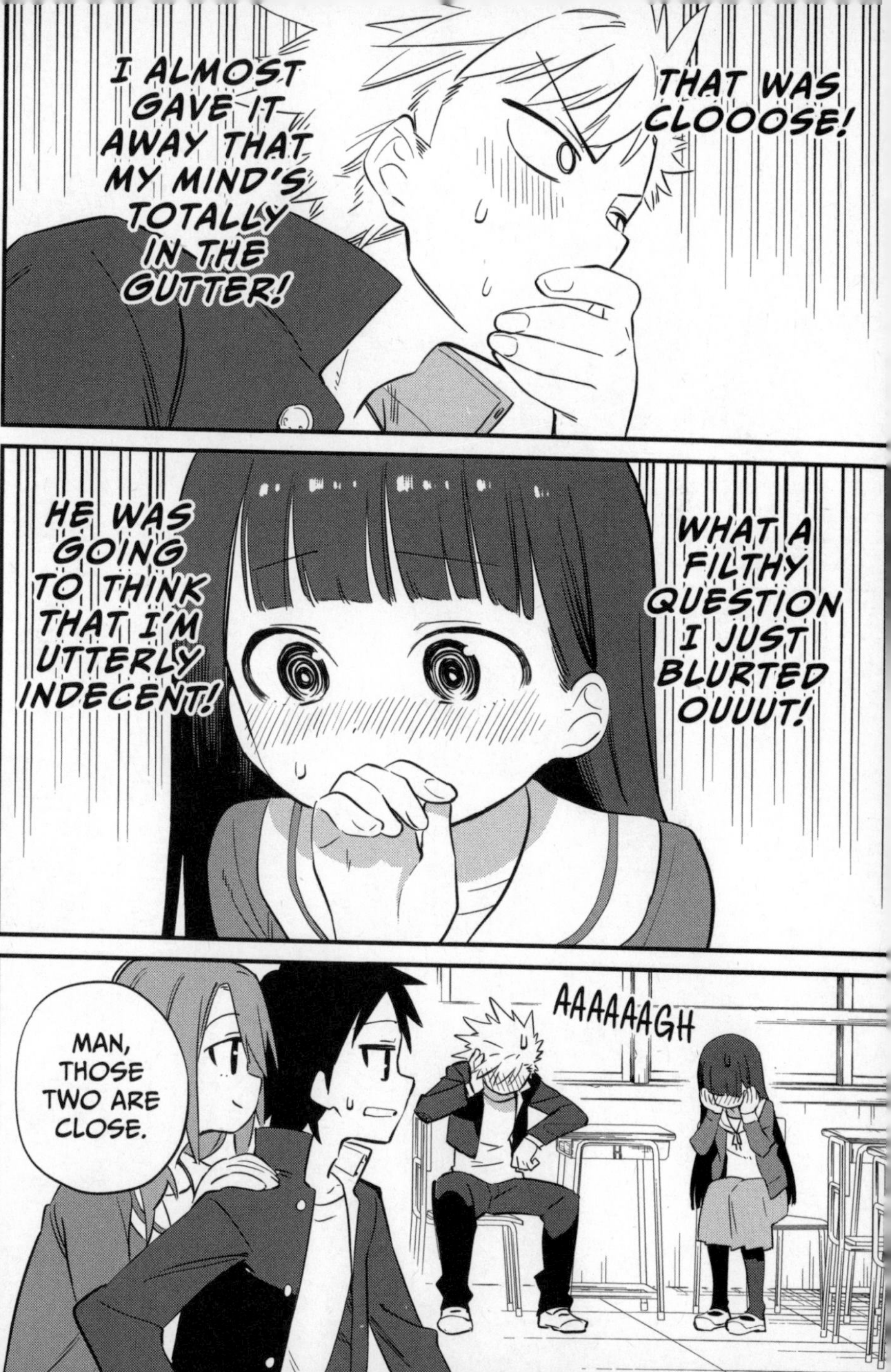
THAT WAS CLOOOSE!
I ALMOST GAVE IT AWAY THAT MY MIND'S TOTALLY IN THE GUTTER!
WHAT A FILTHY QUESTION I JUST BLURTED OUUUT!
HE WAS GOING TO THINK THAT I'M UTTERLY INDECENT!
AAAAAAGH
MAN, THOSE TWO ARE CLOSE.

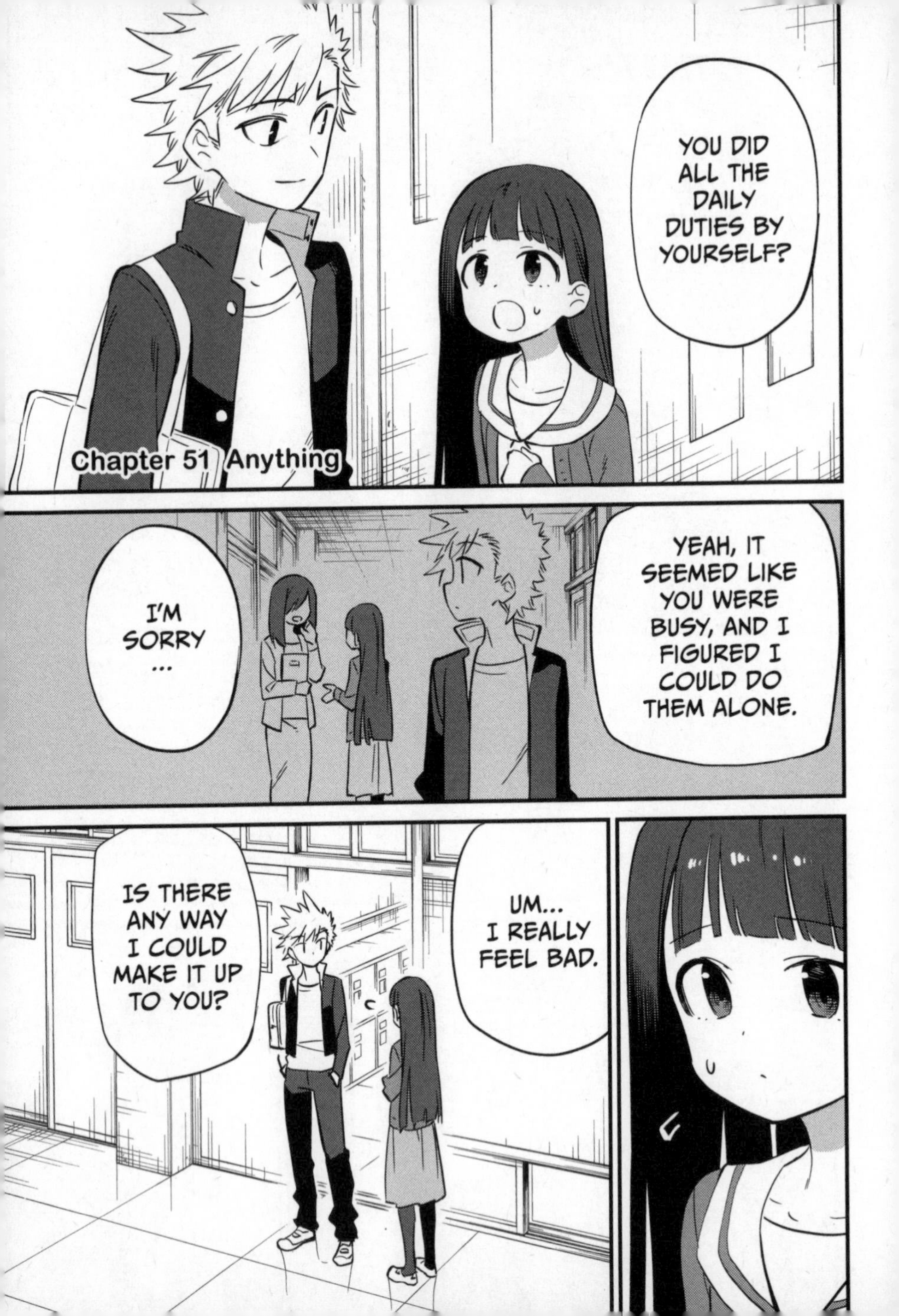
YOU DID ALL THE DAILY DUTIES BY YOURSELF?
Chapter 51 Anything
YEAH, IT SEEMED LIKE YOU WERE BUSY, AND I FIGURED I COULD DO THEM ALONE.
I'M SORRY ...
UM... I REALLY FEEL BAD.
IS THERE ANY WAY I COULD MAKE IT UP TO YOU?

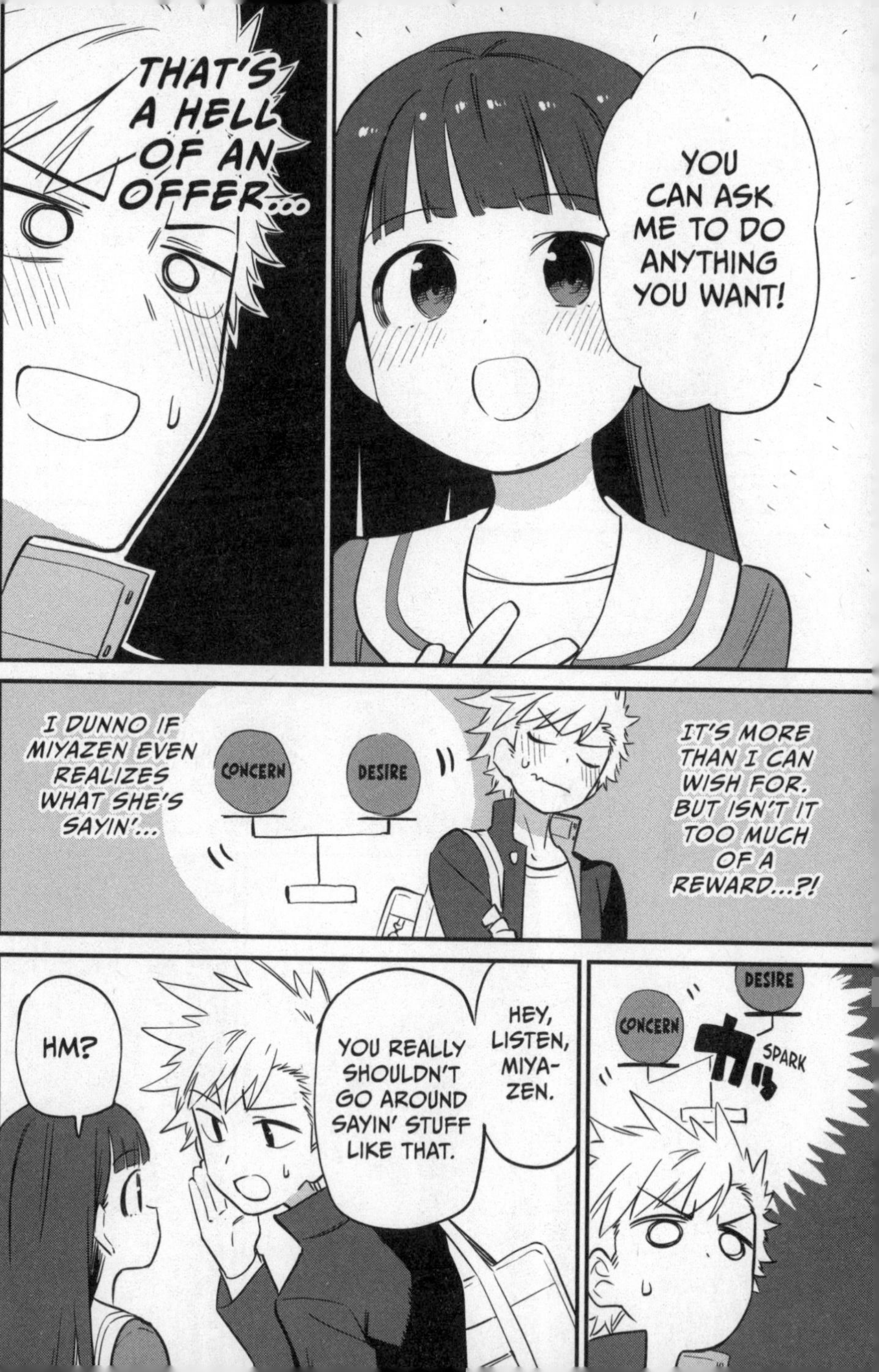
YOU CAN ASK ME TO DO ANYTHING YOU WANT!
THAT'S A HELL OF AN OFFER...
IT'S MORE THAN I CAN WISH FOR. BUT ISN'T IT TOO MUCH OF A REWARD...?!
DESIRE
CONCERN
I DUNNO IF MIYAZEN EVEN REALIZES WHAT SHE'S SAYIN'...
DESIRE
CONCERN
SPARK
HEY, LISTEN, MIYA-ZEN.
YOU REALLY SHOULDN'T GO AROUND SAYIN' STUFF LIKE THAT.
HM?

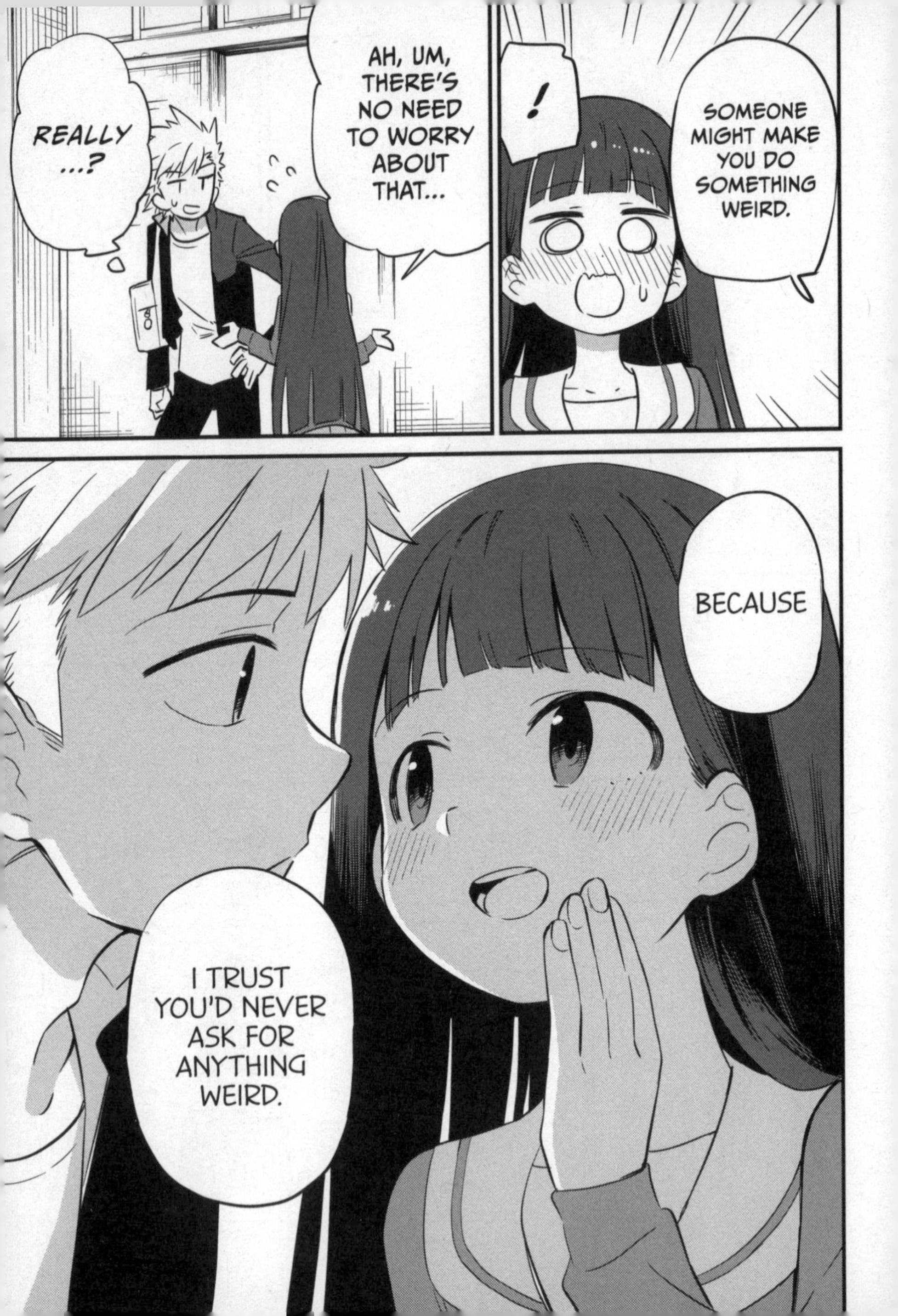
SOMEONE MIGHT MAKE YOU DO SOMETHING WEIRD.
!
AH, UM, THERE'S NO NEED TO WORRY ABOUT THAT...
REALLY ...?
BECAUSE
I TRUST YOU'D NEVER ASK FOR ANYTHING WEIRD.

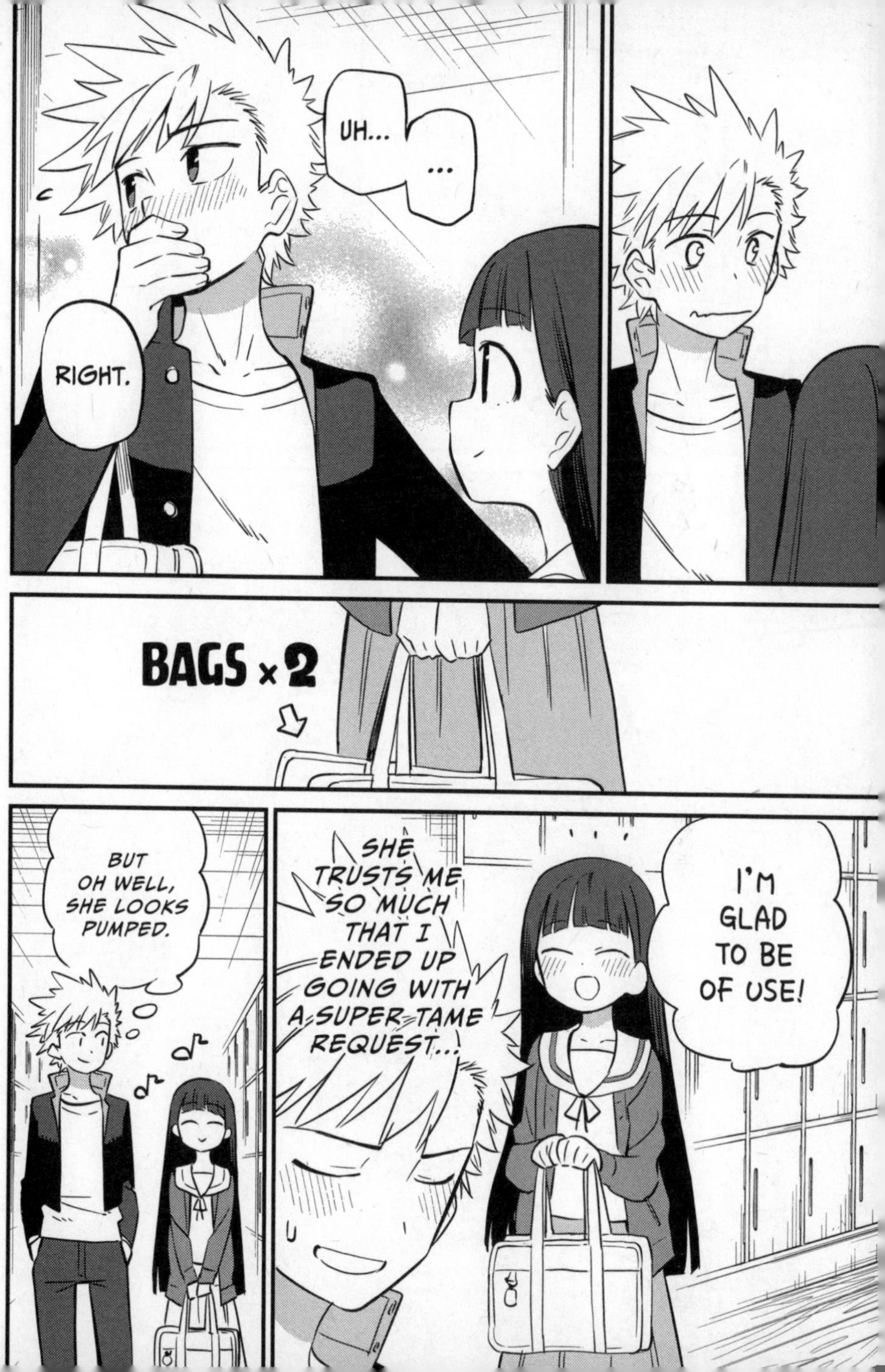
UH...
...
RIGHT.
BAGS x 2
I'M GLAD TO BE OF USE!
SHE TRUSTS ME SO MUCH THAT I ENDED UP GOING WITH A SUPER-TAME REQUEST...
BUT OH WELL, SHE LOOKS PUMPED.

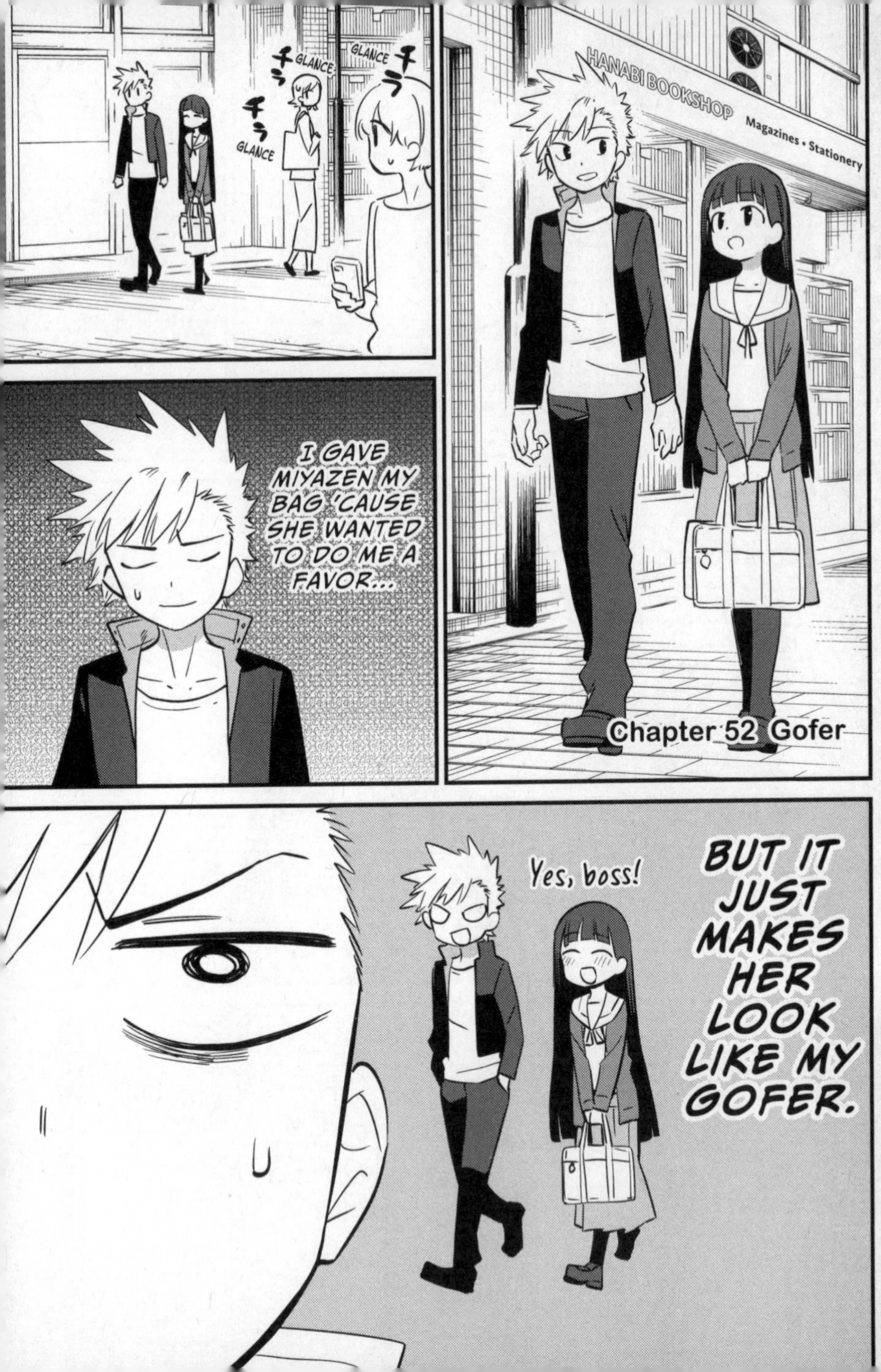
HANABI BOOKSHOP
Magazines • Stationery
Chapter 52 Gofer
チラ
GLANCE
チラ
GLANCE
チラ
GLANCE
I GAVE MIYAZEN MY BAG 'CAUSE SHE WANTED TO DO ME A FAVOR...
BUT IT JUST MAKES HER LOOK LIKE MY GOFER.
Yes, boss!

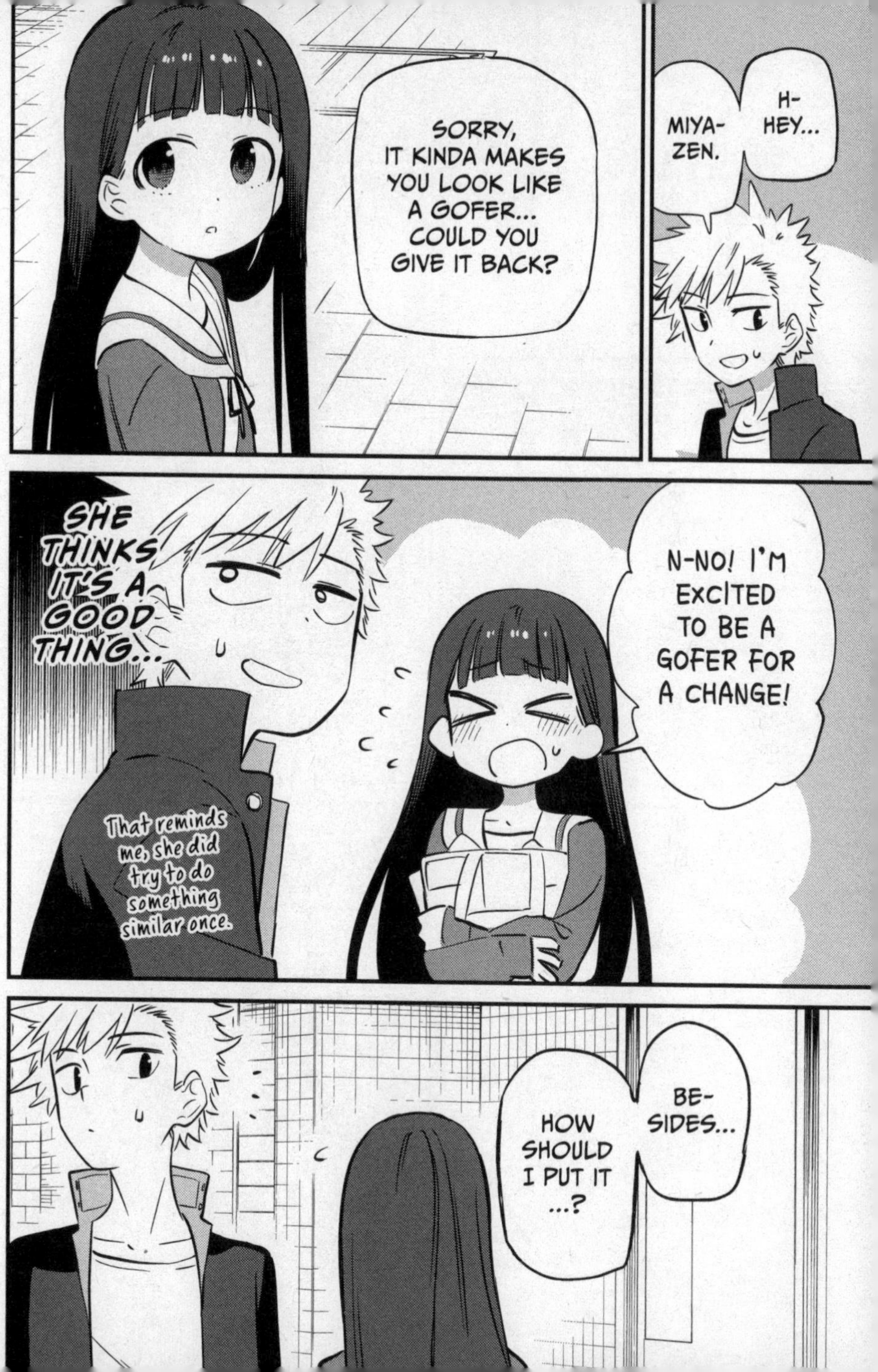
H-HEY...
MIYA-ZEN.
SORRY, IT KINDA MAKES YOU LOOK LIKE A GOFER... COULD YOU GIVE IT BACK?
N-NO! I'M EXCITED TO BE A GOFER FOR A CHANGE!
SHE THINKS IT'S A GOOD THING...
That reminds me, she did try to do something similar once.
BE-SIDES...
HOW SHOULD I PUT IT ...?

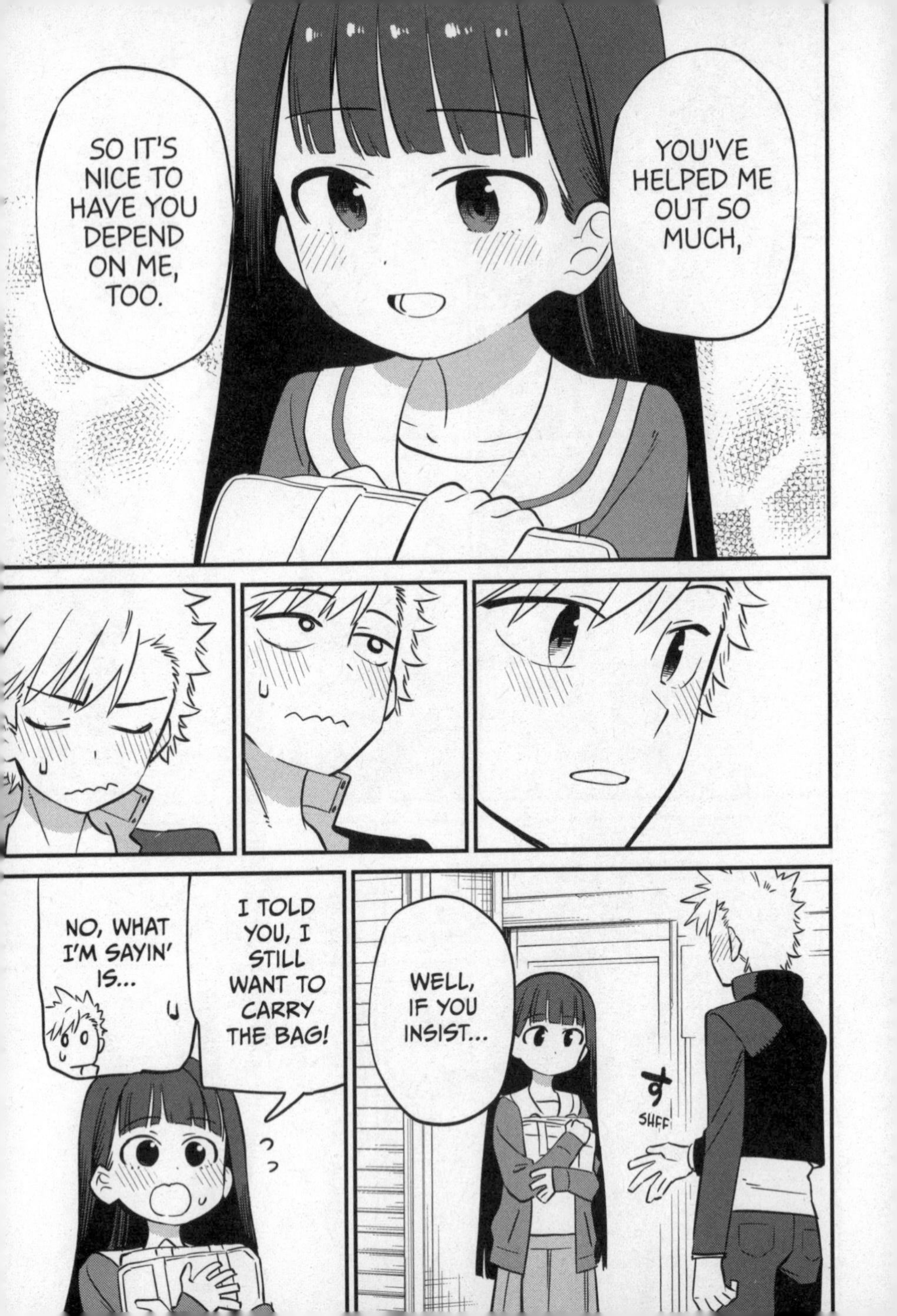
YOU'VE HELPED ME OUT SO MUCH,
SO IT'S NICE TO HAVE YOU DEPEND ON ME, TOO.
WELL, IF YOU INSIST...
す
SHFF
I TOLD YOU, I STILL WANT TO CARRY THE BAG!
NO, WHAT I'M SAYIN' IS...

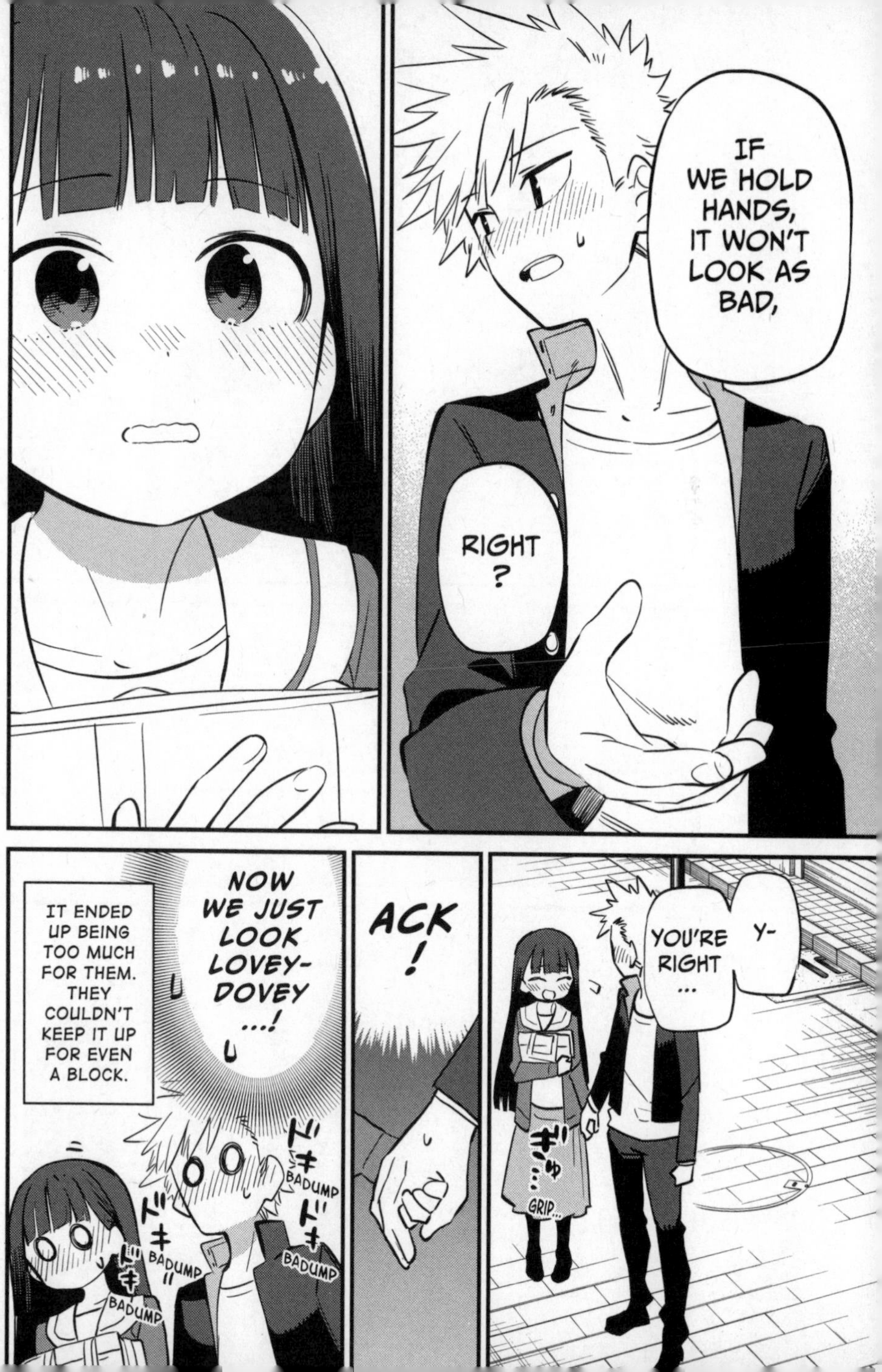
IF WE HOLD HANDS, IT WON'T LOOK AS BAD,
RIGHT?
Y-
YOU'RE RIGHT ...
ぎゅ...
GRIP...
ACK!
NOW WE JUST LOOK LOVEY-DOVEY ...!
IT ENDED UP BEING TOO MUCH FOR THEM. THEY COULDN'T KEEP IT UP FOR EVEN A BLOCK.
ドキ
BADUMP
ドキ
BADUMP
ドキ
BADUMP
ドキ
BADUMP

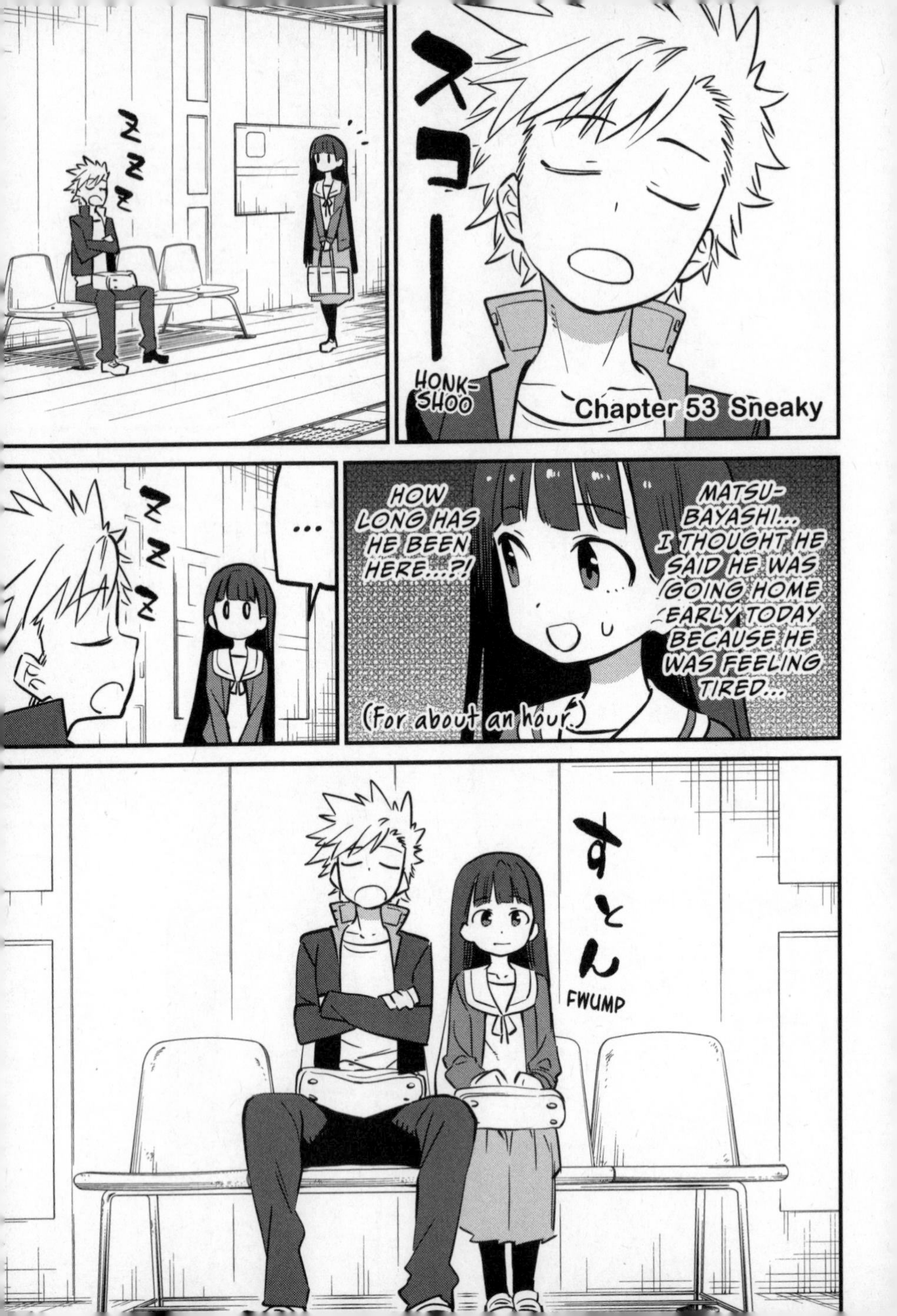
スコー
HONK-SHOO
Chapter 53 Sneaky
Z Z Z
MATSU-BAYASHI... I THOUGHT HE SAID HE WAS GOING HOME EARLY TODAY BECAUSE HE WAS FEELING TIRED...
HOW LONG HAS HE BEEN HERE...?!
(For about an hour.)
...
Z Z Z
すとん
FWUMP

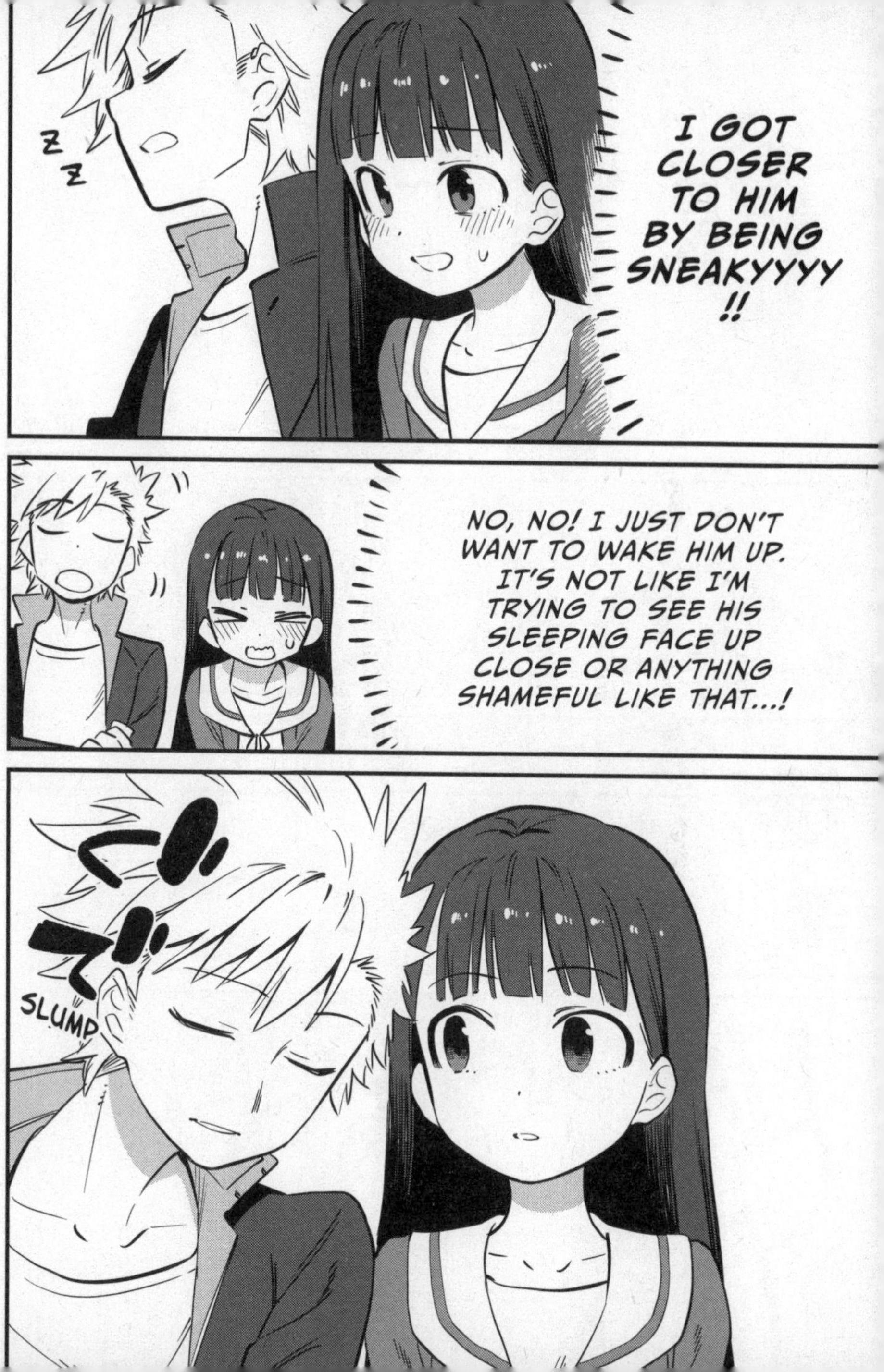
I GOT CLOSER TO HIM BY BEING SNEAKYYYY!!
Z Z
NO, NO! I JUST DON'T WANT TO WAKE HIM UP. IT'S NOT LIKE I'M TRYING TO SEE HIS SLEEPING FACE UP CLOSE OR ANYTHING SHAMEFUL LIKE THAT...!
SLUMP

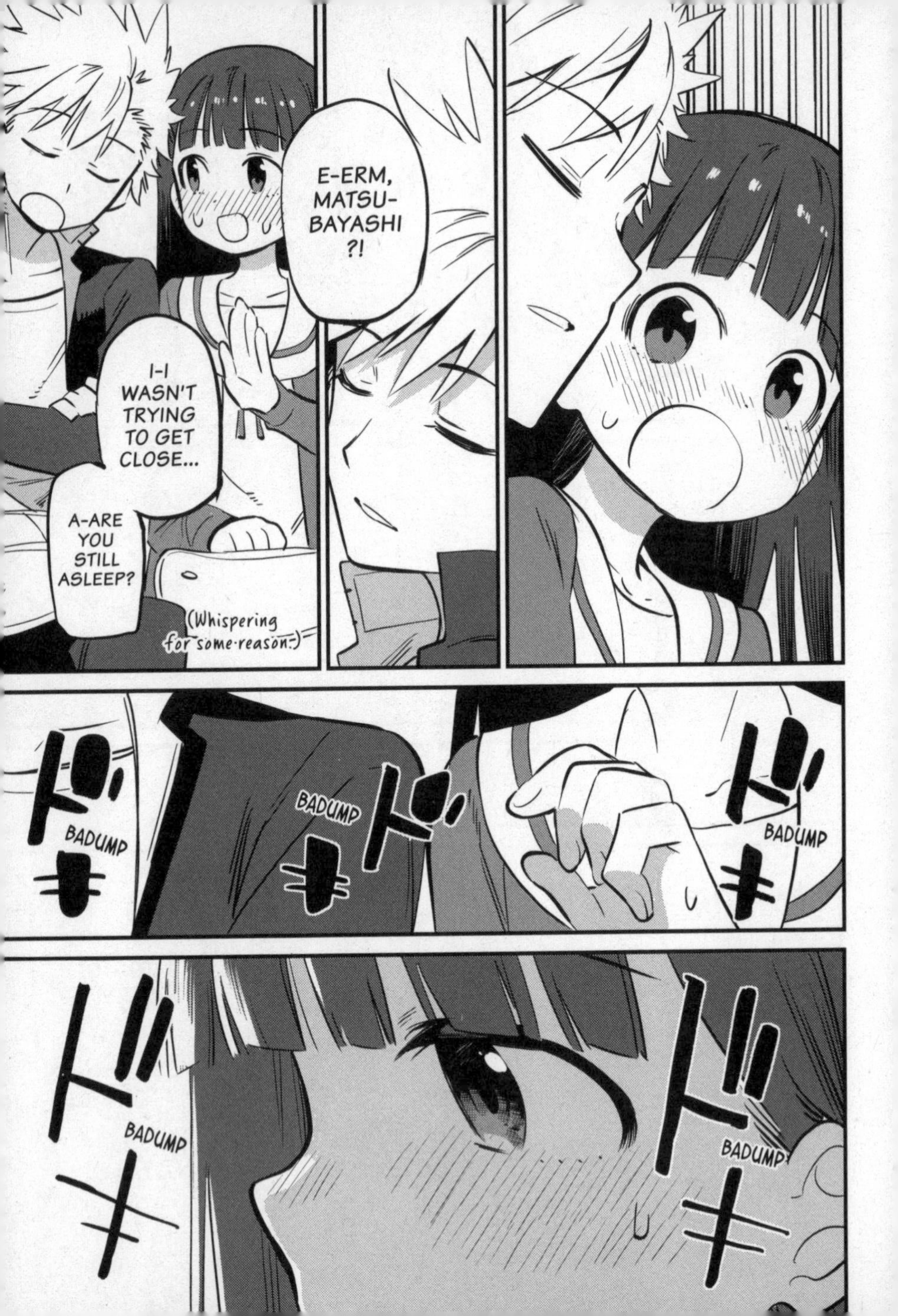
E-ERM, MATSU-BAYASHI ?!
I-I WASN'T TRYING TO GET CLOSE...
A-ARE YOU STILL ASLEEP?
(Whispering for some reason.)
BADUMP
BADUMP
BADUMP
BADUMP
BADUMP

BUMP...

I'M SO SOR-RYYY!

WHOAA, I'M SORRY!

HUH? WHAT? MIYAZEN?

OW!

JUMP

AH, THE TRAIN'S HERE! HURRY UP!

THUNK

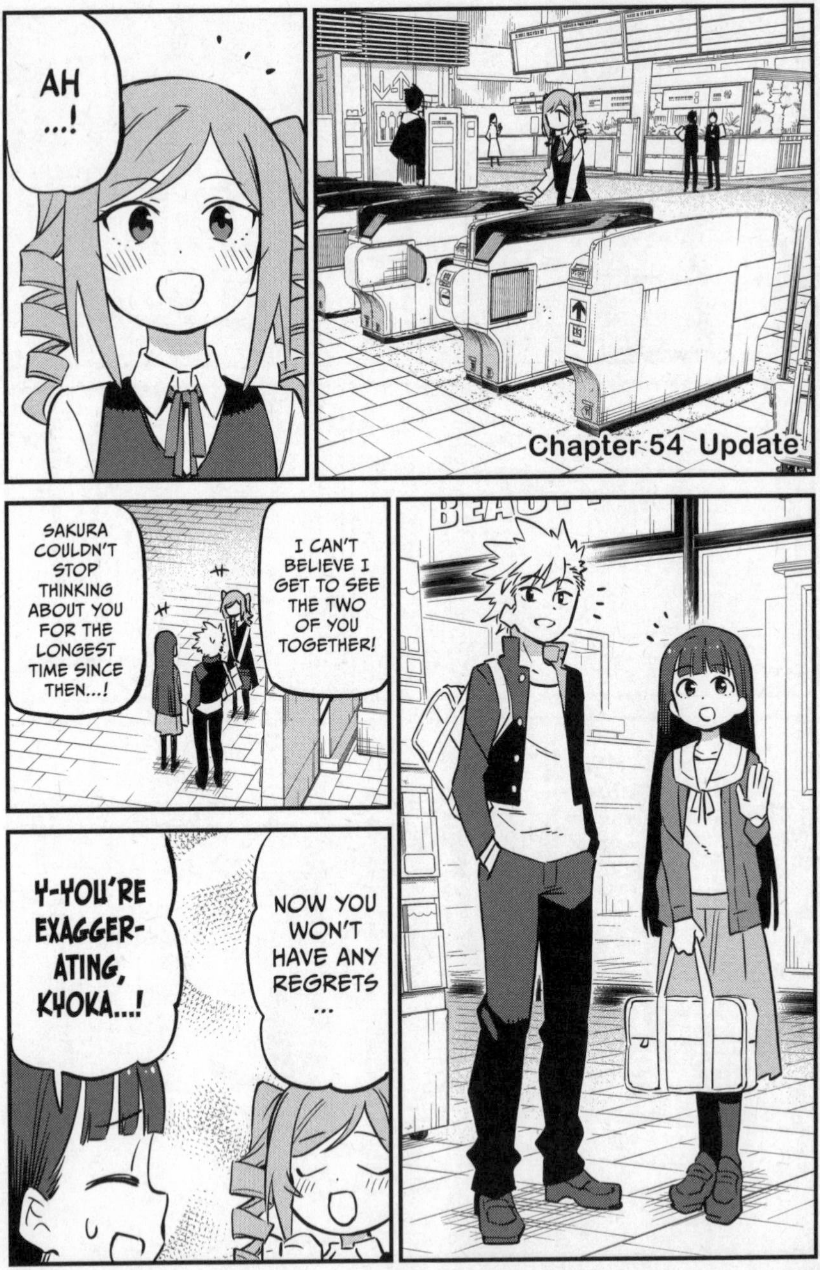
Chapter 54 Update
AH ...!
I CAN'T BELIEVE I GET TO SEE THE TWO OF YOU TOGETHER!
SAKURA COULDN'T STOP THINKING ABOUT YOU FOR THE LONGEST TIME SINCE THEN...!
NOW YOU WON'T HAVE ANY REGRETS ...
Y-YOU'RE EXAGGER-ATING, KYOKA...!

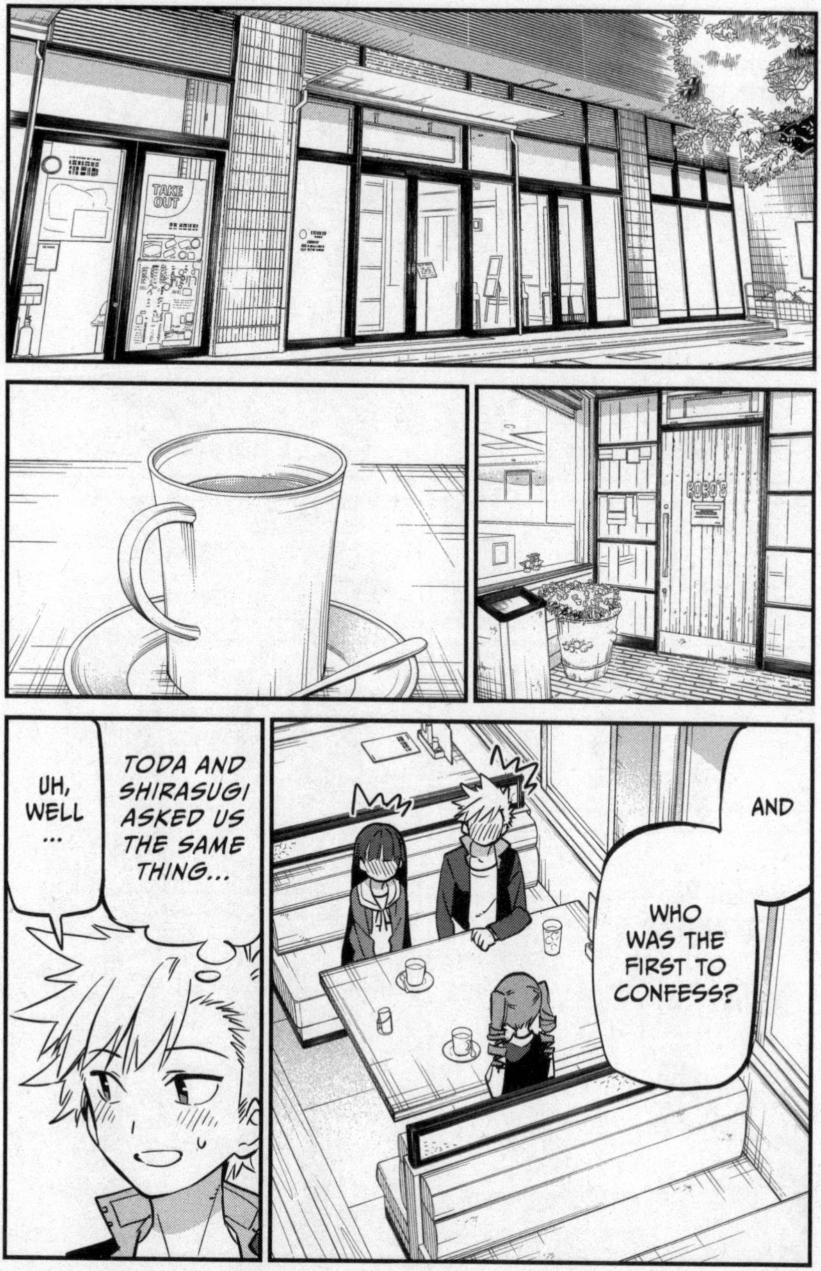
TAKE OUT
AND
WHO WAS THE FIRST TO CONFESS?
TODA AND SHIRASUGI ASKED US THE SAME THING...
UH, WELL ...

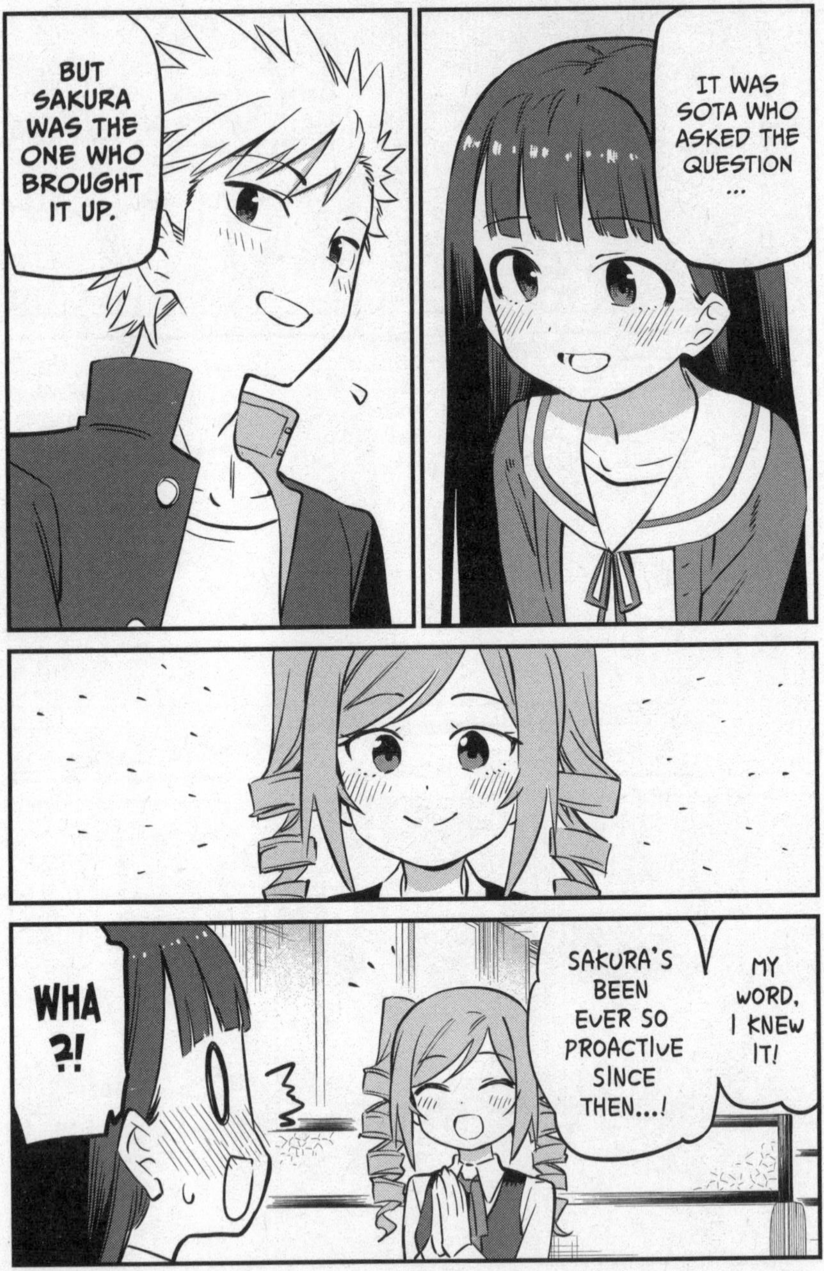
IT WAS SOTA WHO ASKED THE QUESTION ...
BUT SAKURA WAS THE ONE WHO BROUGHT IT UP.
MY WORD, I KNEW IT!
SAKURA'S BEEN EVER SO PROACTIVE SINCE THEN...!
WHA ?!

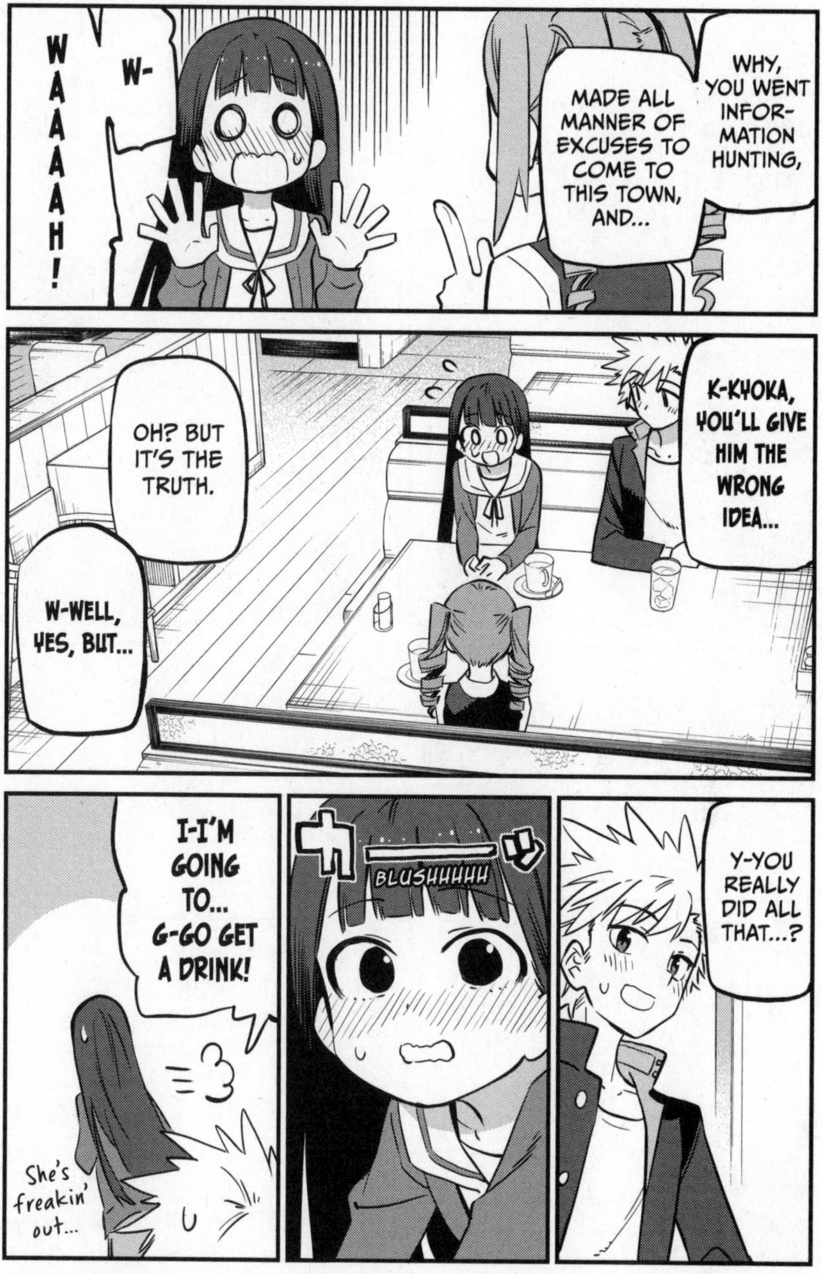
WHY, YOU WENT INFORMATION HUNTING,
MADE ALL MANNER OF EXCUSES TO COME TO THIS TOWN, AND...
W-
WAAAAH!
K-KYOKA, YOU'LL GIVE HIM THE WRONG IDEA...
OH? BUT IT'S THE TRUTH.
W-WELL, YES, BUT...
Y-YOU REALLY DID ALL THAT...?
BLUSHHHHH
I-I'M GOING TO... G-GO GET A DRINK!
She's freakin' out...

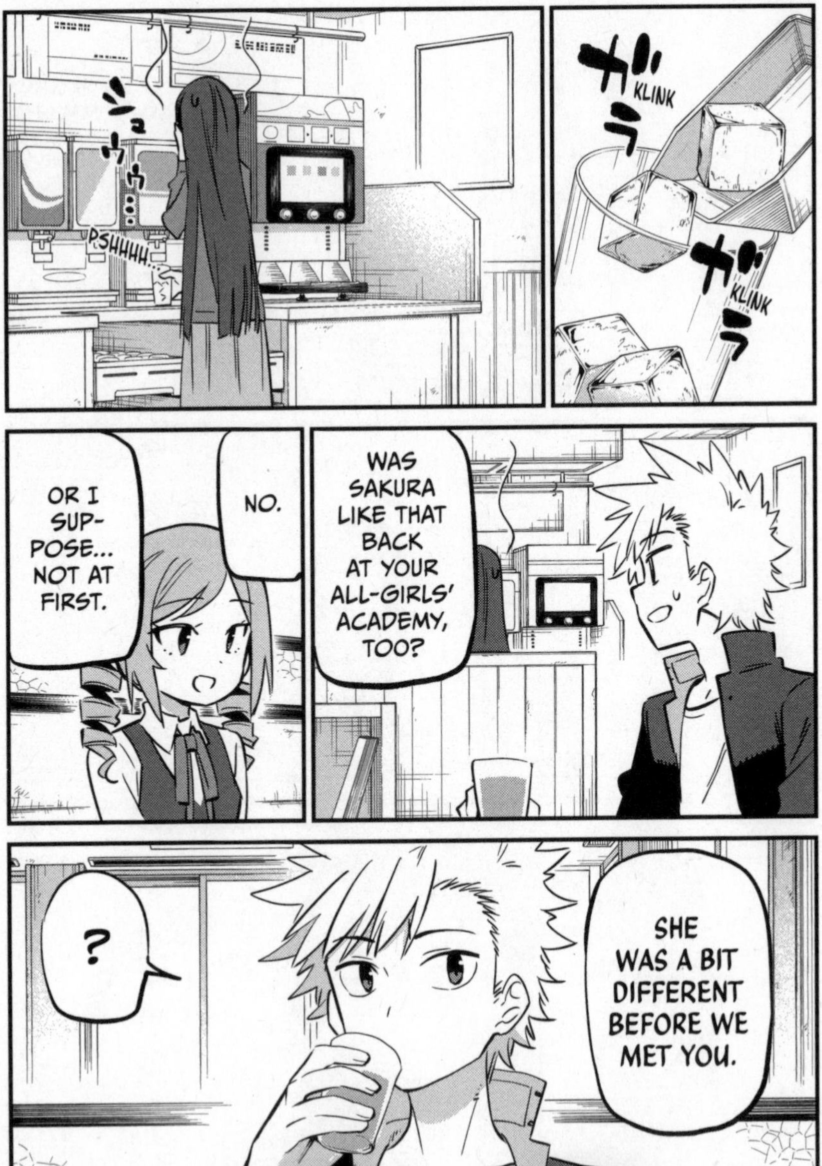
ガラ
KLINK
ガラ
KLINK
シュウウ
PSHHHH...
WAS SAKURA LIKE THAT BACK AT YOUR ALL-GIRLS' ACADEMY, TOO?
NO.
OR I SUPPOSE... NOT AT FIRST.
SHE WAS A BIT DIFFERENT BEFORE WE MET YOU.
?

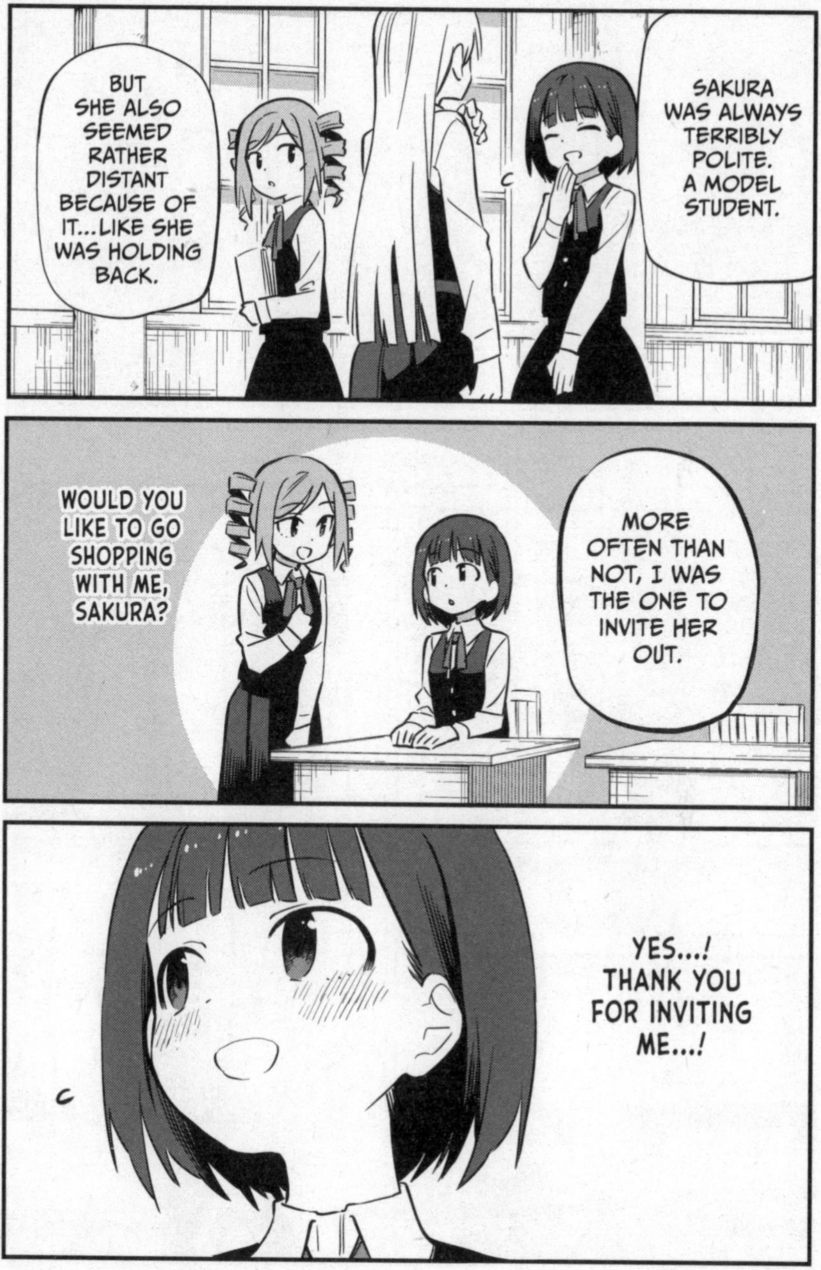
SAKURA WAS ALWAYS TERRIBLY POLITE. A MODEL STUDENT.
BUT SHE ALSO SEEMED RATHER DISTANT BECAUSE OF IT...LIKE SHE WAS HOLDING BACK.
MORE OFTEN THAN NOT, I WAS THE ONE TO INVITE HER OUT.
WOULD YOU LIKE TO GO SHOPPING WITH ME, SAKURA?
YES...! THANK YOU FOR INVITING ME...!

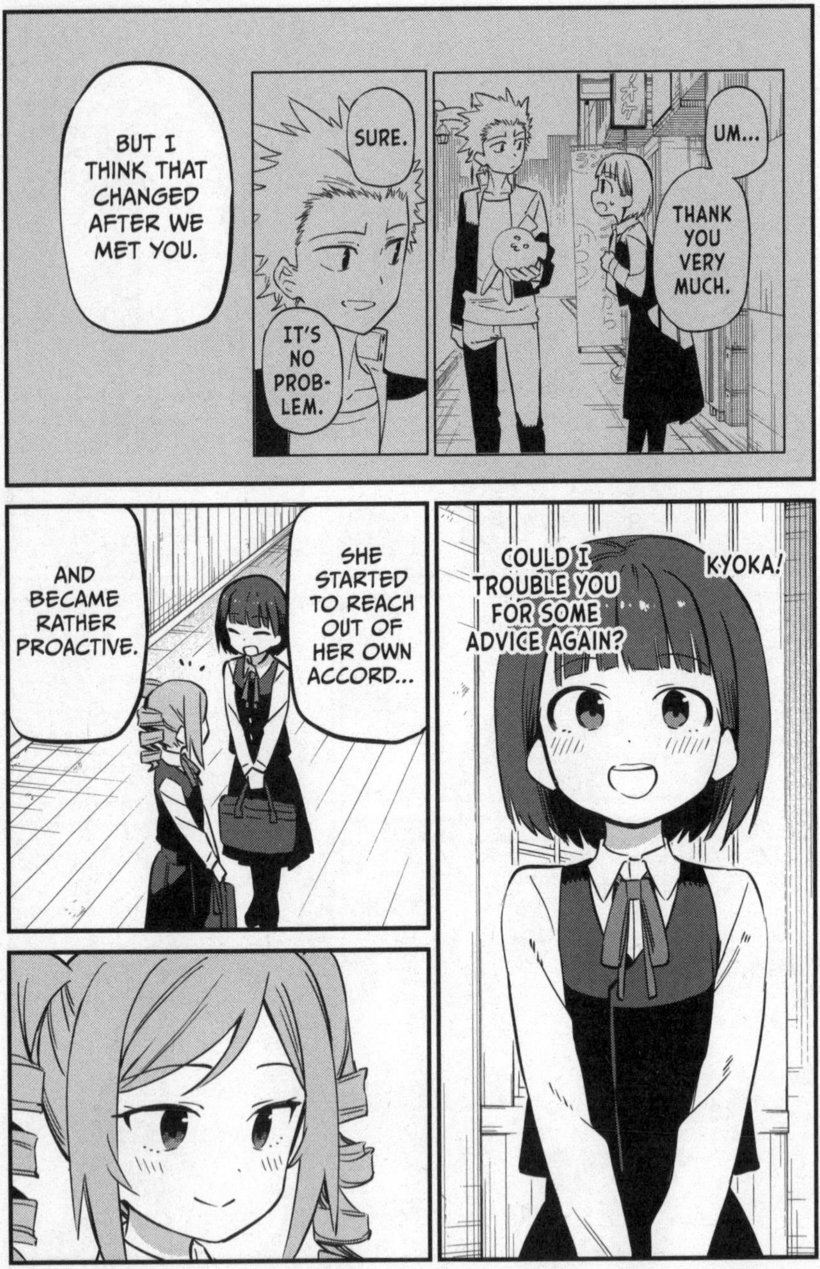
UM...
THANK YOU VERY MUCH.
SURE.
IT'S NO PROB-LEM.
BUT I THINK THAT CHANGED AFTER WE MET YOU.
KYOKA!
COULD I TROUBLE YOU FOR SOME ADVICE AGAIN?
SHE STARTED TO REACH OUT OF HER OWN ACCORD...
AND BECAME RATHER PROACTIVE.

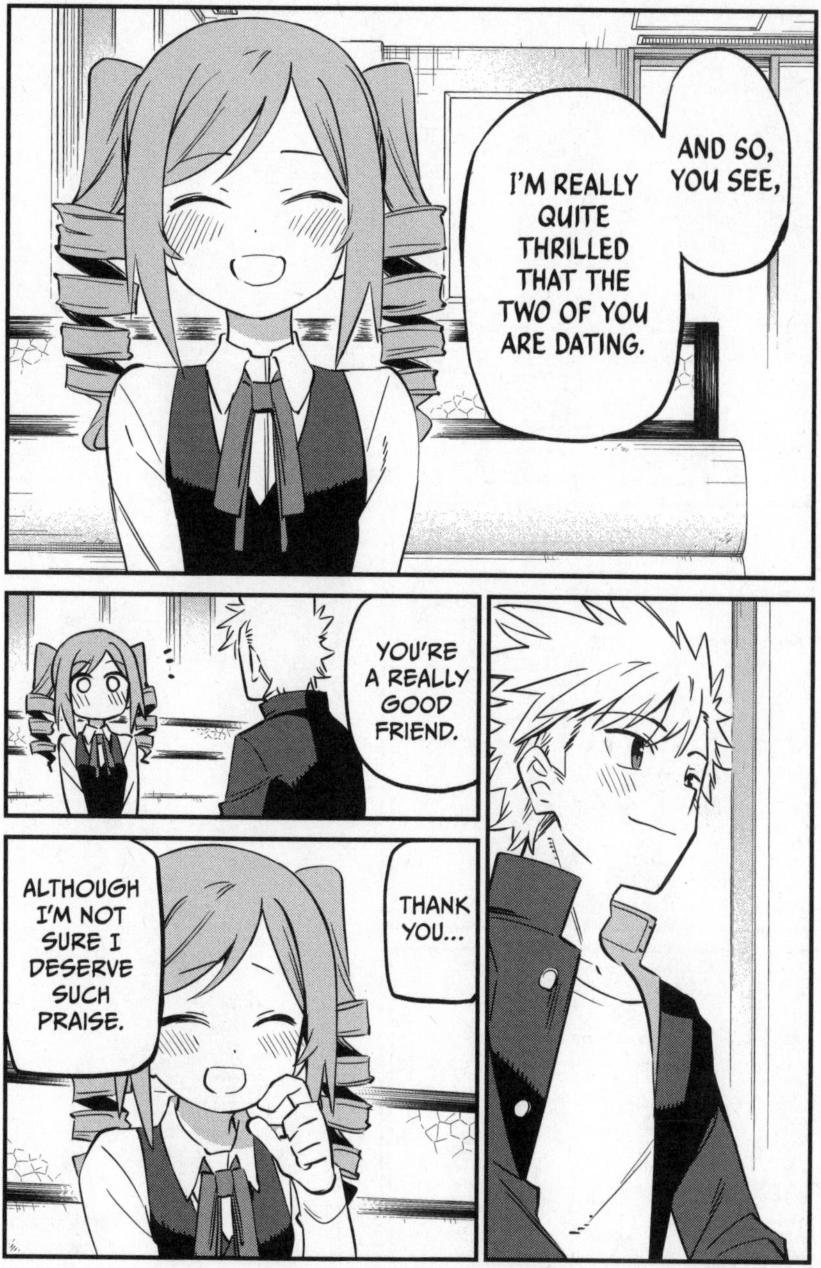
AND SO, YOU SEE,
I'M REALLY QUITE THRILLED THAT THE TWO OF YOU ARE DATING.
YOU'RE A REALLY GOOD FRIEND.
THANK YOU...
ALTHOUGH I'M NOT SURE I DESERVE SUCH PRAISE.

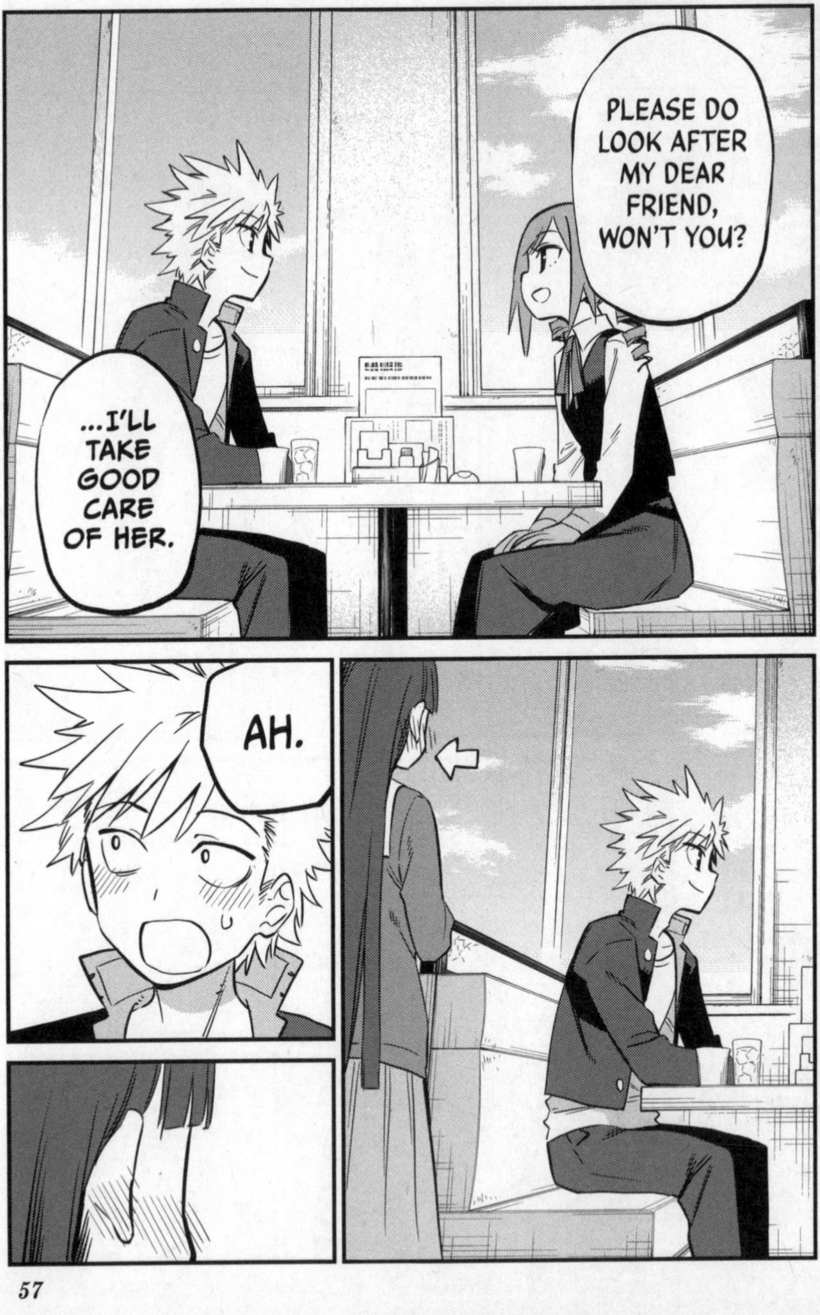
PLEASE DO LOOK AFTER MY DEAR FRIEND, WON'T YOU?
...I'LL TAKE GOOD CARE OF HER.
AH.

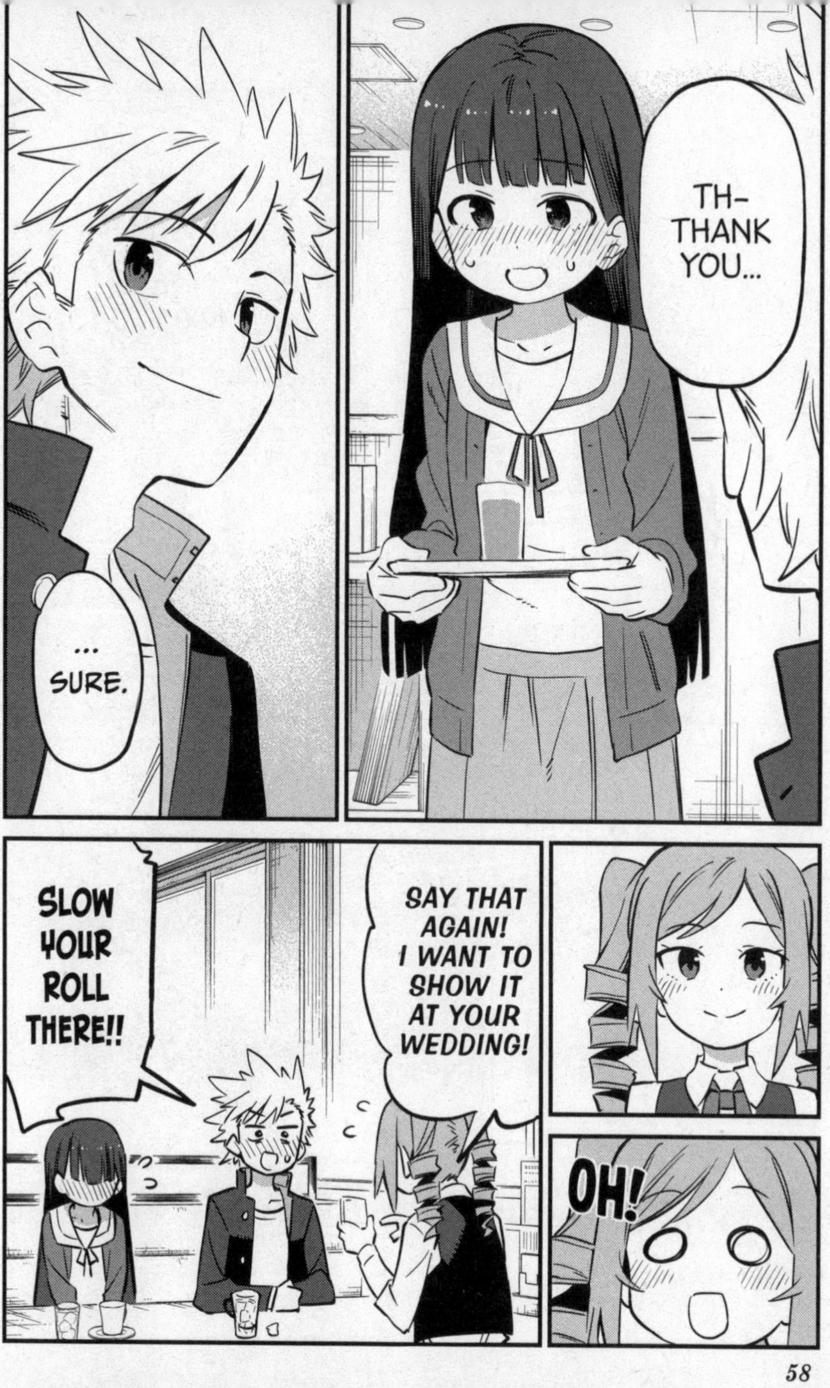
TH-THANK YOU...
... SURE.
OH!
SAY THAT AGAIN! I WANT TO SHOW IT AT YOUR WEDDING!
SLOW YOUR ROLL THERE!!

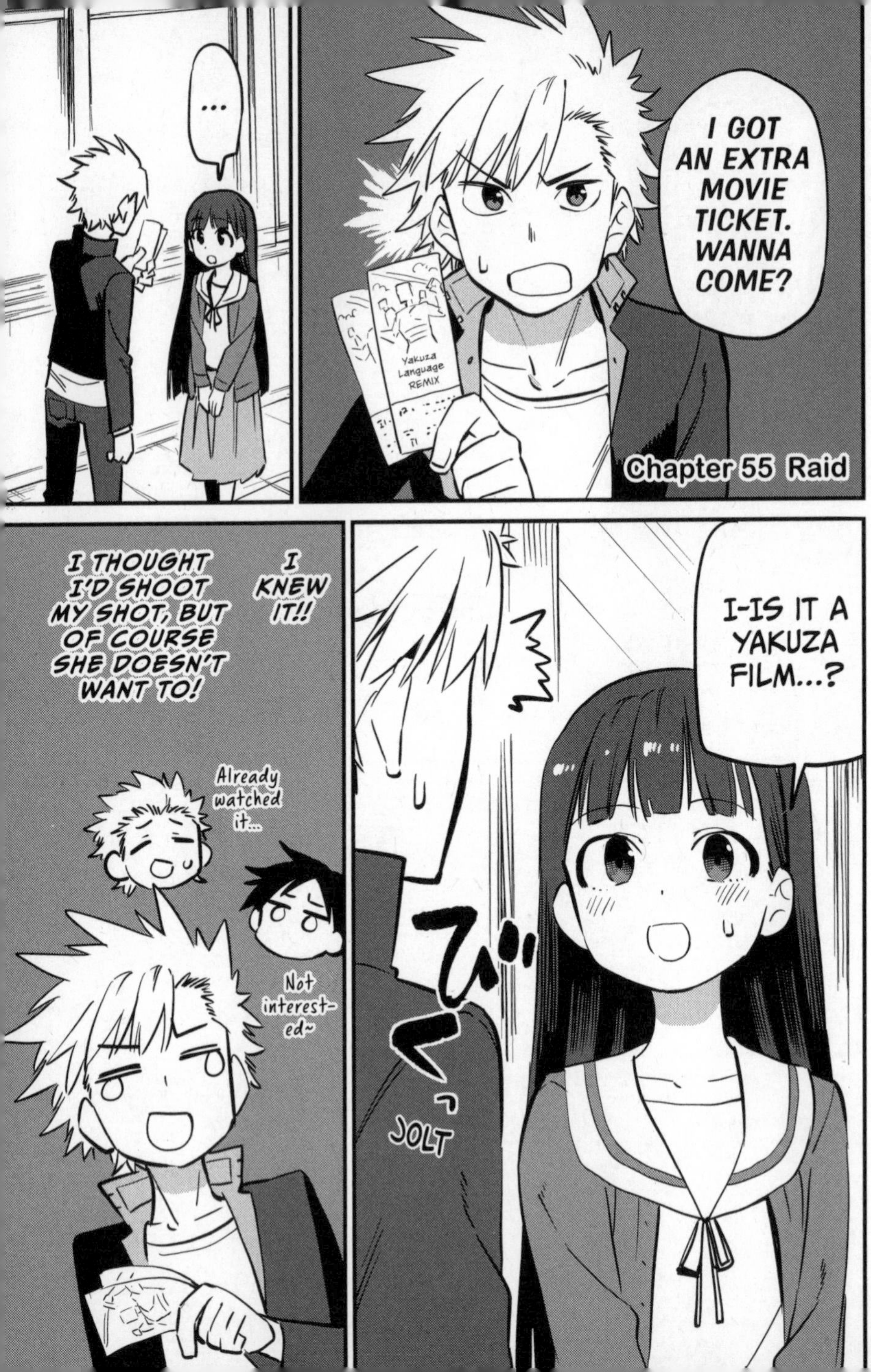
I GOT AN EXTRA MOVIE TICKET. WANNA COME?
Yakuza Language REMIX
Chapter 55 Raid
...
I-IS IT A YAKUZA FILM...?
JOLT
I KNEW IT!!
I THOUGHT I'D SHOOT MY SHOT, BUT OF COURSE SHE DOESN'T WANT TO!
Already watched it...
Not interest-ed~

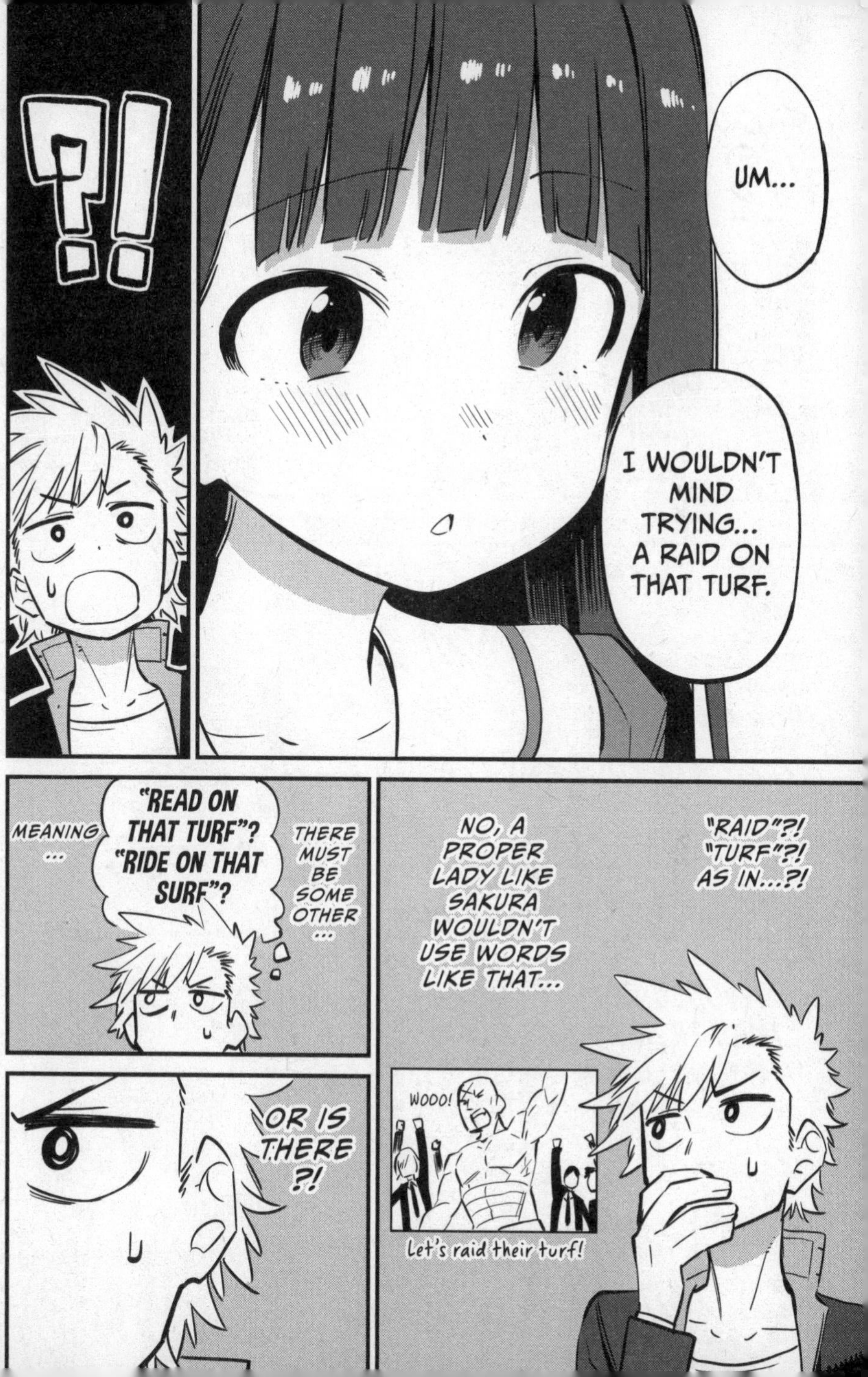
UM...
I WOULDN'T MIND TRYING... A RAID ON THAT TURF.
?!
"RAID"?! "TURF"?! AS IN...?!
NO, A PROPER LADY LIKE SAKURA WOULDN'T USE WORDS LIKE THAT...
THERE MUST BE SOME OTHER ...
MEANING ...
"READ ON THAT TURF"? "RIDE ON THAT SURF"?
WOOO!
Let's raid their turf!
OR IS THERE ?!

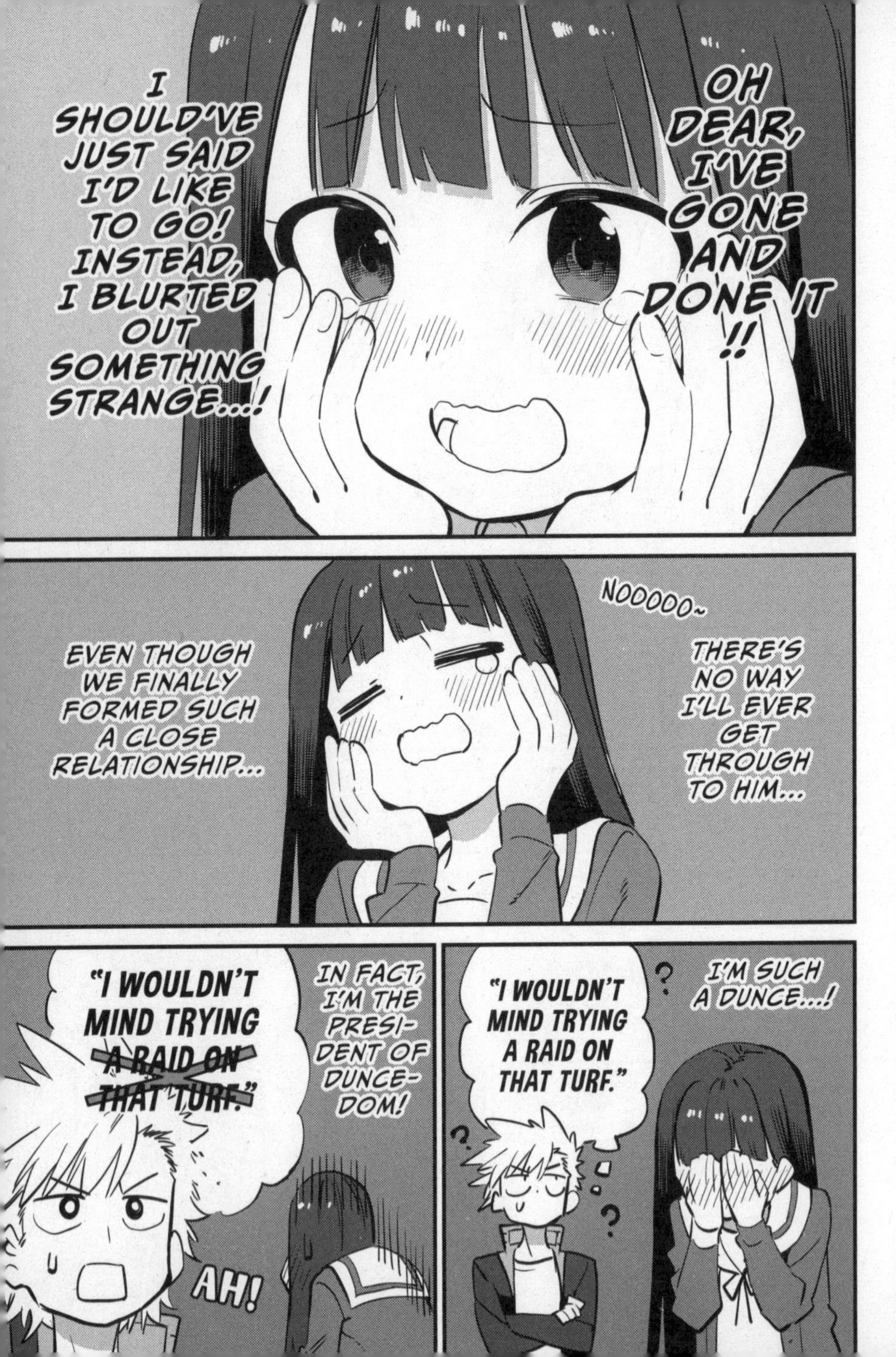
OH DEAR, I'VE GONE AND DONE IT!!
I SHOULD'VE JUST SAID I'D LIKE TO GO! INSTEAD, I BLURTED OUT SOMETHING STRANGE...!
NOOOOO~
THERE'S NO WAY I'LL EVER GET THROUGH TO HIM...
EVEN THOUGH WE FINALLY FORMED SUCH A CLOSE RELATIONSHIP...
I'M SUCH A DUNCE...!
"I WOULDN'T MIND TRYING A RAID ON THAT TURF."
IN FACT, I'M THE PRESI-DENT OF DUNCE-DOM!
"I WOULDN'T MIND TRYING A RAID ON THAT TURF."
AH!

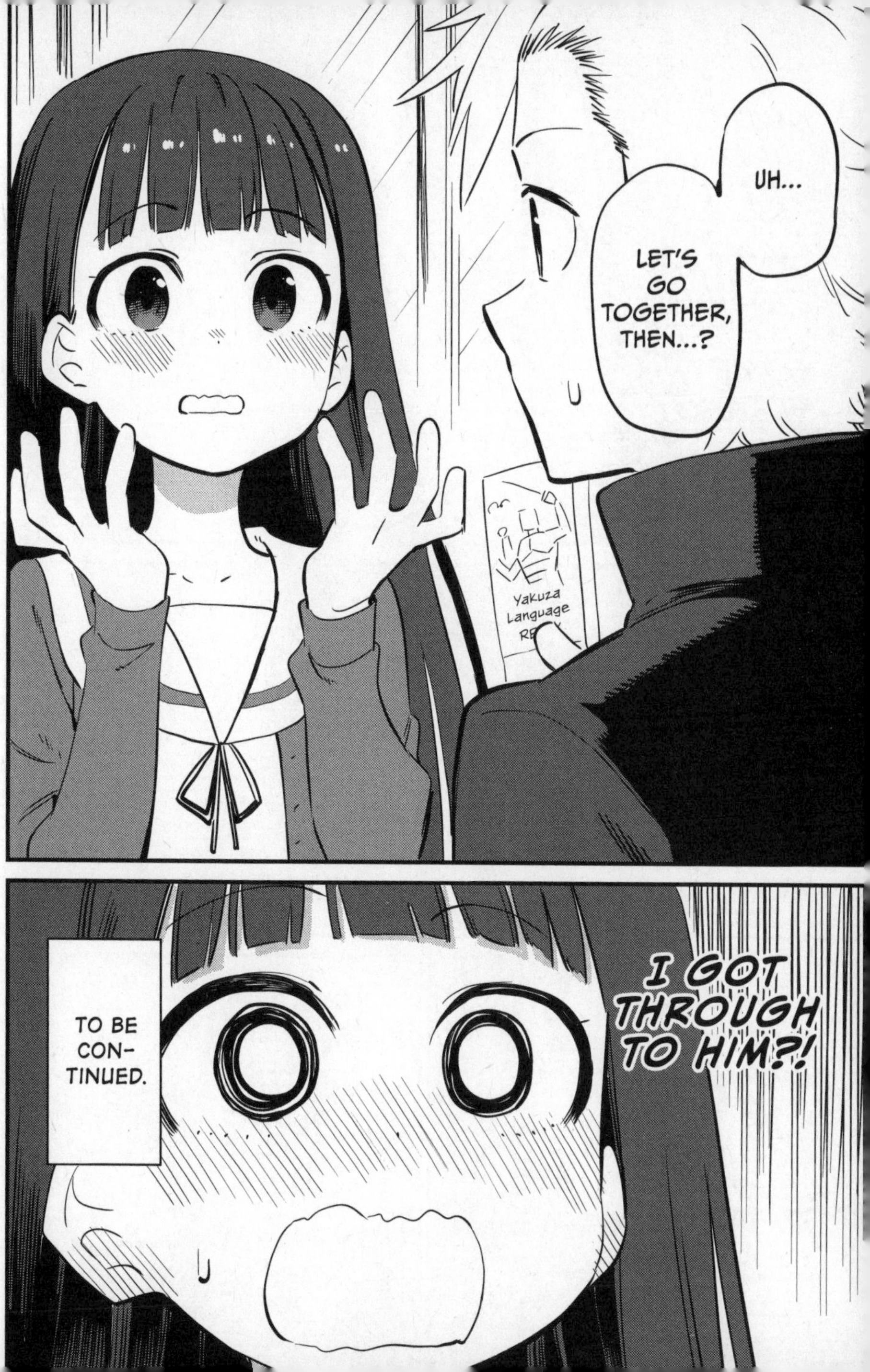
UH...
LET'S GO TOGETHER, THEN...?
Yakuza Language
I GOT THROUGH TO HIM?!
TO BE CON-TINUED.

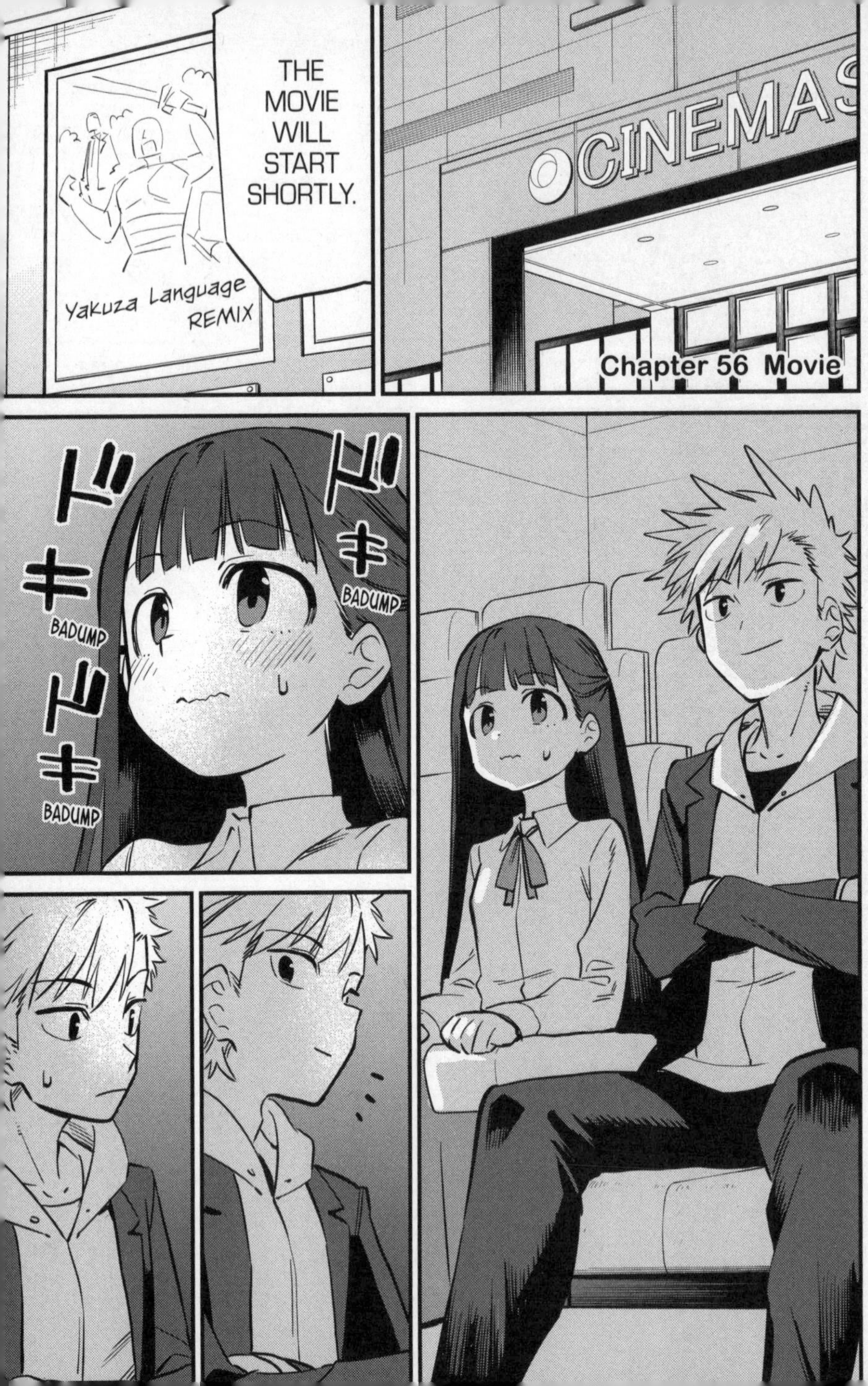
CINEMAS
Chapter 56 Movie
THE MOVIE WILL START SHORTLY.
Yakuza Language REMIX
ドキ
BADUMP
ドキ
BADUMP
ドキ
BADUMP

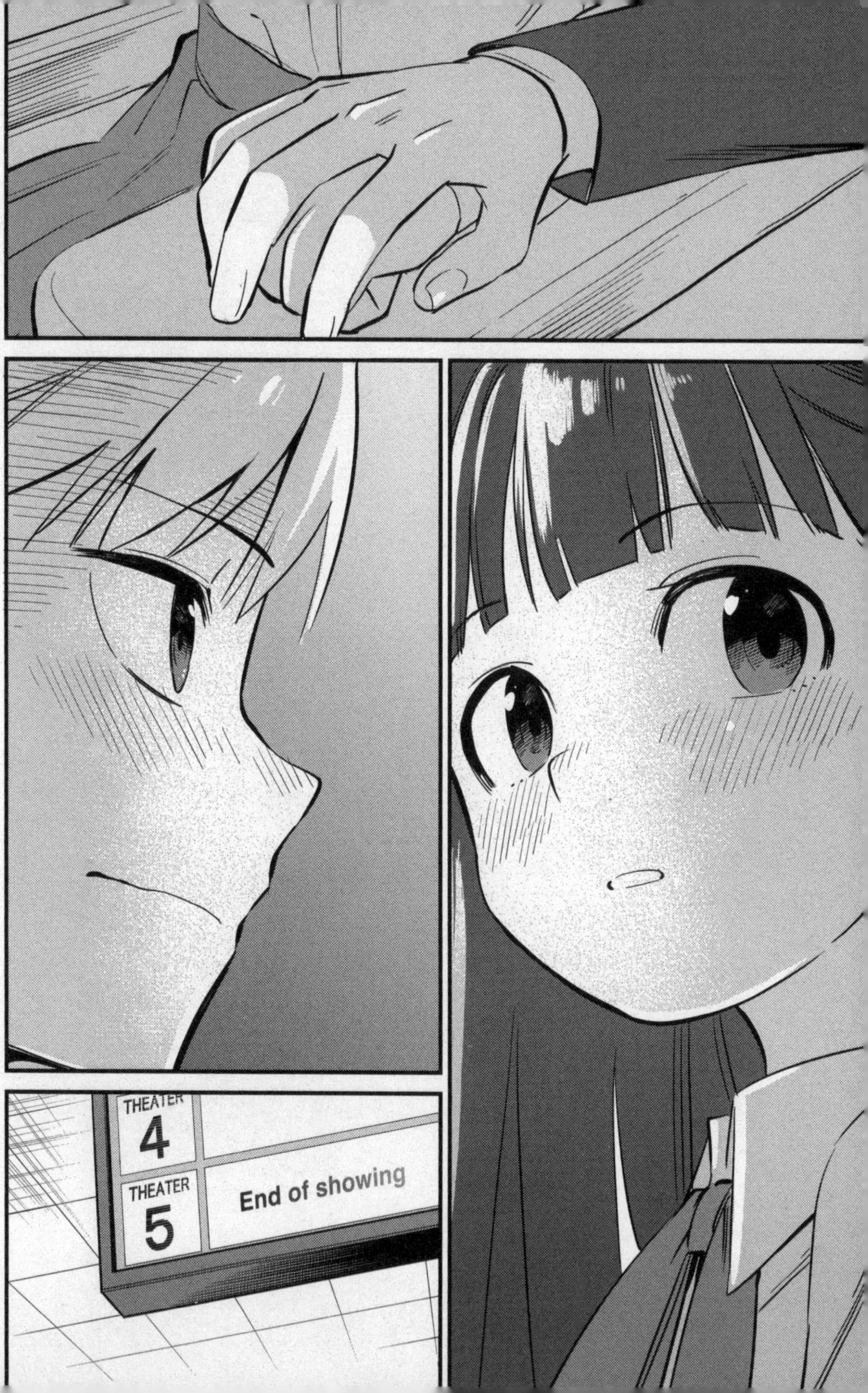
THEATER
4
THEATER
5
End of showing

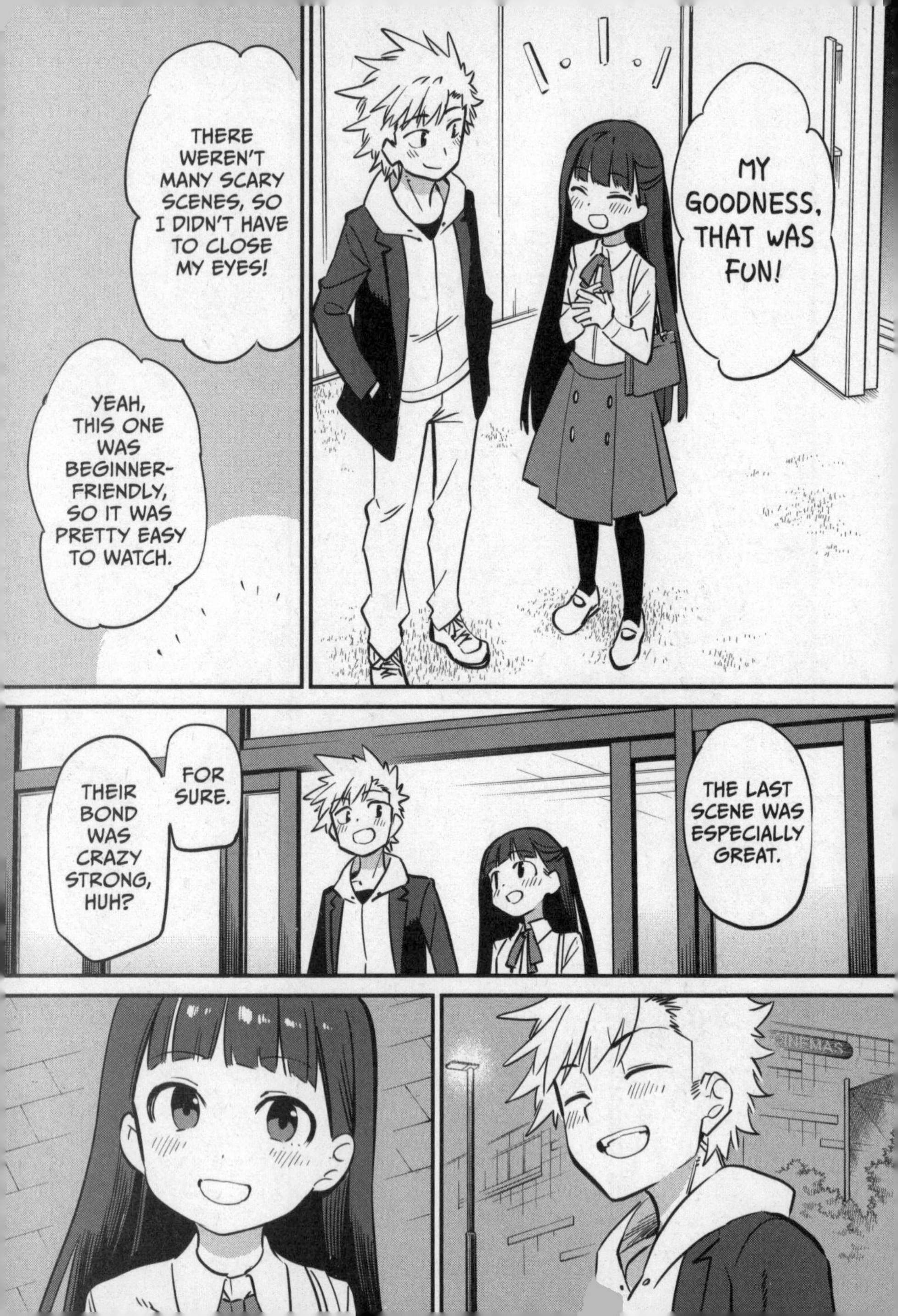
MY GOODNESS, THAT WAS FUN!
THERE WEREN'T MANY SCARY SCENES, SO I DIDN'T HAVE TO CLOSE MY EYES!
YEAH, THIS ONE WAS BEGINNER-FRIENDLY, SO IT WAS PRETTY EASY TO WATCH.
THE LAST SCENE WAS ESPECIALLY GREAT.
FOR SURE.
THEIR BOND WAS CRAZY STRONG, HUH?

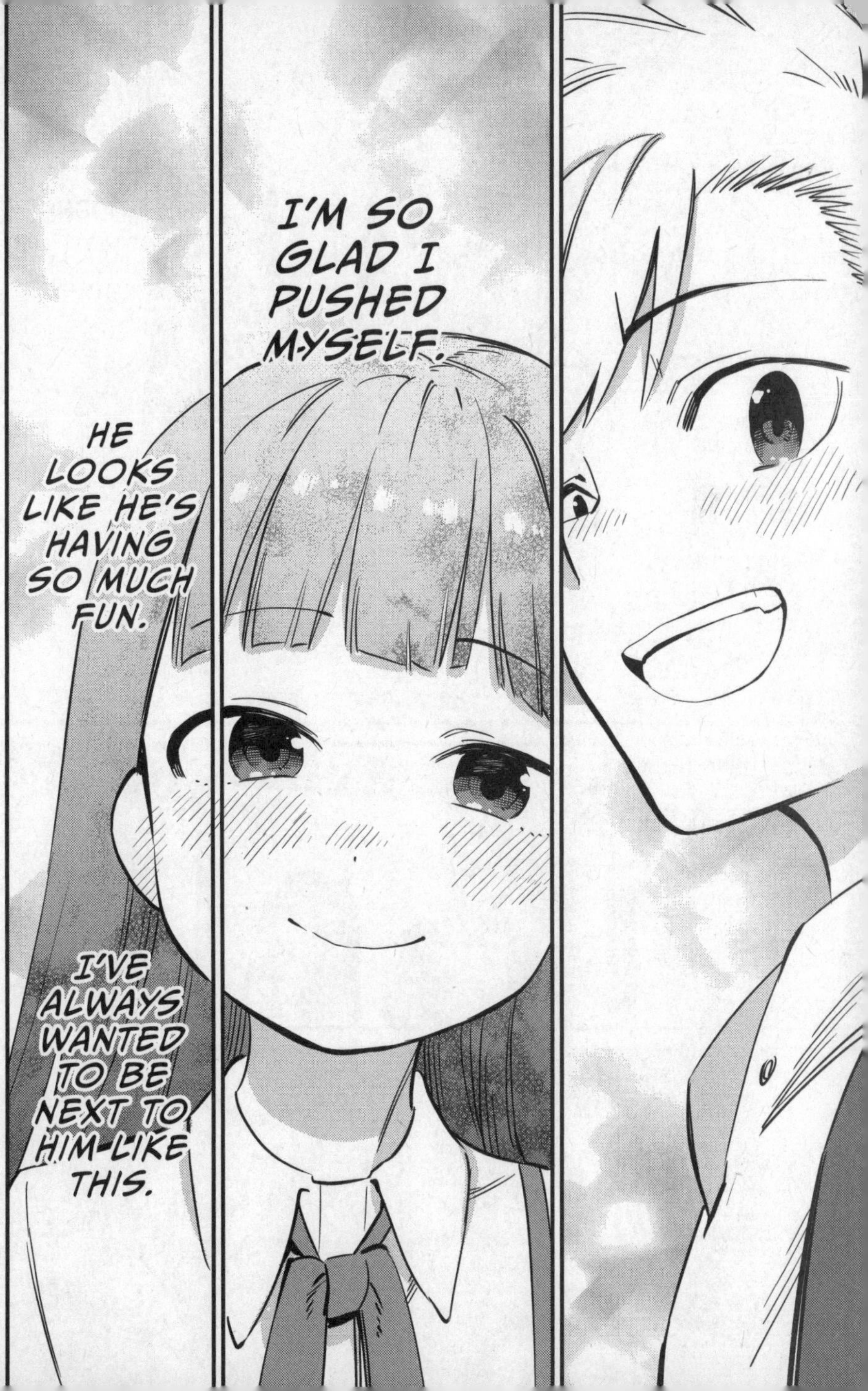
I'M SO GLAD I PUSHED MYSELF.
HE LOOKS LIKE HE'S HAVING SO MUCH FUN.
I'VE ALWAYS WANTED TO BE NEXT TO HIM LIKE THIS.

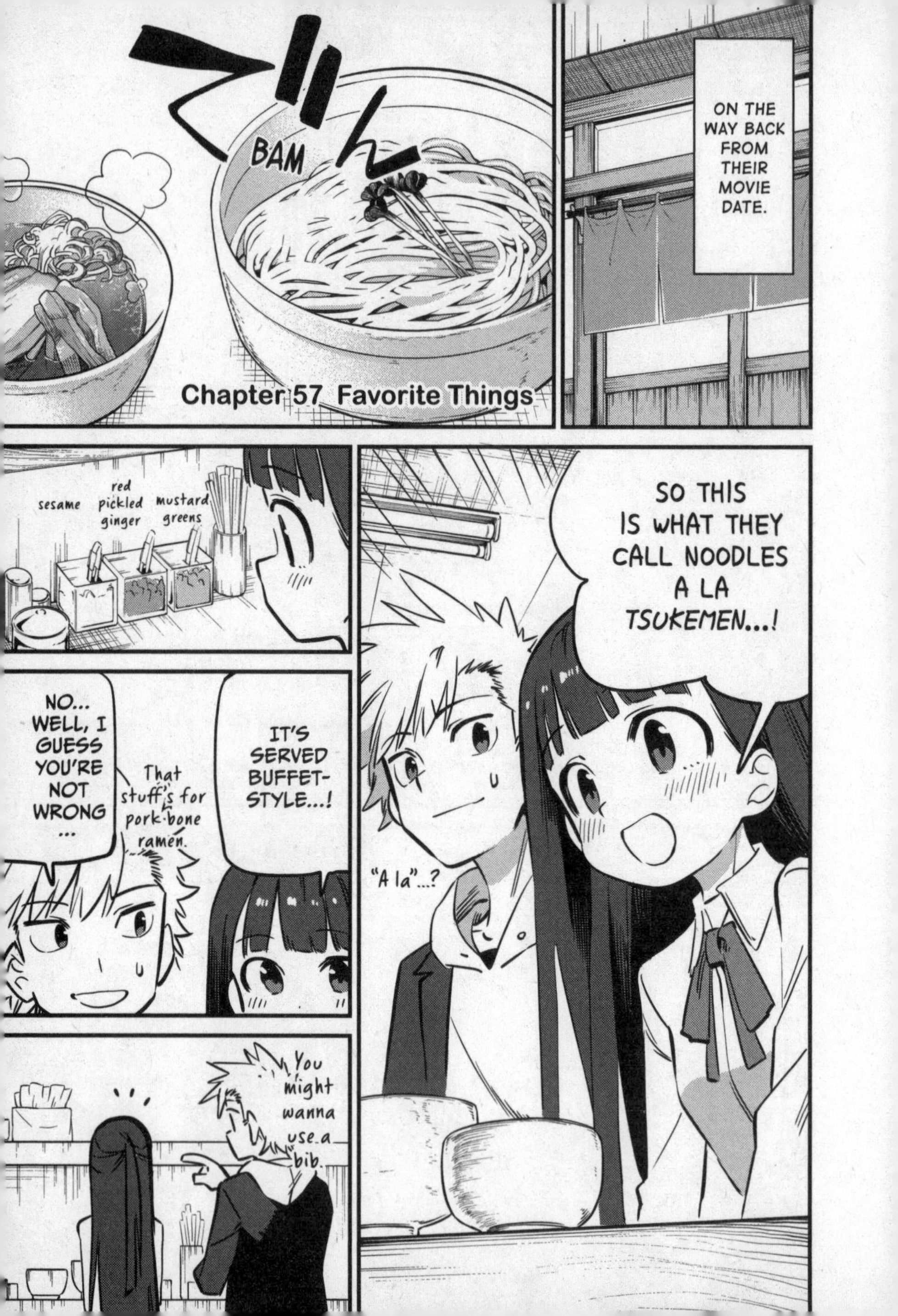
ON THE WAY BACK FROM THEIR MOVIE DATE.
BAM
Chapter 57 Favorite Things
SO THIS IS WHAT THEY CALL NOODLES A LA TSUKEMEN...!
"A la"...?
mustard greens
red pickled ginger
sesame
IT'S SERVED BUFFET-STYLE...!
NO... WELL, I GUESS YOU'RE NOT WRONG...
That stuff's for pork-bone ramen.
You might wanna use a bib.

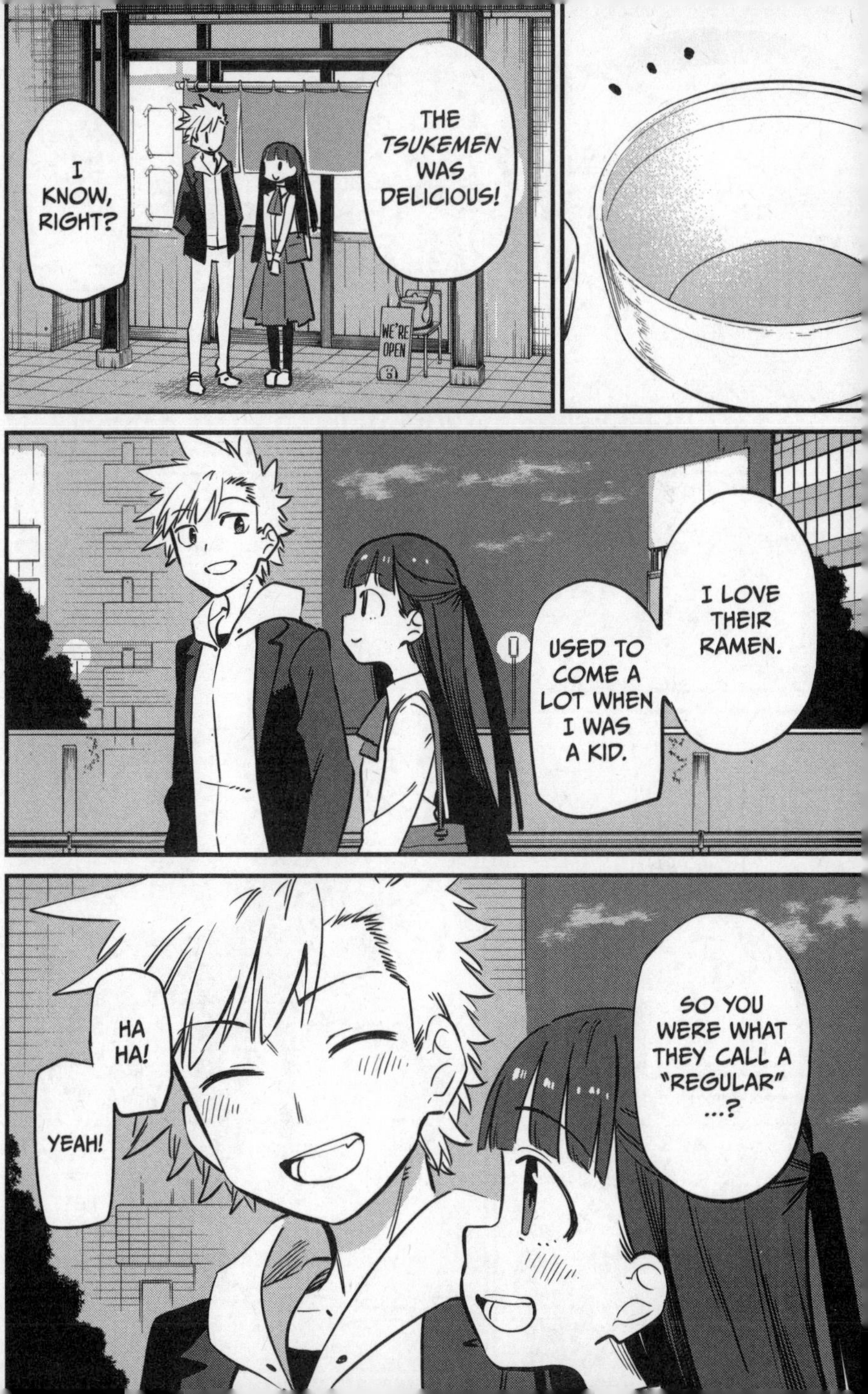
THE TSUKEMEN WAS DELICIOUS!
I KNOW, RIGHT?
WE'RE OPEN
I LOVE THEIR RAMEN.
USED TO COME A LOT WHEN I WAS A KID.
SO YOU WERE WHAT THEY CALL A "REGULAR" ...?
HA HA!
YEAH!

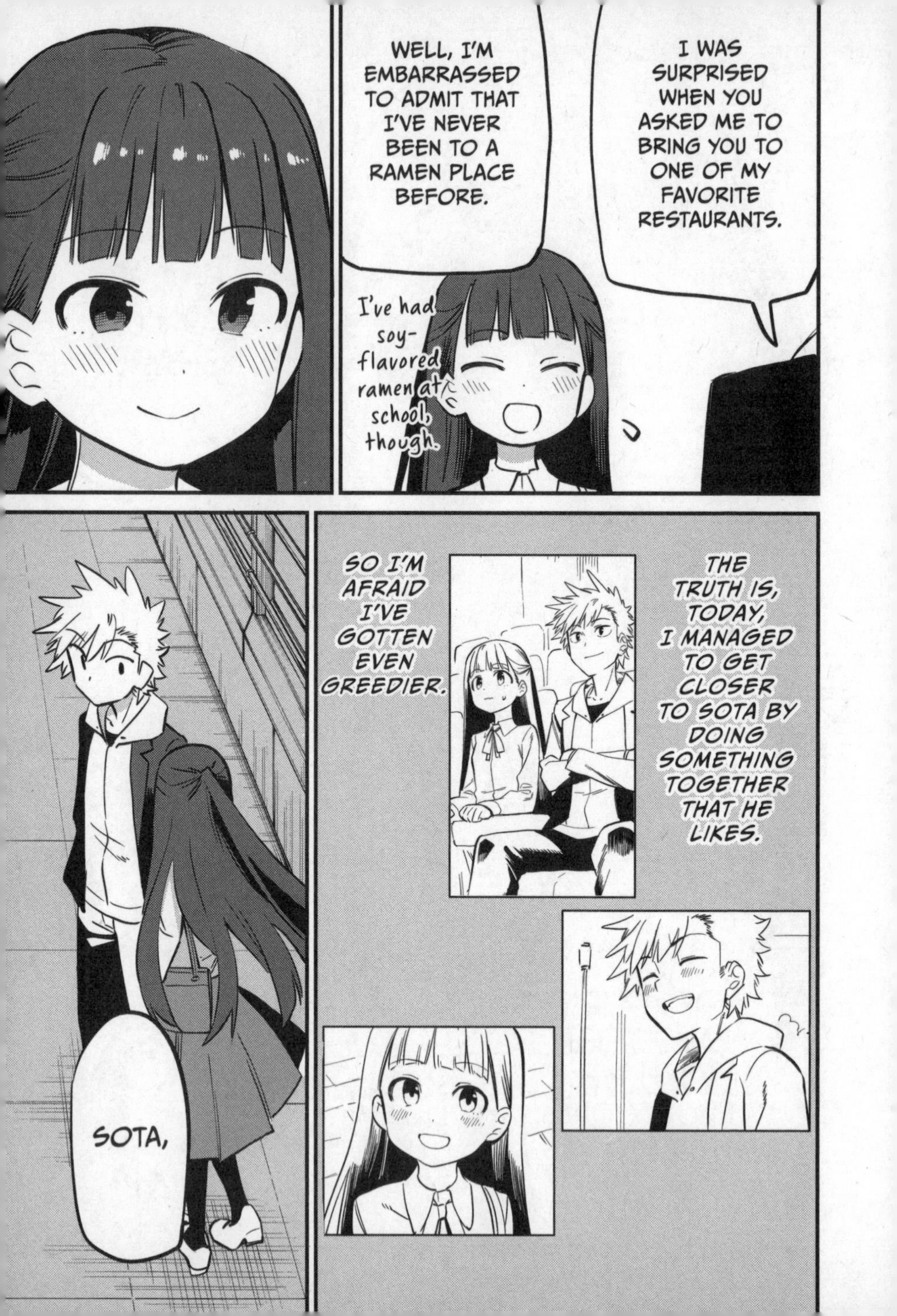
I WAS SURPRISED WHEN YOU ASKED ME TO BRING YOU TO ONE OF MY FAVORITE RESTAURANTS.
WELL, I'M EMBARRASSED TO ADMIT THAT I'VE NEVER BEEN TO A RAMEN PLACE BEFORE.
I've had soy-flavored ramen at school, though.
THE TRUTH IS, TODAY, I MANAGED TO GET CLOSER TO SOTA BY DOING SOMETHING TOGETHER THAT HE LIKES.
SO I'M AFRAID I'VE GOTTEN EVEN GREEDIER.
SOTA,

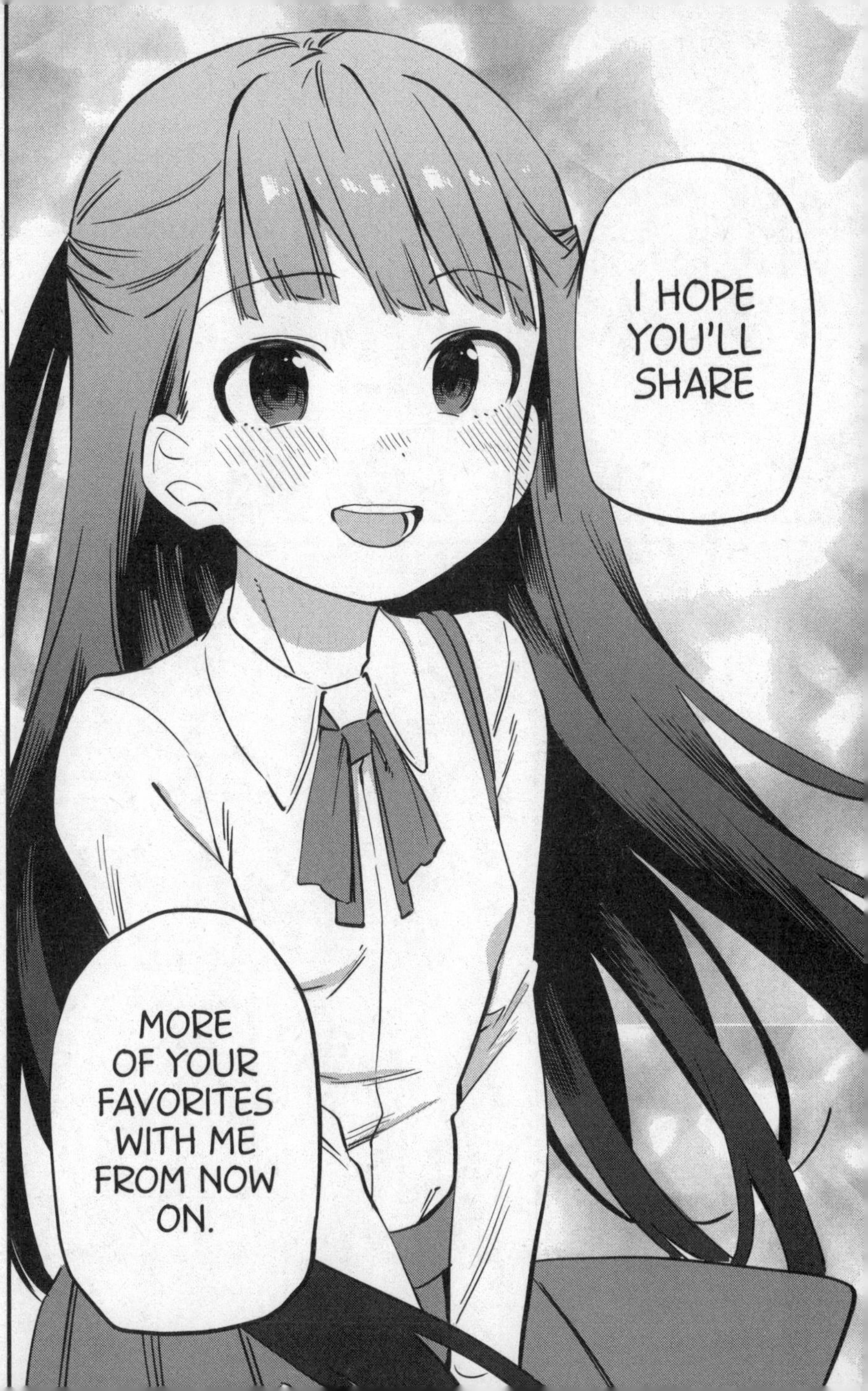
I HOPE YOU'LL SHARE
MORE OF YOUR FAVORITES WITH ME FROM NOW ON.

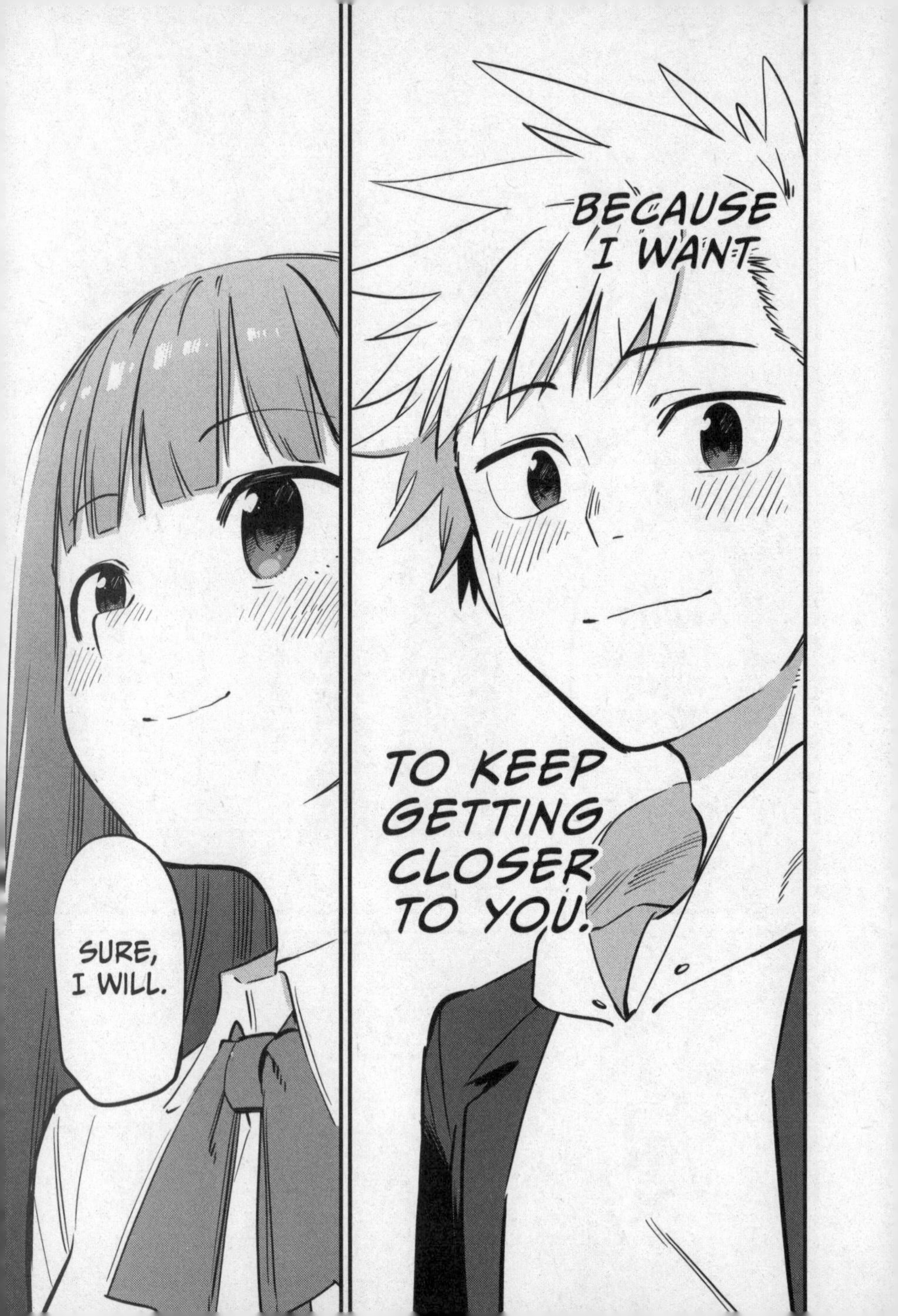
BECAUSE I WANT
TO KEEP GETTING CLOSER TO YOU.
SURE, I WILL.

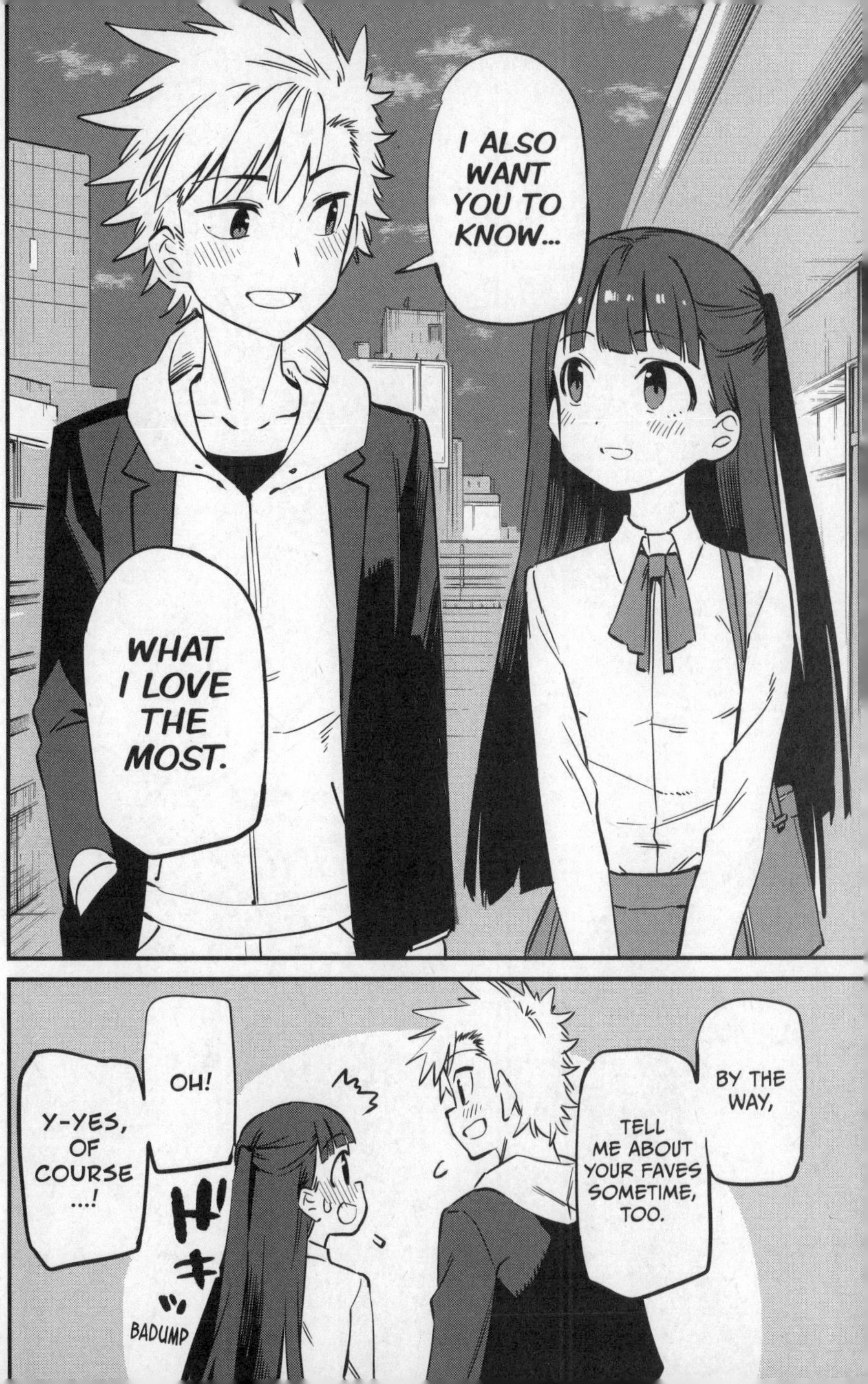
I ALSO WANT YOU TO KNOW...
WHAT I LOVE THE MOST.
BY THE WAY,
TELL ME ABOUT YOUR FAVES SOMETIME, TOO.
OH!
Y-YES, OF COURSE ...!
BADUMP

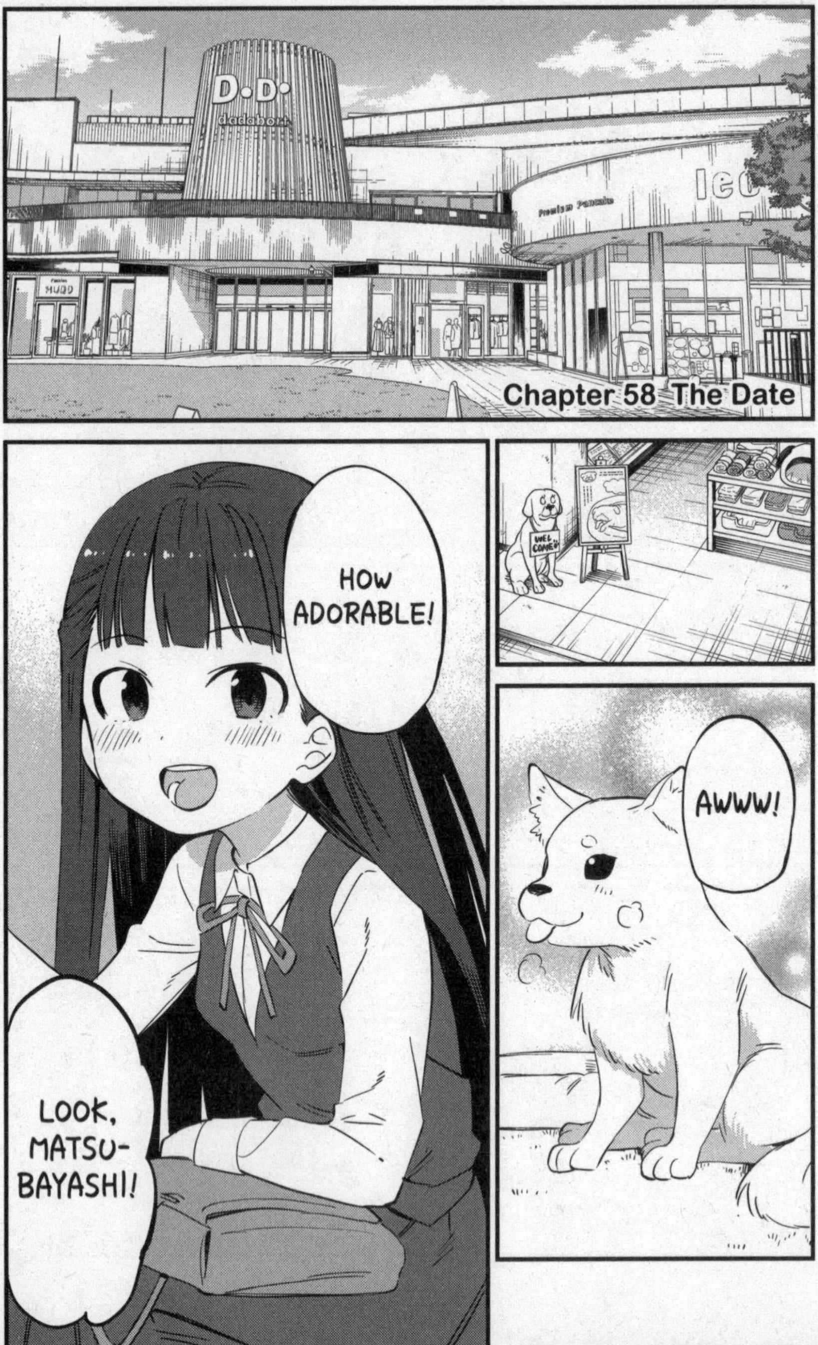
Chapter 58 The Date
AWWW!
HOW ADORABLE!
LOOK, MATSU-BAYASHI!

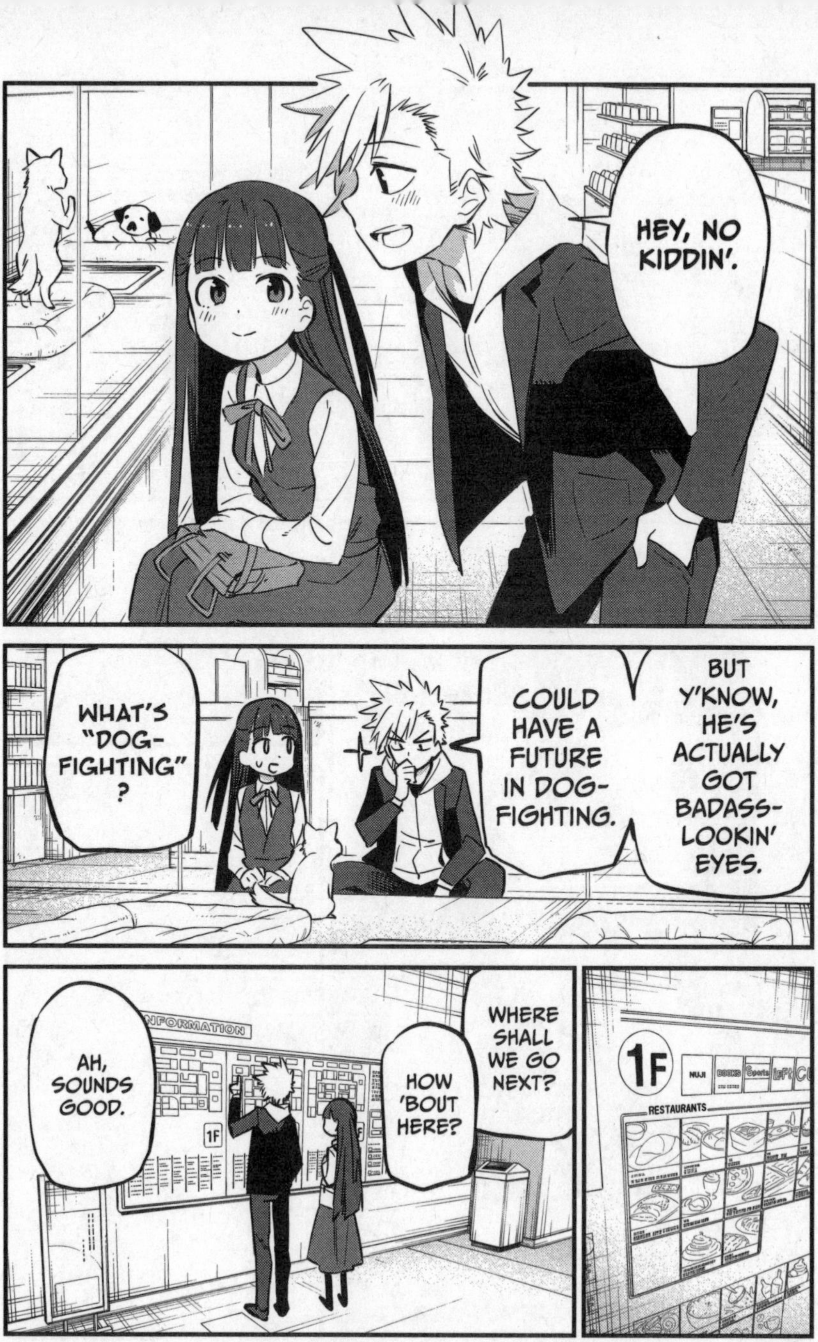
HEY, NO KIDDIN'.
BUT Y'KNOW, HE'S ACTUALLY GOT BADASS-LOOKIN' EYES.
COULD HAVE A FUTURE IN DOG-FIGHTING.
WHAT'S "DOG-FIGHTING"?
1F
NUJI
BOOKS
RESTAURANTS
WHERE SHALL WE GO NEXT?
HOW 'BOUT HERE?
AH, SOUNDS GOOD.
1F

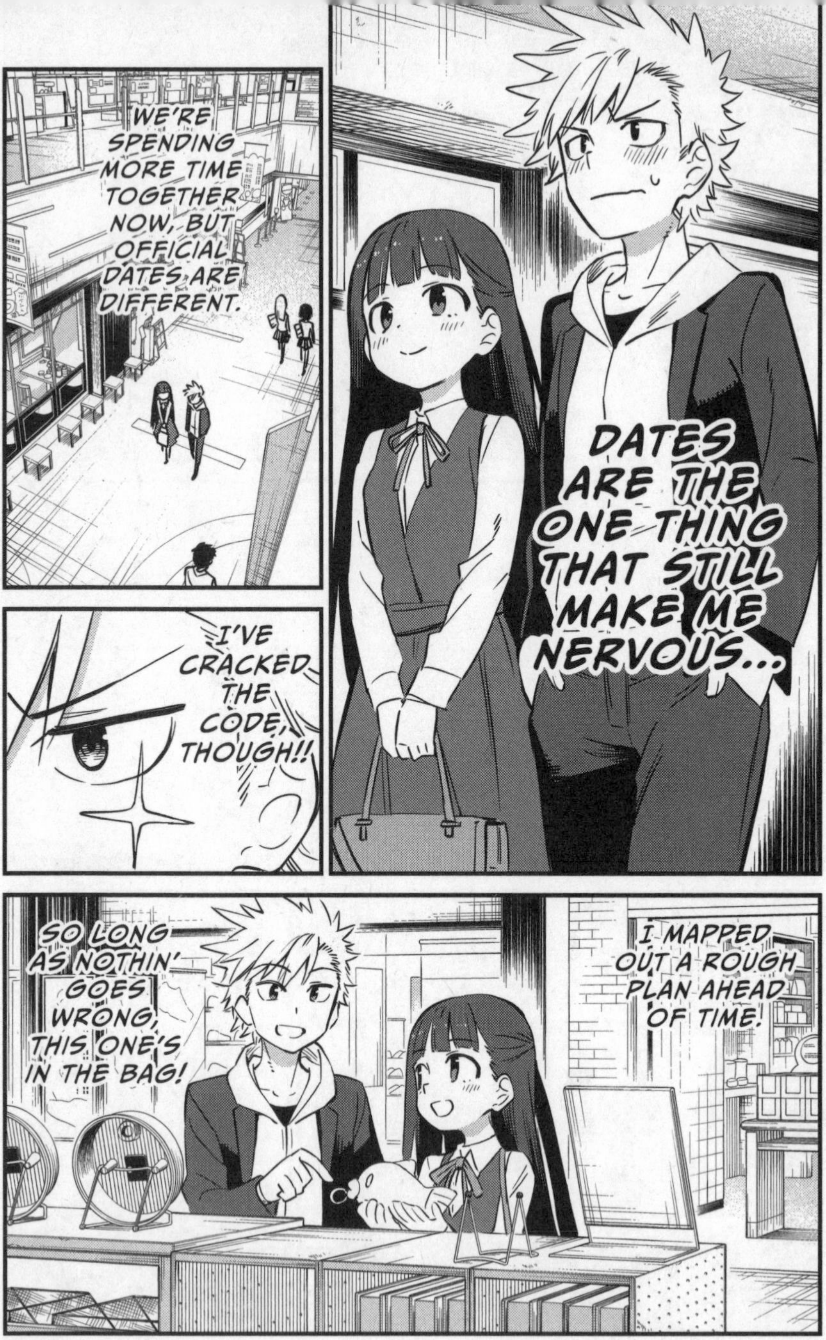
DATES ARE THE ONE THING THAT STILL MAKE ME NERVOUS...
WE'RE SPENDING MORE TIME TOGETHER NOW, BUT OFFICIAL DATES ARE DIFFERENT.
I'VE CRACKED THE CODE, THOUGH!!
I MAPPED OUT A ROUGH PLAN AHEAD OF TIME!
SO LONG AS NOTHIN' GOES WRONG, THIS ONE'S IN THE BAG!

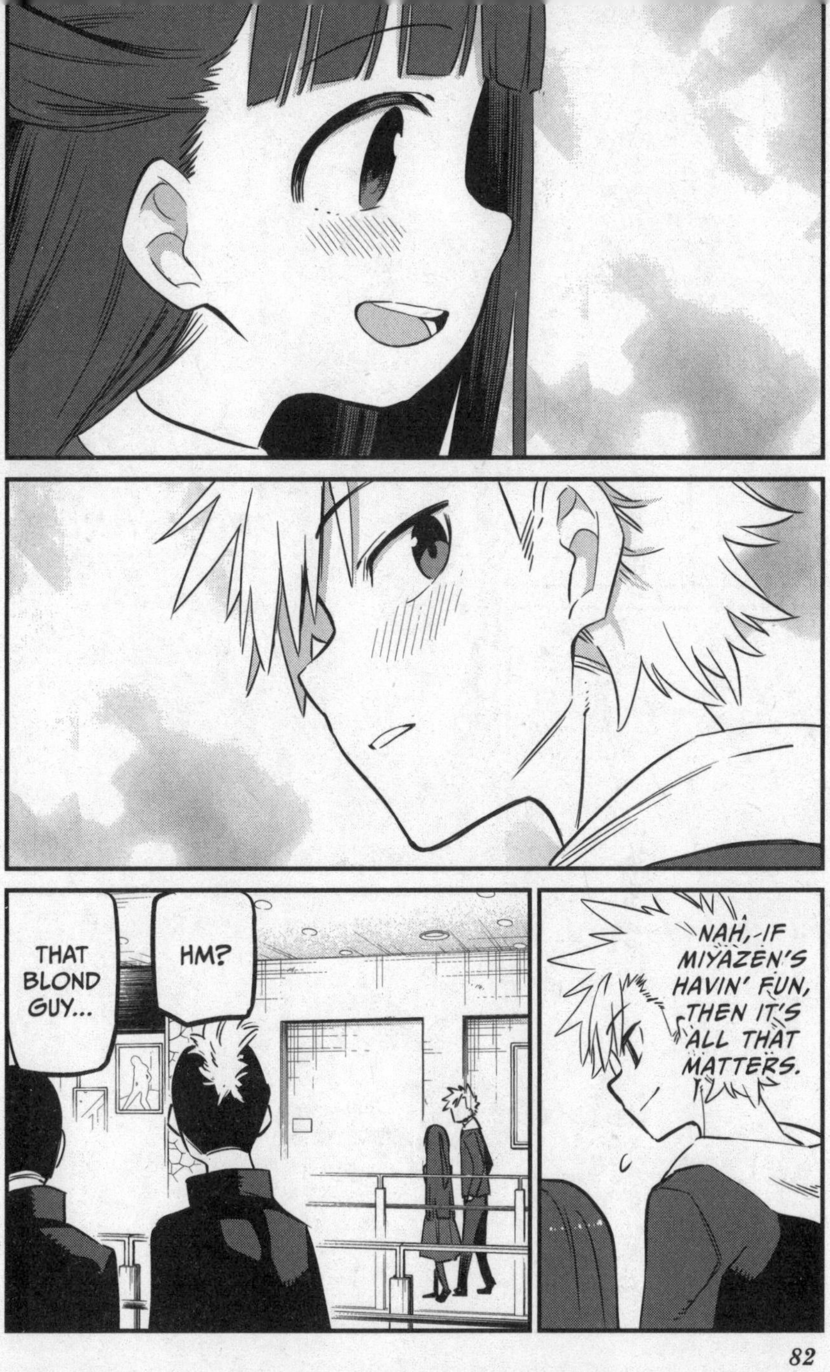
NAH, IF MIYAZEN'S HAVIN' FUN, THEN IT'S ALL THAT MATTERS.
HM?
THAT BLOND GUY...

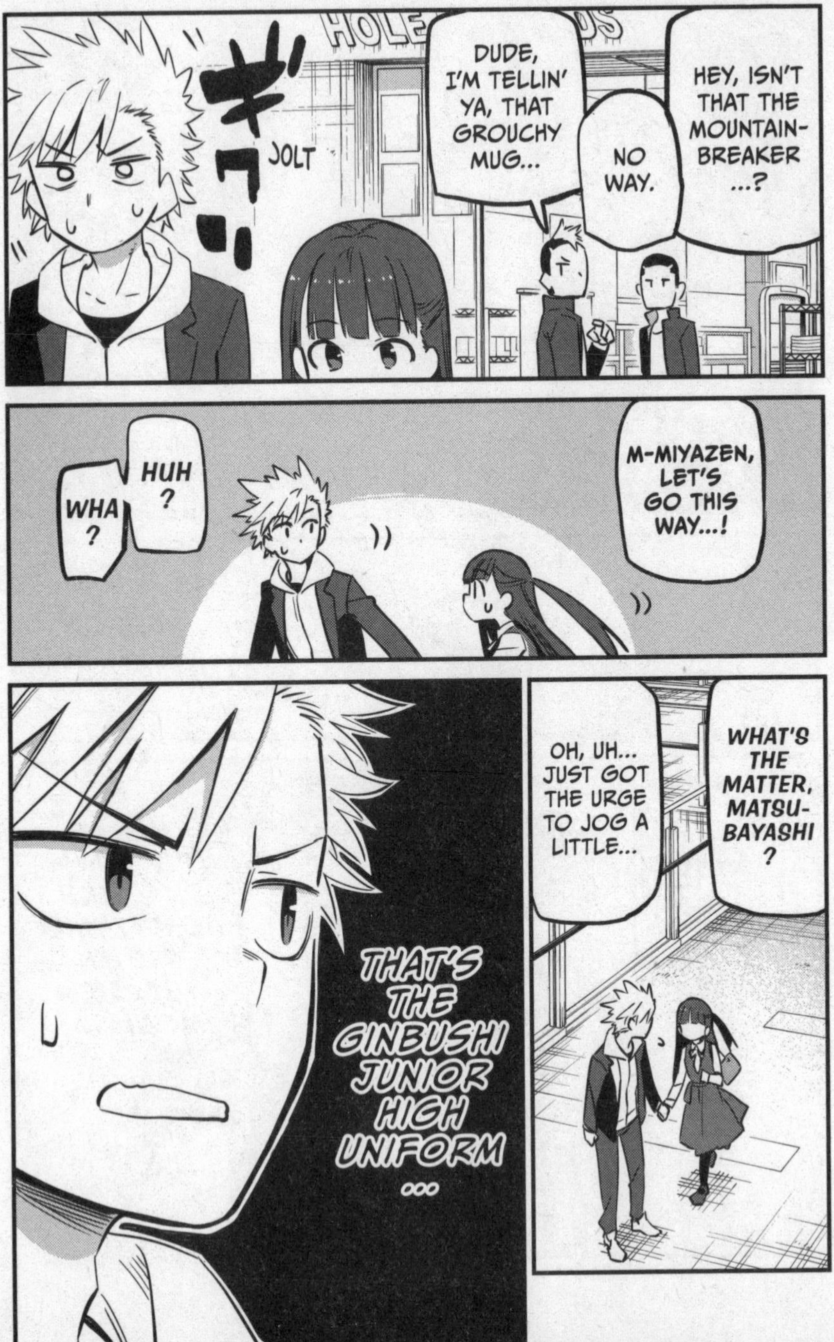
HEY, ISN'T THAT THE MOUNTAIN-BREAKER ...?
NO WAY.
DUDE, I'M TELLIN' YA, THAT GROUCHY MUG...
JOLT
ギクッ
M-MIYAZEN, LET'S GO THIS WAY...!
HUH ?
WHA ?
WHAT'S THE MATTER, MATSU-BAYASHI ?
OH, UH... JUST GOT THE URGE TO JOG A LITTLE...
THAT'S THE GINBUSHI JUNIOR HIGH UNIFORM ...

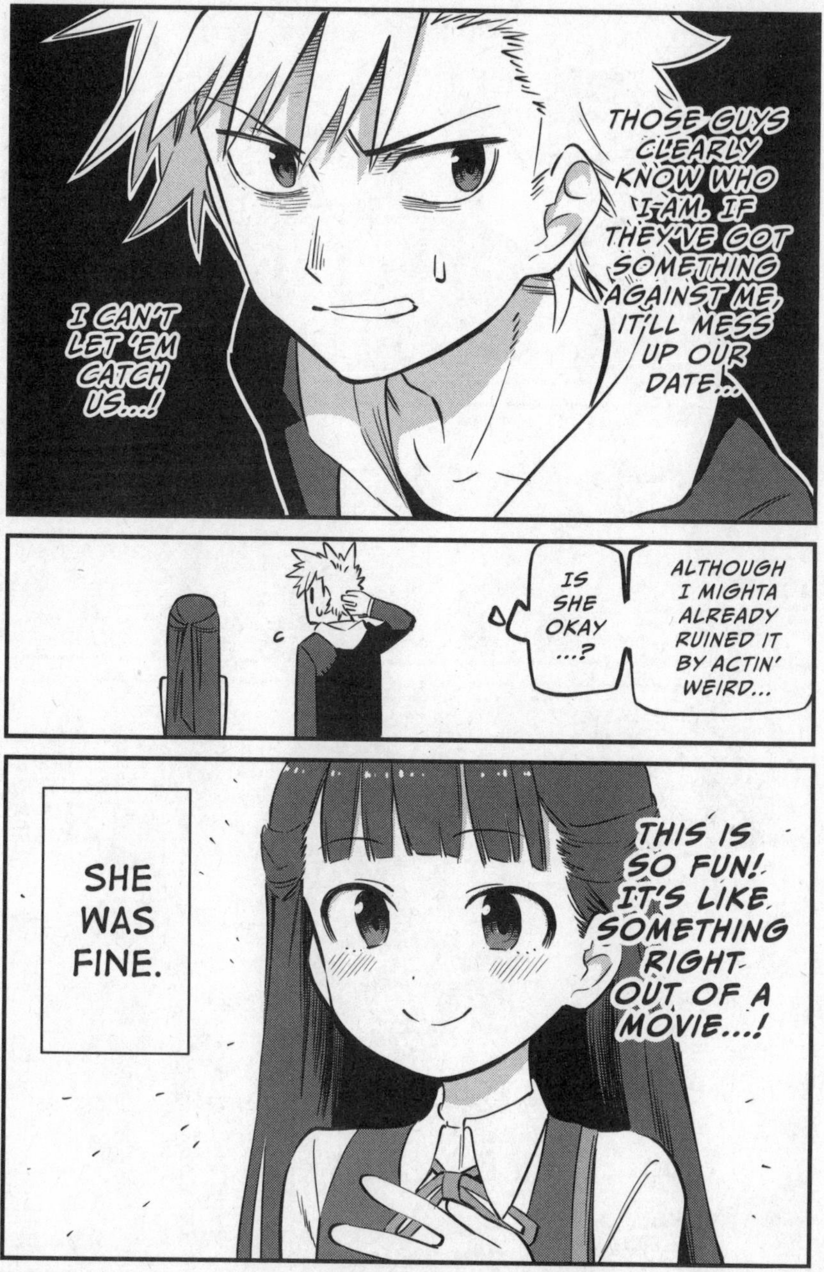
THOSE GUYS CLEARLY KNOW WHO I AM. IF THEY'VE GOT SOMETHING AGAINST ME, IT'LL MESS UP OUR DATE...
I CAN'T LET 'EM CATCH US...!
ALTHOUGH I MIGHTA ALREADY RUINED IT BY ACTIN' WEIRD...
IS SHE OKAY ...?
THIS IS SO FUN! IT'S LIKE SOMETHING RIGHT OUT OF A MOVIE...!
SHE WAS FINE.

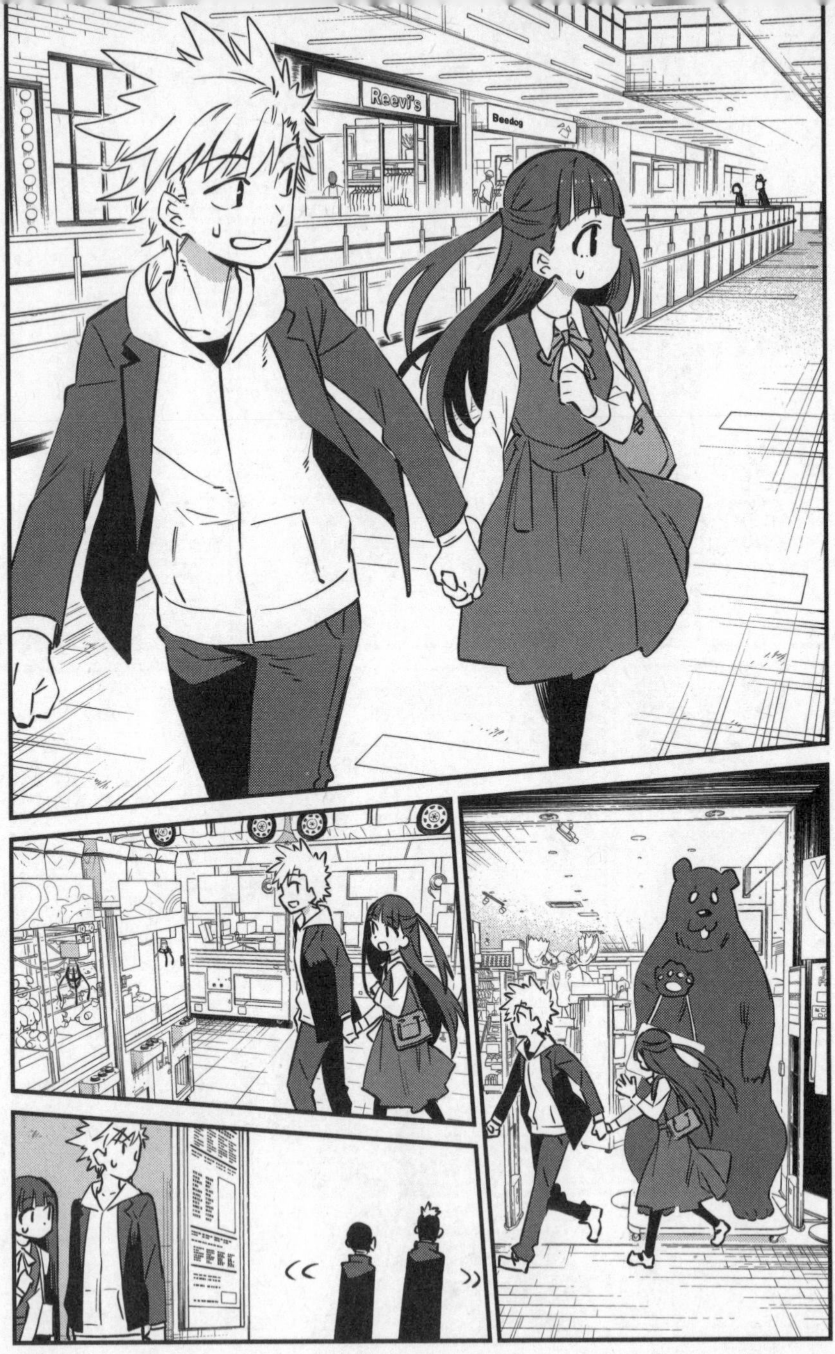
Reevi's
Beedog

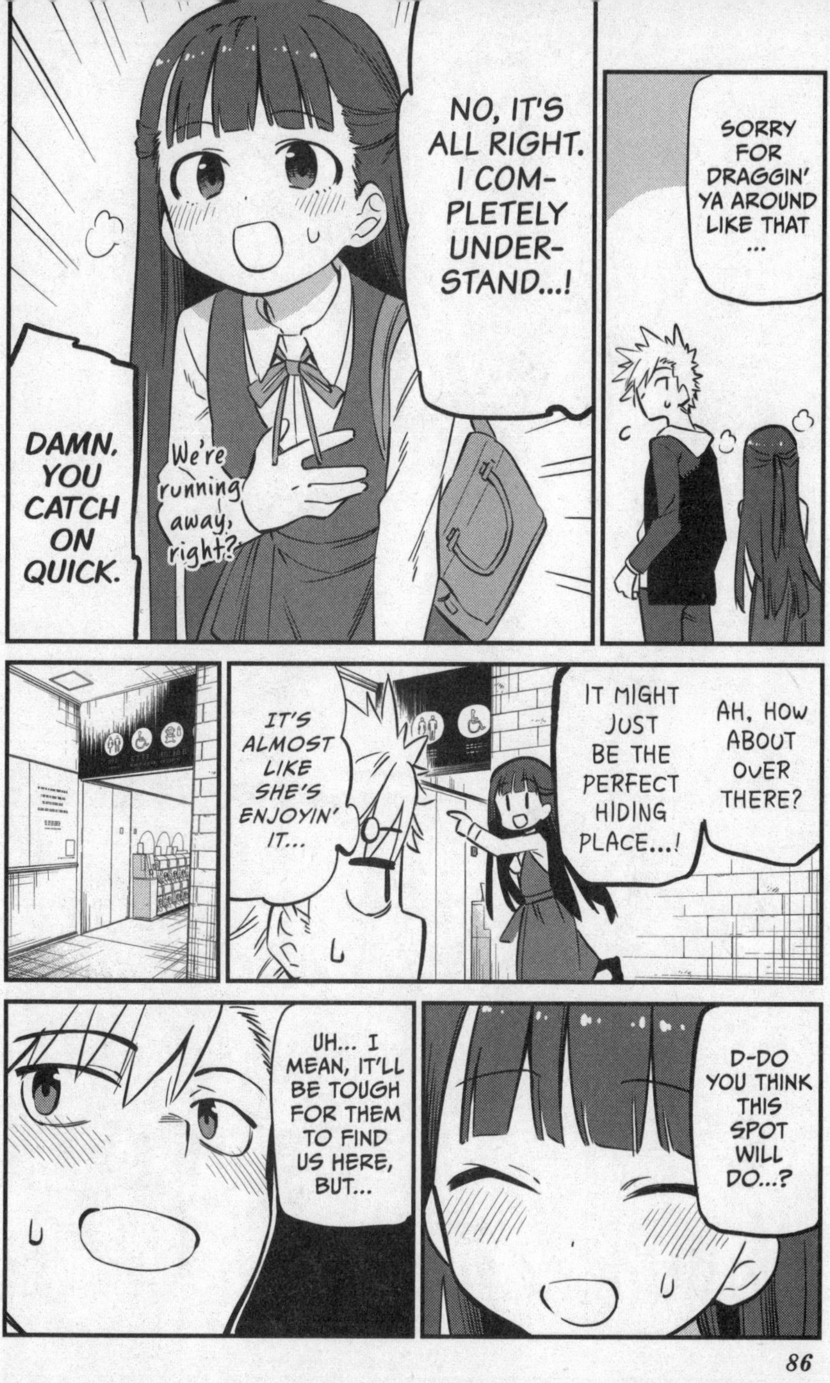
SORRY FOR DRAGGIN' YA AROUND LIKE THAT ...
NO, IT'S ALL RIGHT. I COMPLETELY UNDERSTAND...!
We're running away, right?
DAMN. YOU CATCH ON QUICK.
AH, HOW ABOUT OVER THERE?
IT MIGHT JUST BE THE PERFECT HIDING PLACE...!
IT'S ALMOST LIKE SHE'S ENJOYIN' IT...
D-DO YOU THINK THIS SPOT WILL DO...?
UH... I MEAN, IT'LL BE TOUGH FOR THEM TO FIND US HERE, BUT...

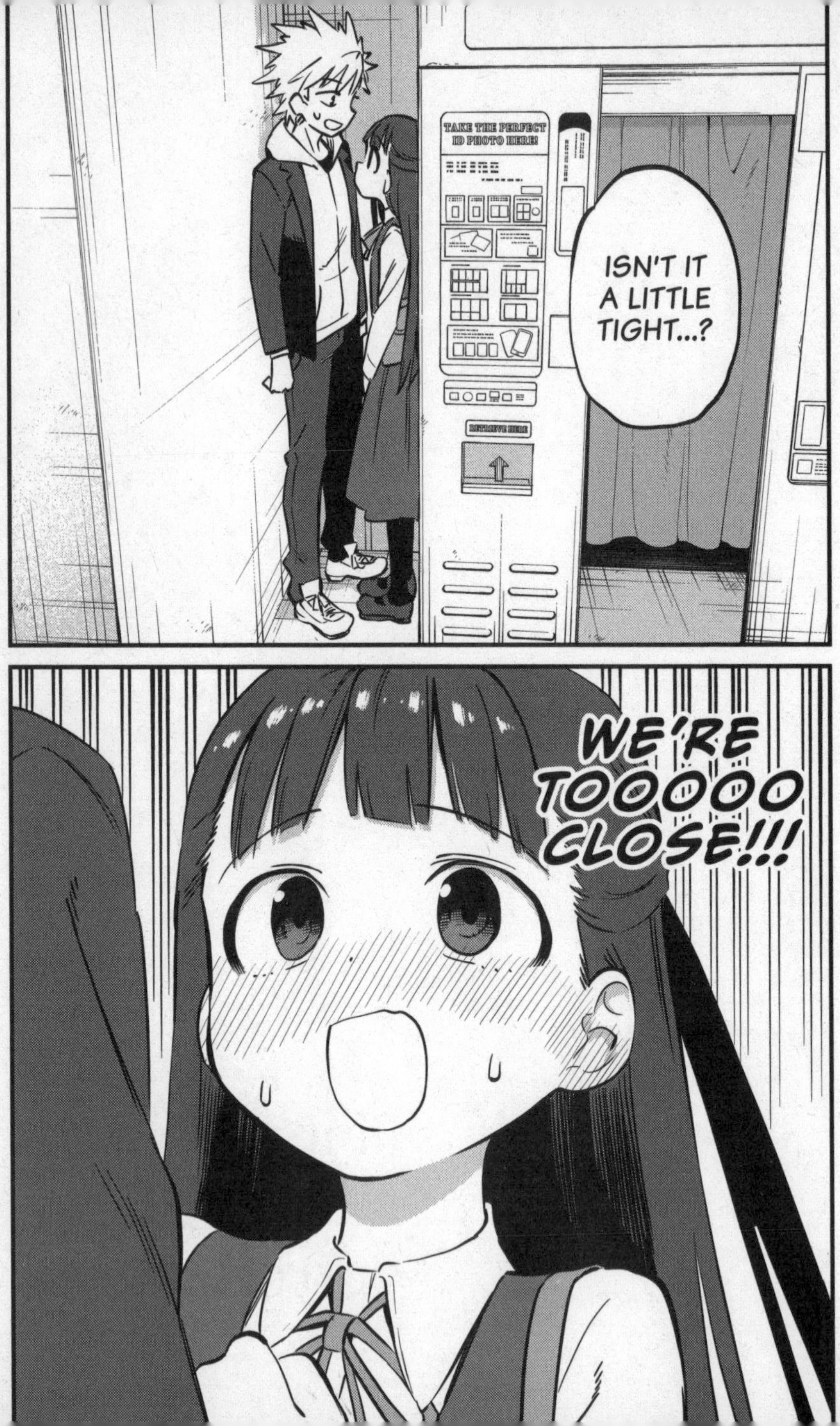
TAKE THE PERFECT ID PHOTO HERE!
ISN'T IT A LITTLE TIGHT...?
RETRIEVE HERE
WE'RE TOOOOO CLOSE!!!

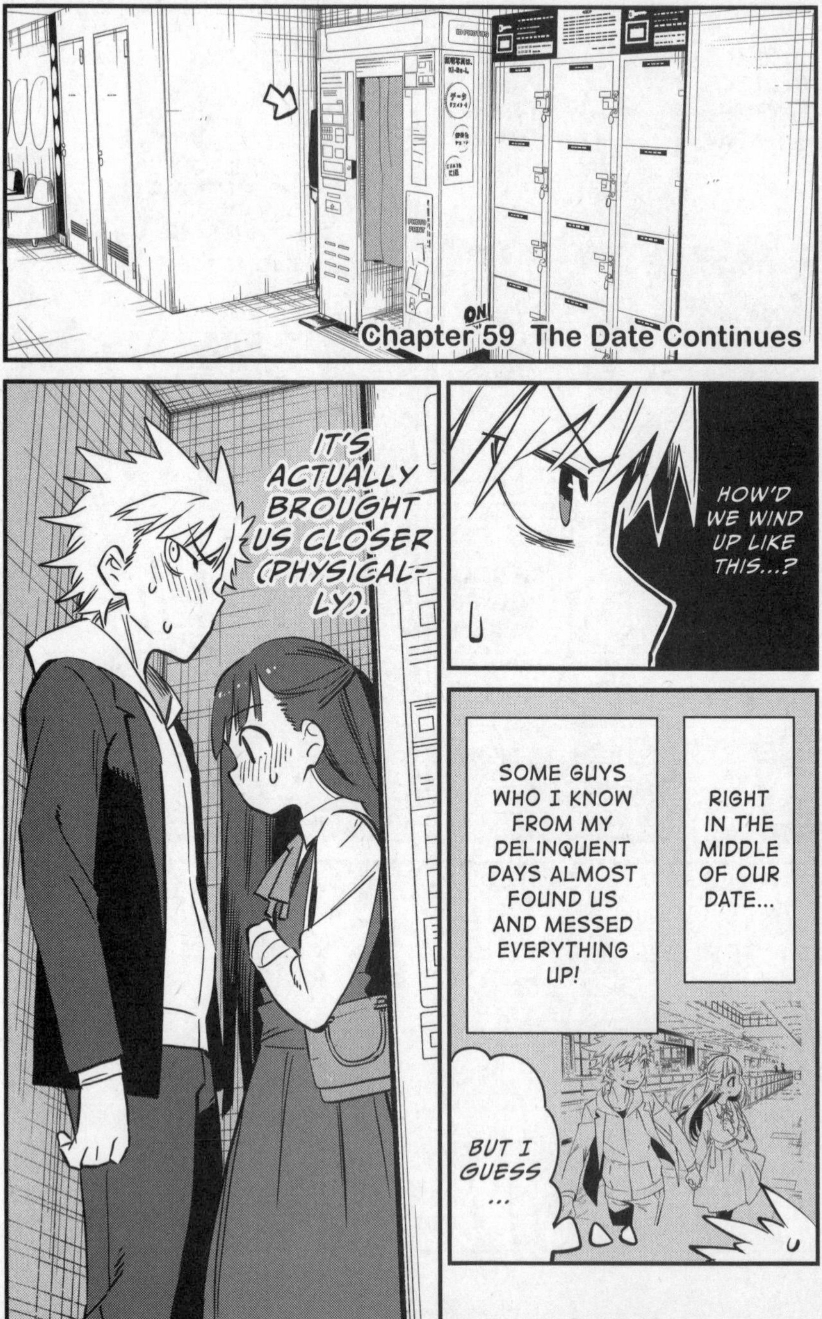
Chapter 59 The Date Continues
HOW'D WE WIND UP LIKE THIS...?
RIGHT IN THE MIDDLE OF OUR DATE...
SOME GUYS WHO I KNOW FROM MY DELINQUENT DAYS ALMOST FOUND US AND MESSED EVERYTHING UP!
BUT I GUESS...
IT'S ACTUALLY BROUGHT US CLOSER (PHYSICAL-LY).

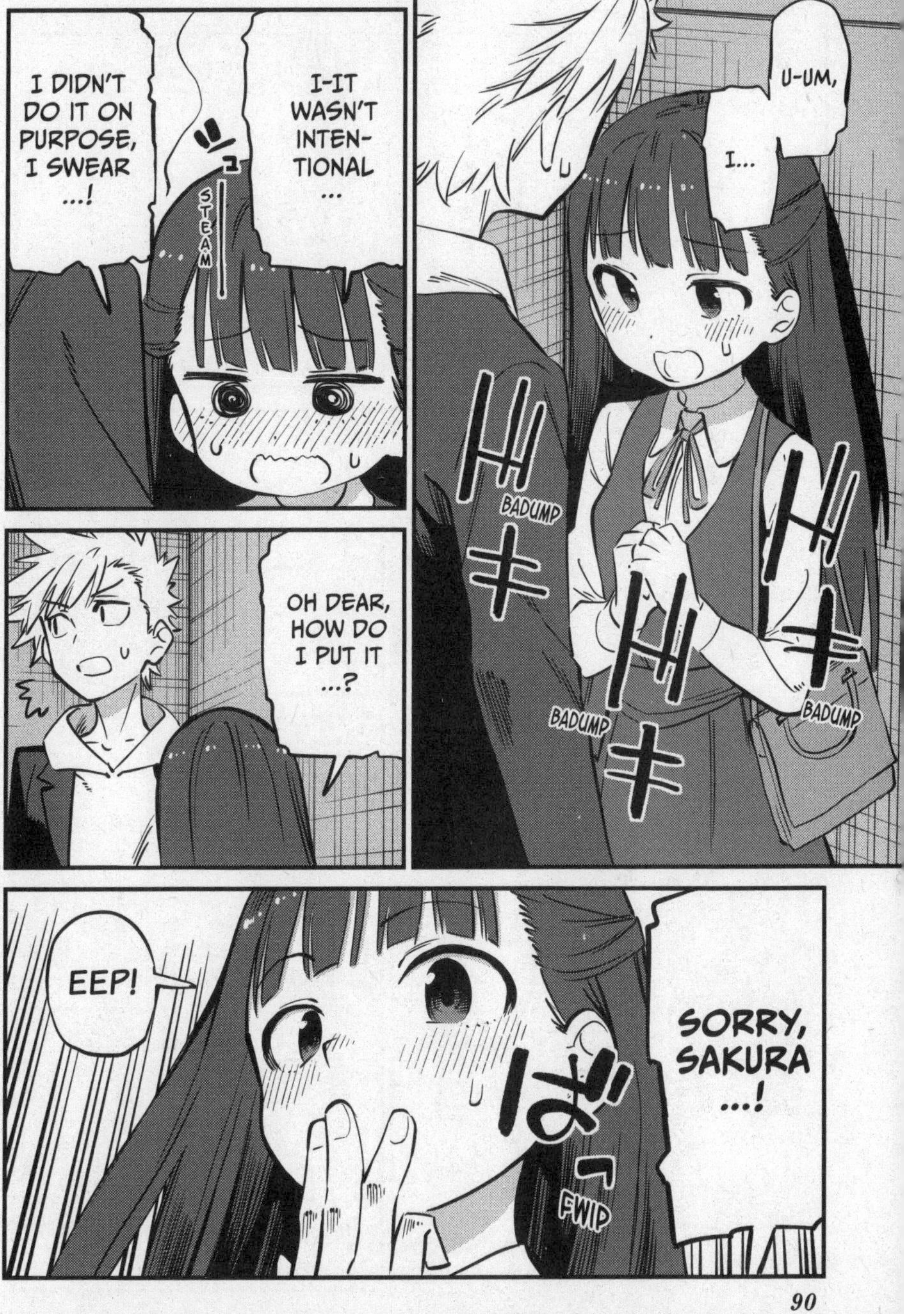
U-UM,
I...
BADUMP
BADUMP
BADUMP
I-IT WASN'T INTENTIONAL ...
I DIDN'T DO IT ON PURPOSE, I SWEAR ...!
STEAM
OH DEAR, HOW DO I PUT IT ...?
SORRY, SAKURA ...!
FWIP
EEP!

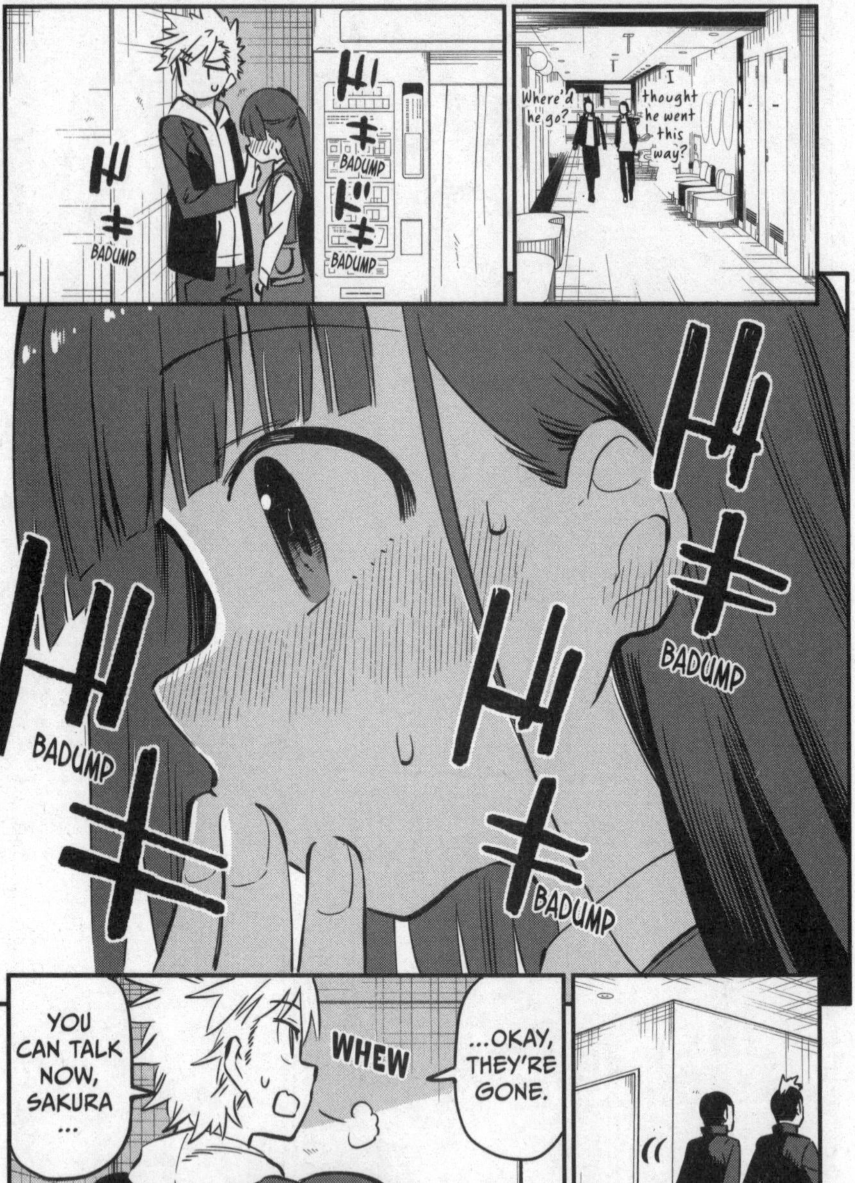
I thought he went this way?
Where'd he go?
BADUMP
BADUMP
BADUMP
BADUMP
BADUMP
BADUMP
BADUMP
...OKAY, THEY'RE GONE.
WHEW
YOU CAN TALK NOW, SAKURA ...

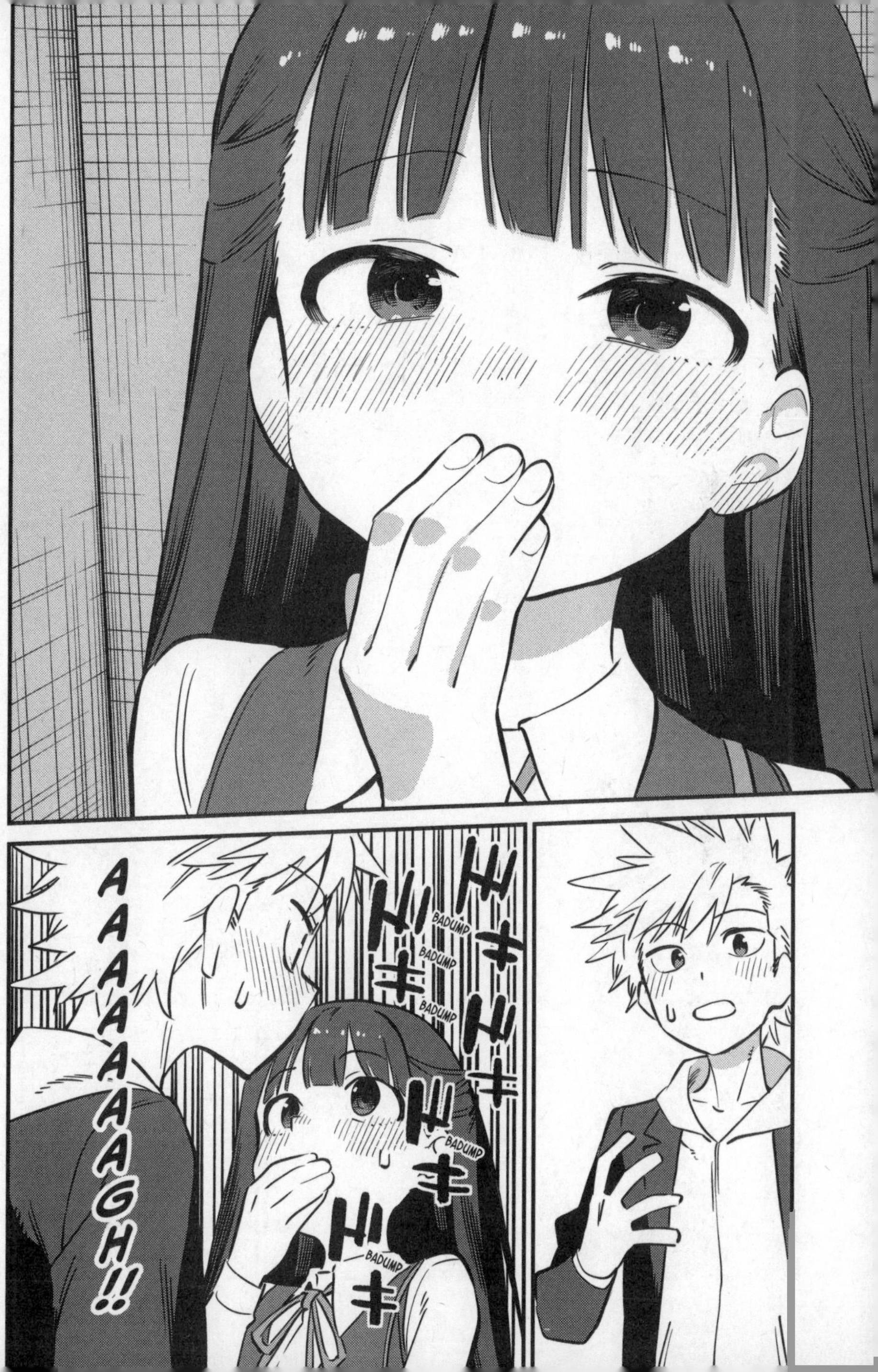
BADUMP
BADUMP
BADUMP
BADUMP
BADUMP
AAAAAAAGH!!

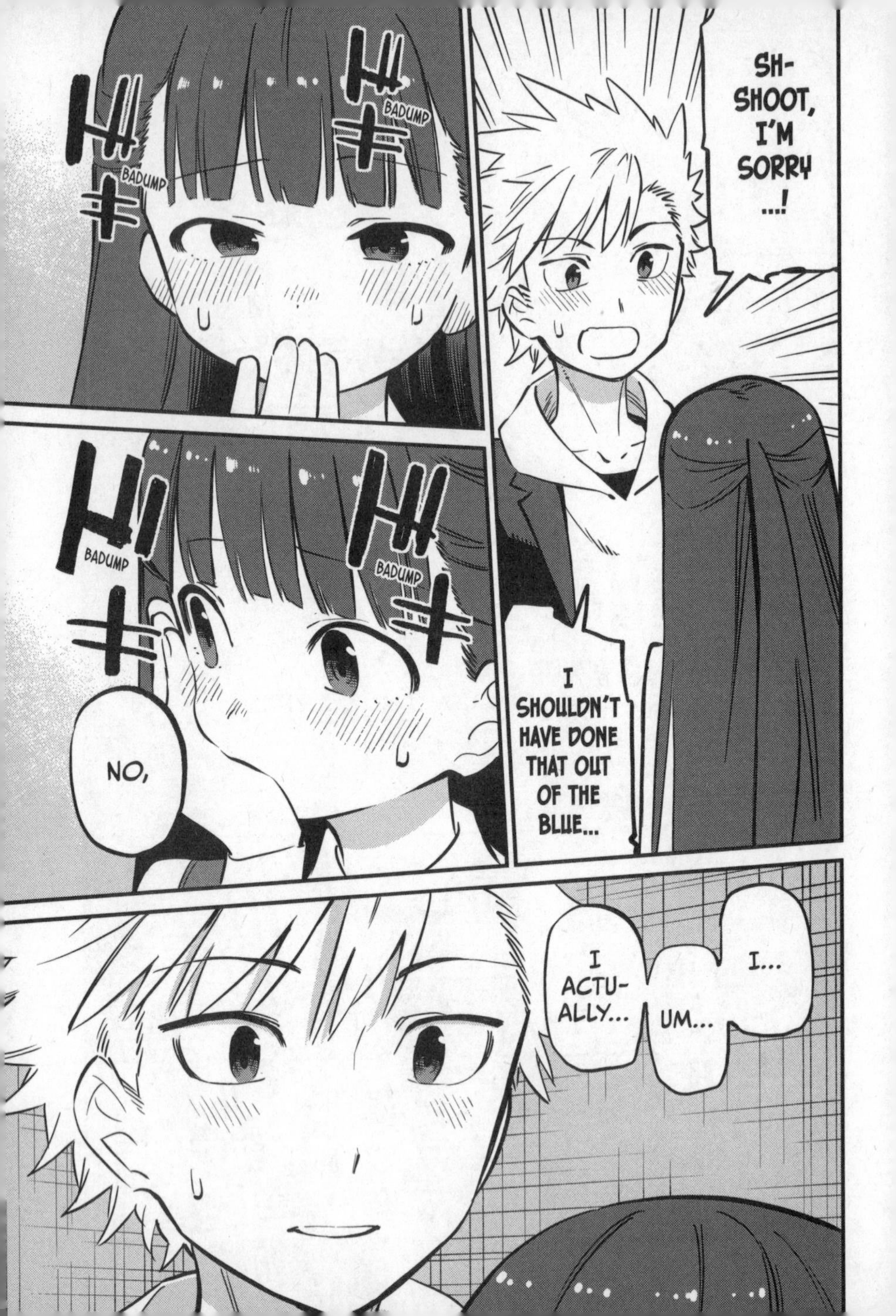
SH-SHOOT, I'M SORRY ...!
I SHOULDN'T HAVE DONE THAT OUT OF THE BLUE...
BADUMP
BADUMP
BADUMP
BADUMP
NO,
I...
UM...
I ACTU-ALLY...

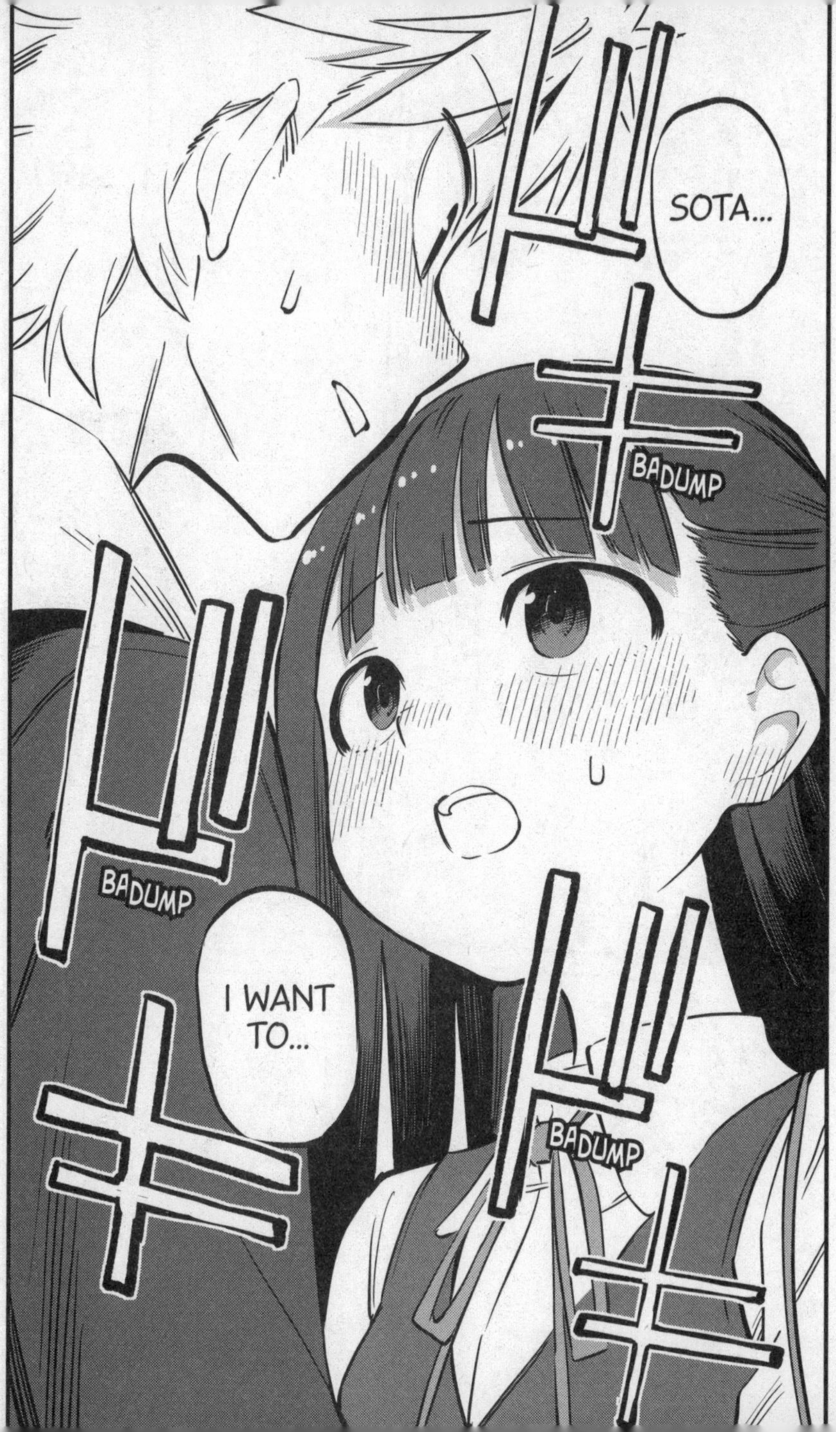
SOTA...
BADUMP
I WANT TO...
BADUMP
BADUMP

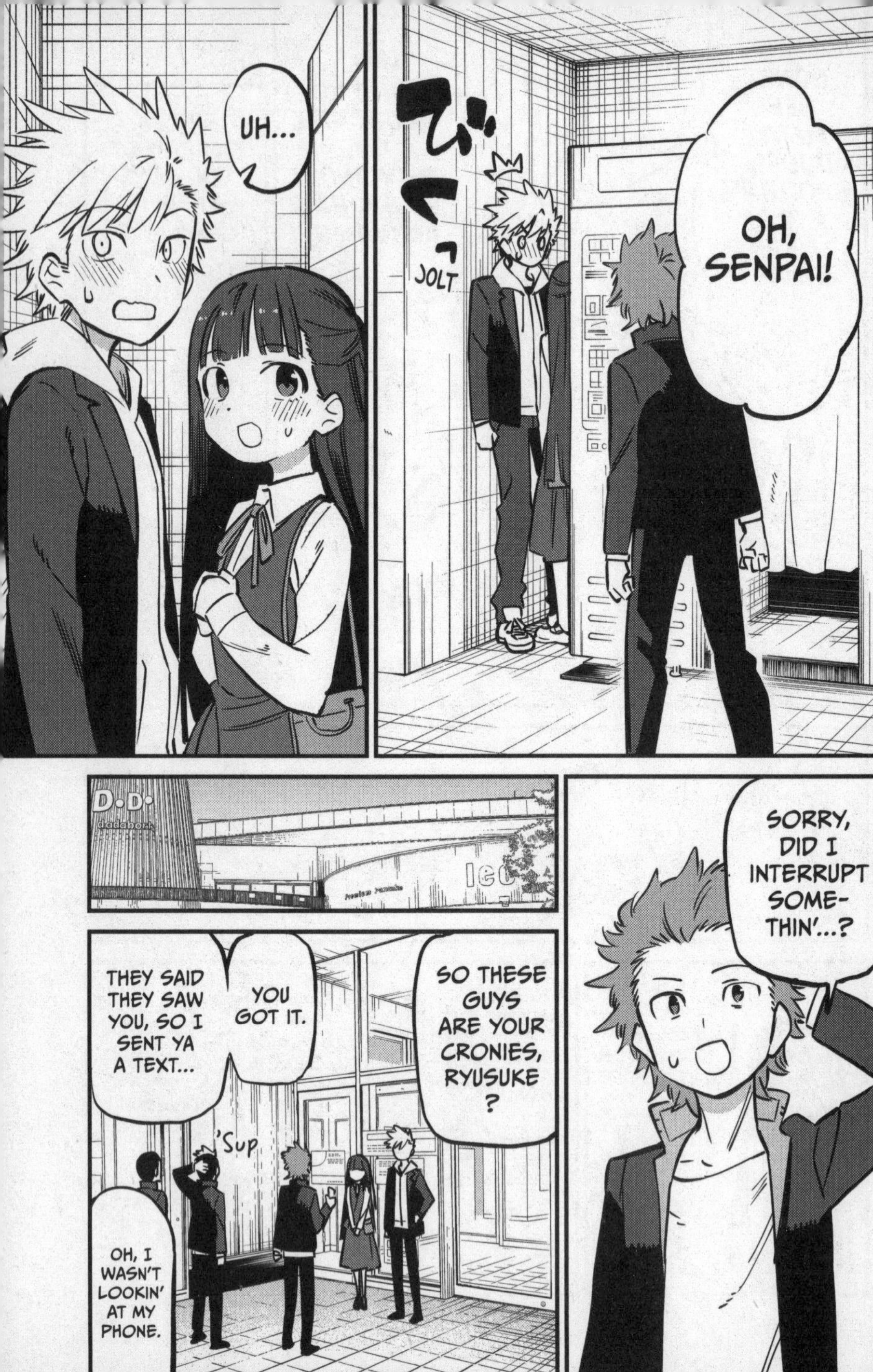
OH, SENPAI!
びくっ
JOLT
UH...
SORRY, DID I INTERRUPT SOME-THIN'...?
SO THESE GUYS ARE YOUR CRONIES, RYUSUKE ?
YOU GOT IT.
THEY SAID THEY SAW YOU, SO I SENT YA A TEXT...
'Sup
OH, I WASN'T LOOKIN' AT MY PHONE.

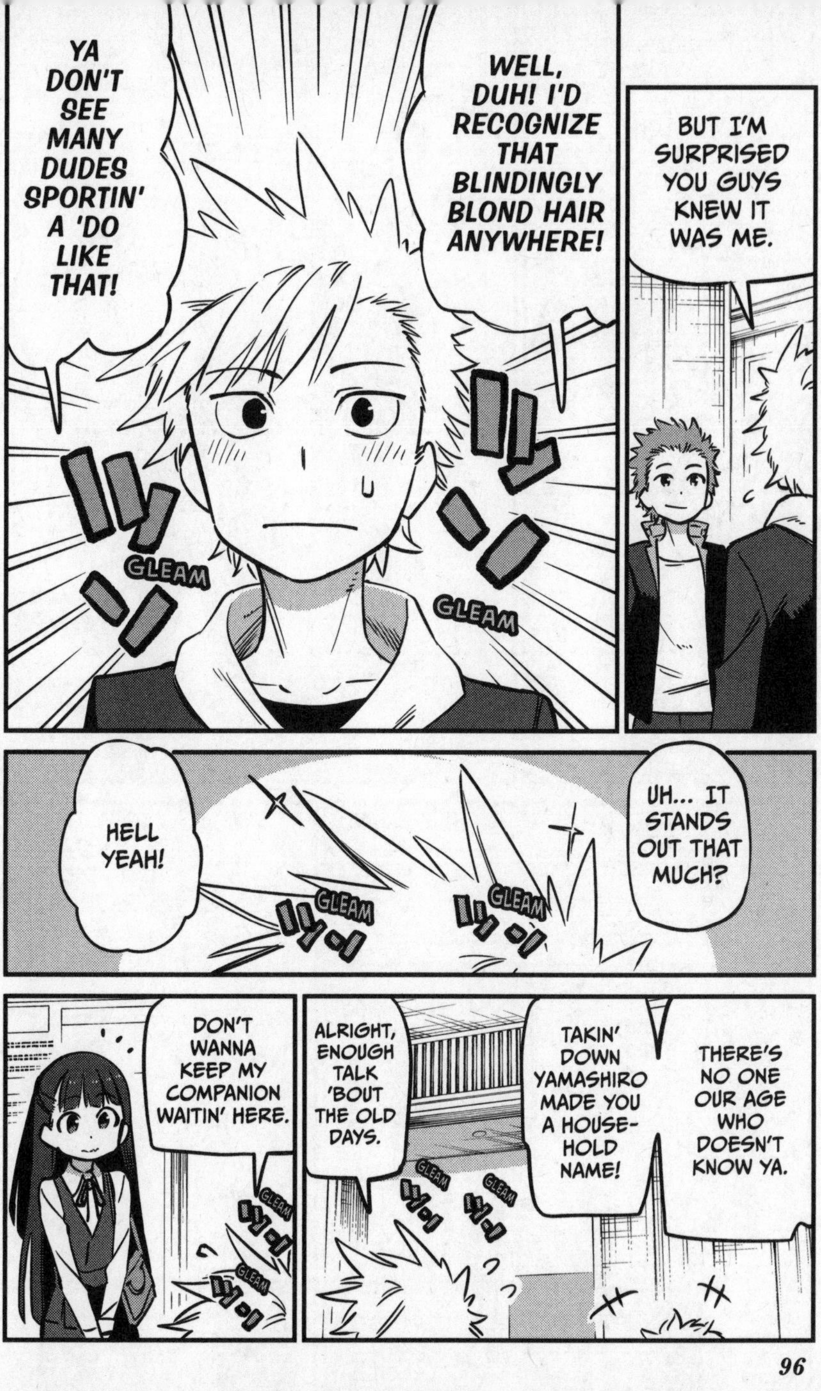
BUT I'M SURPRISED YOU GUYS KNEW IT WAS ME.
WELL, DUH! I'D RECOGNIZE THAT BLINDINGLY BLOND HAIR ANYWHERE!
YA DON'T SEE MANY DUDES SPORTIN' A 'DO LIKE THAT!
GLEAM
GLEAM
UH... IT STANDS OUT THAT MUCH?
GLEAM
GLEAM
HELL YEAH!
THERE'S NO ONE OUR AGE WHO DOESN'T KNOW YA.
TAKIN' DOWN YAMASHIRO MADE YOU A HOUSE-HOLD NAME!
ALRIGHT, ENOUGH TALK 'BOUT THE OLD DAYS.
GLEAM
GLEAM
DON'T WANNA KEEP MY COMPANION WAITIN' HERE.
GLEAM
GLEAM

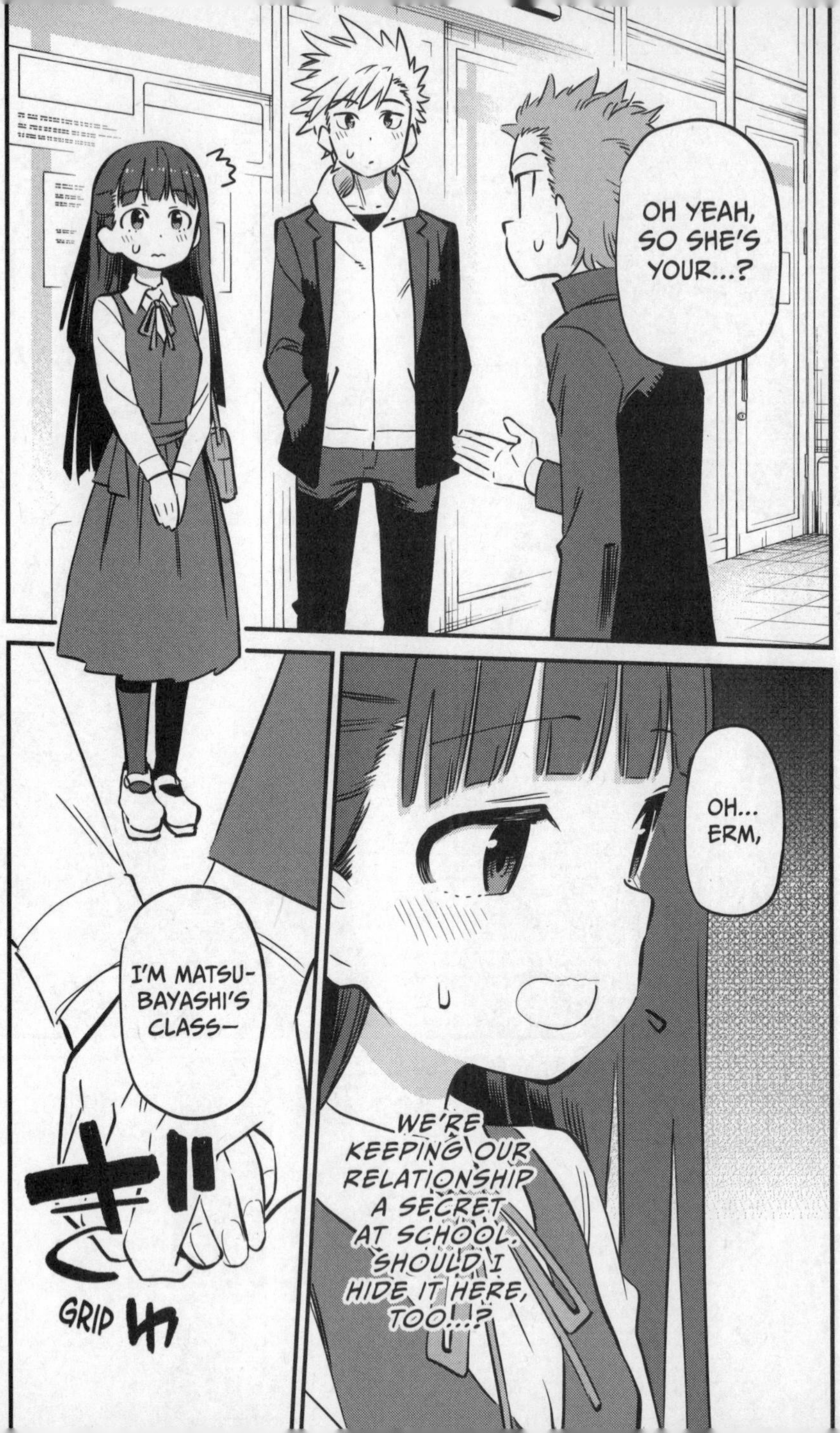
OH YEAH, SO SHE'S YOUR...?
OH... ERM,
WE'RE KEEPING OUR RELATIONSHIP A SECRET AT SCHOOL. SHOULD I HIDE IT HERE, TOO...?
I'M MATSU-BAYASHI'S CLASS—
GRIP

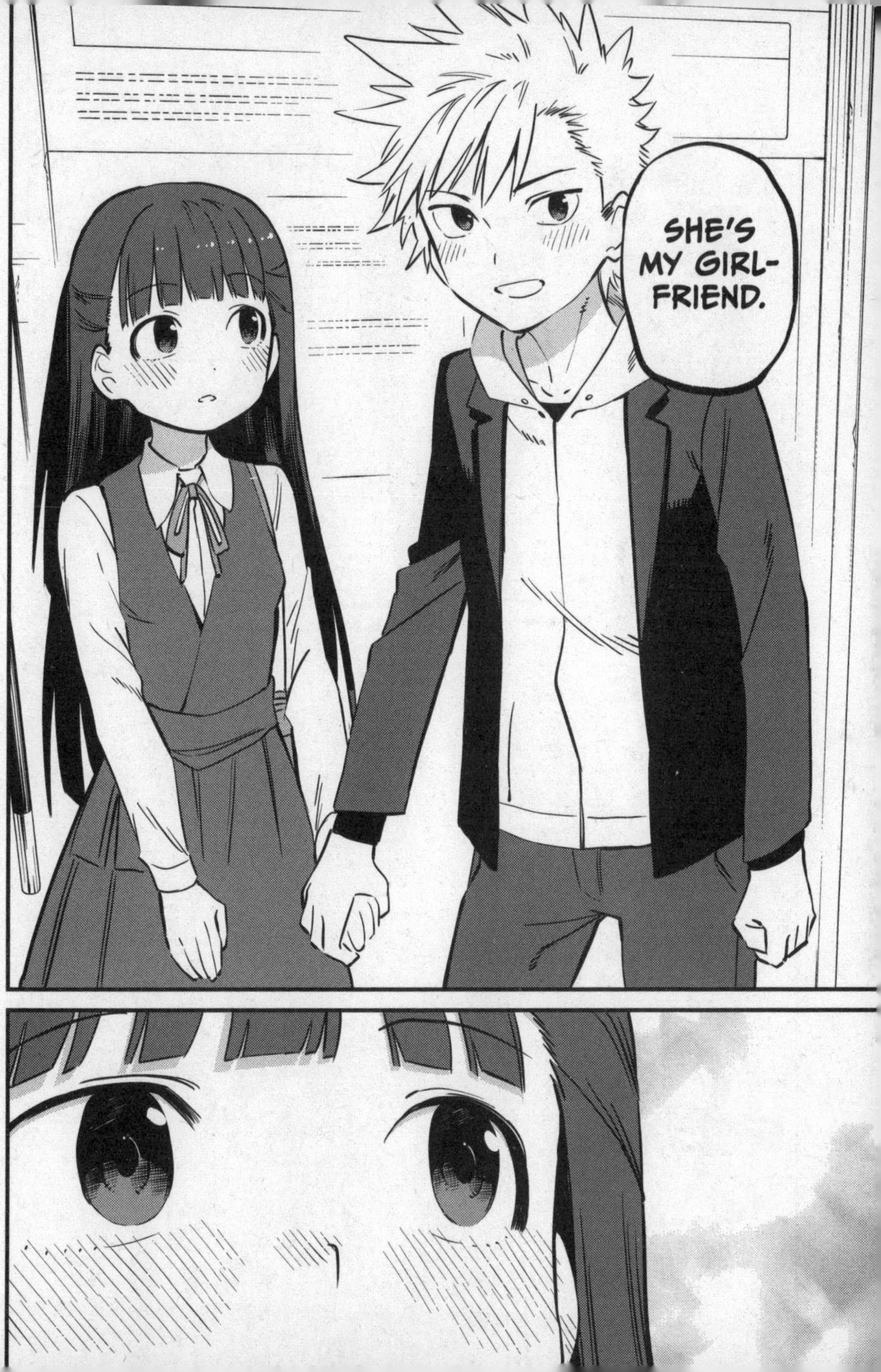
SHE'S MY GIRL-FRIEND.

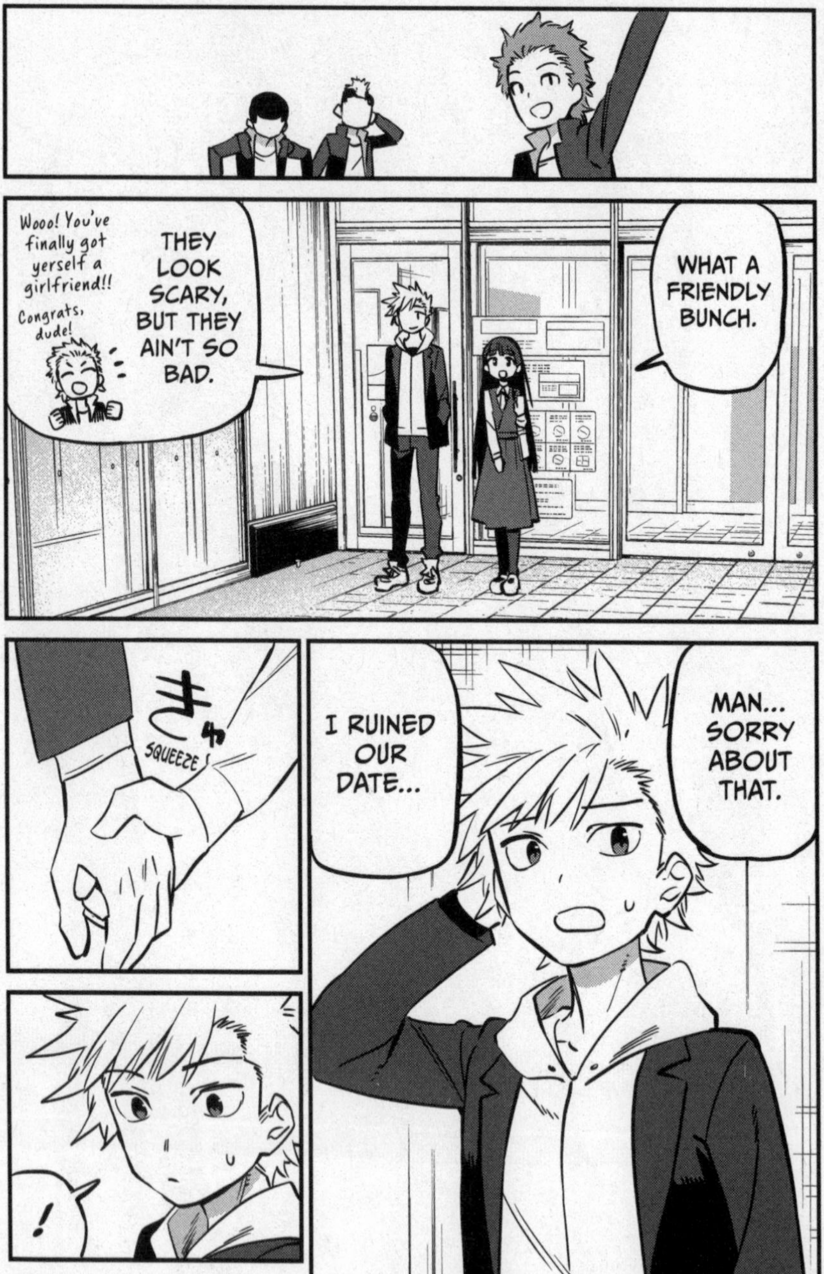
WHAT A FRIENDLY BUNCH.
THEY LOOK SCARY, BUT THEY AIN'T SO BAD.
Wooo! You've finally got yerself a girlfriend!!
Congrats, dude!
MAN... SORRY ABOUT THAT.
I RUINED OUR DATE...
きゅ
SQUEEZE
!

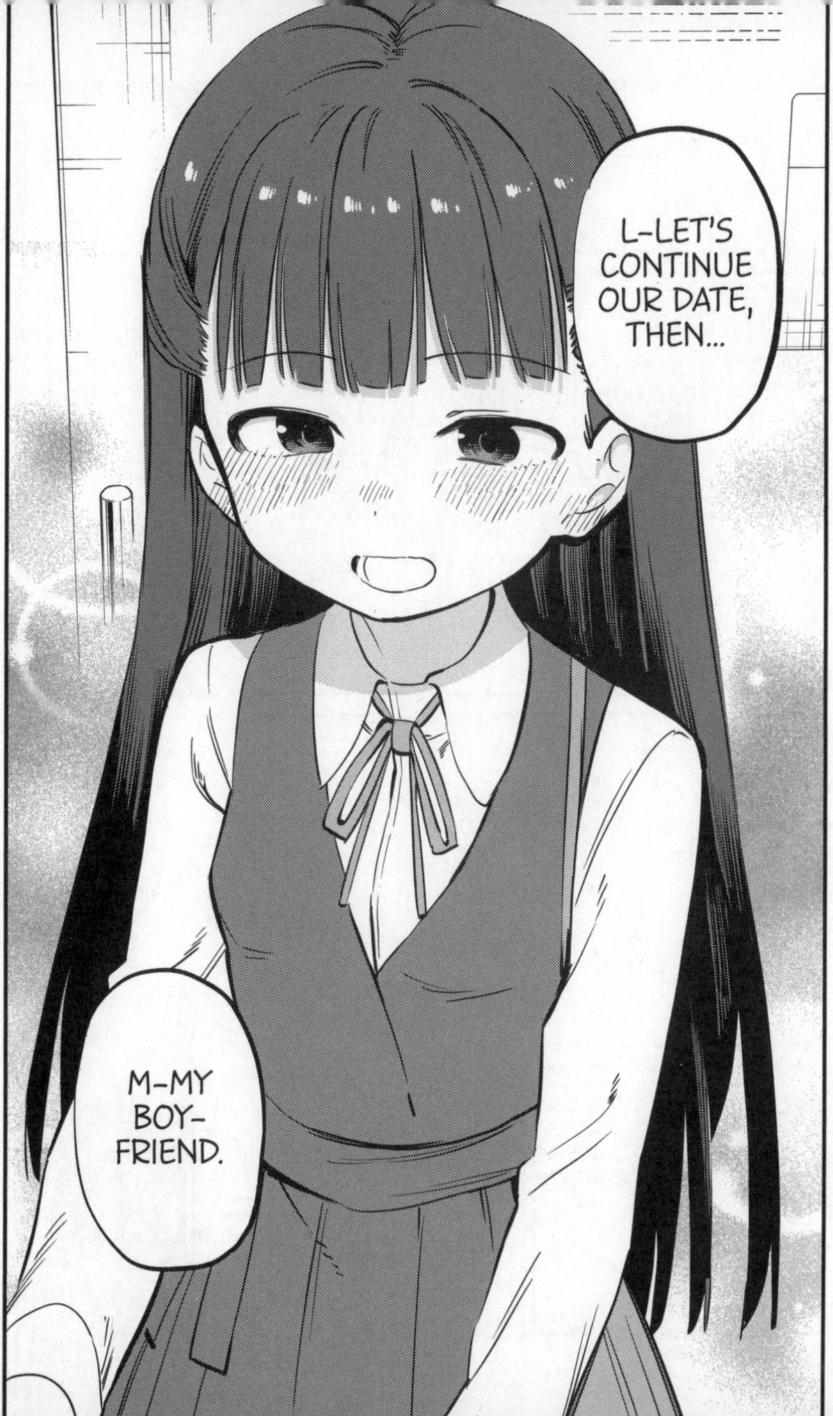
L-LET'S CONTINUE OUR DATE, THEN...
M-MY BOY-FRIEND.

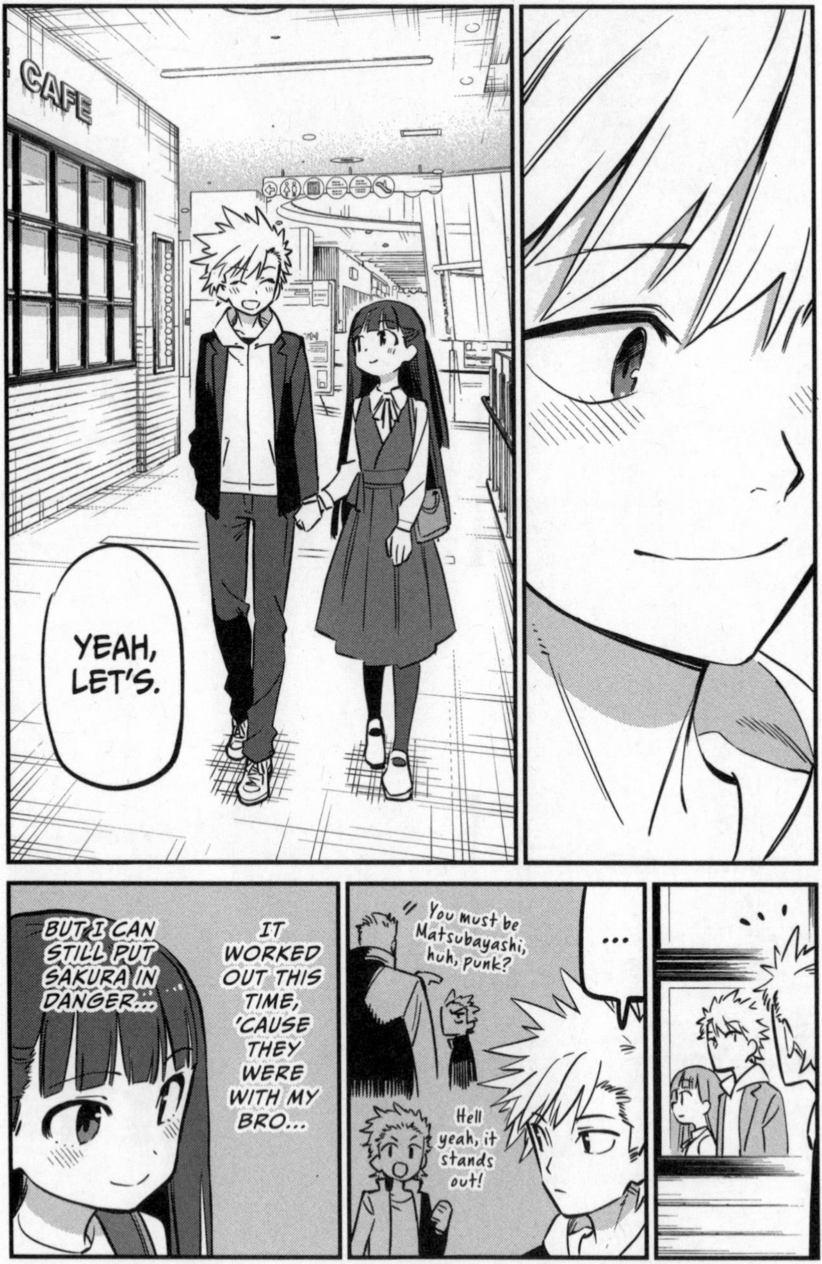
CAFE
YEAH, LET'S.
...
You must be Matsubayashi, huh, punk?
Hell yeah, it stands out!
IT WORKED OUT THIS TIME, 'CAUSE THEY WERE WITH MY BRO...
BUT I CAN STILL PUT SAKURA IN DANGER...

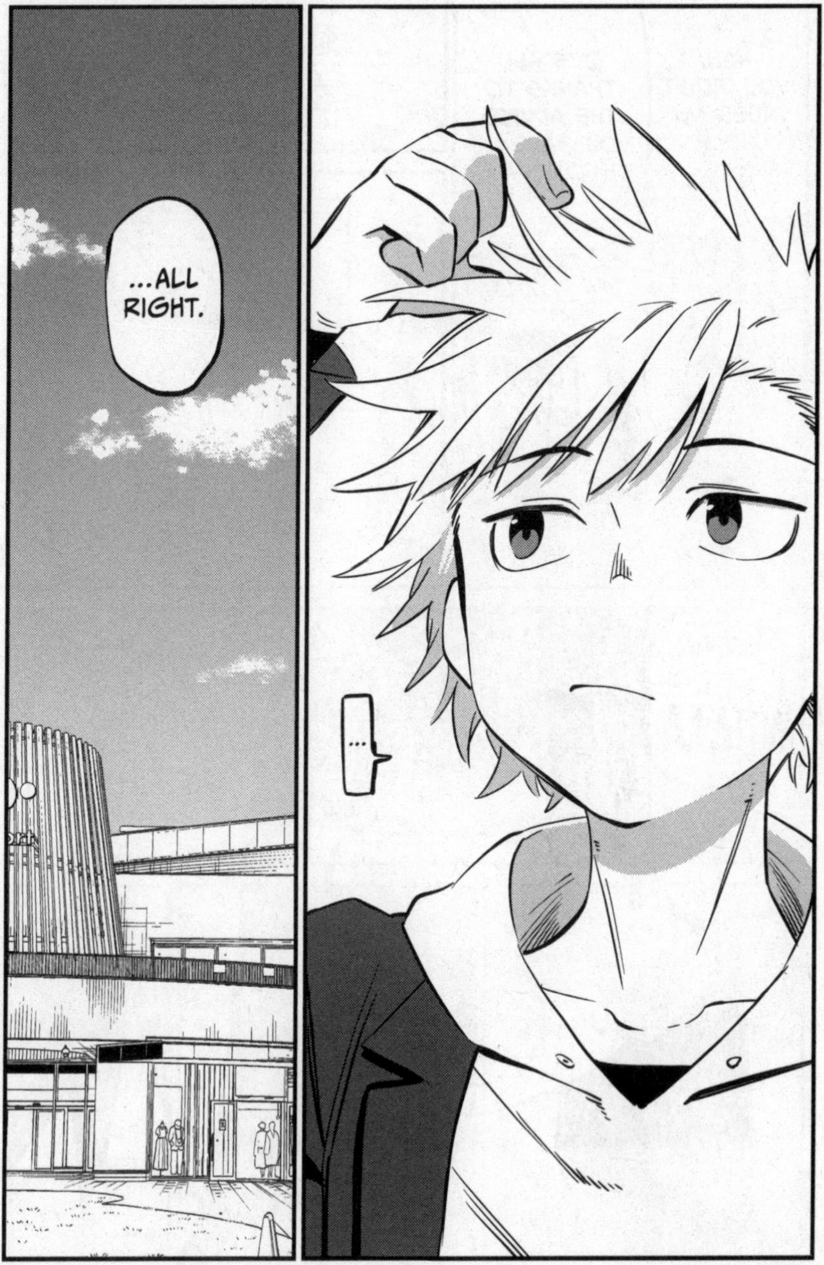
...
...ALL RIGHT.

Chapter 60 I Want to Talk

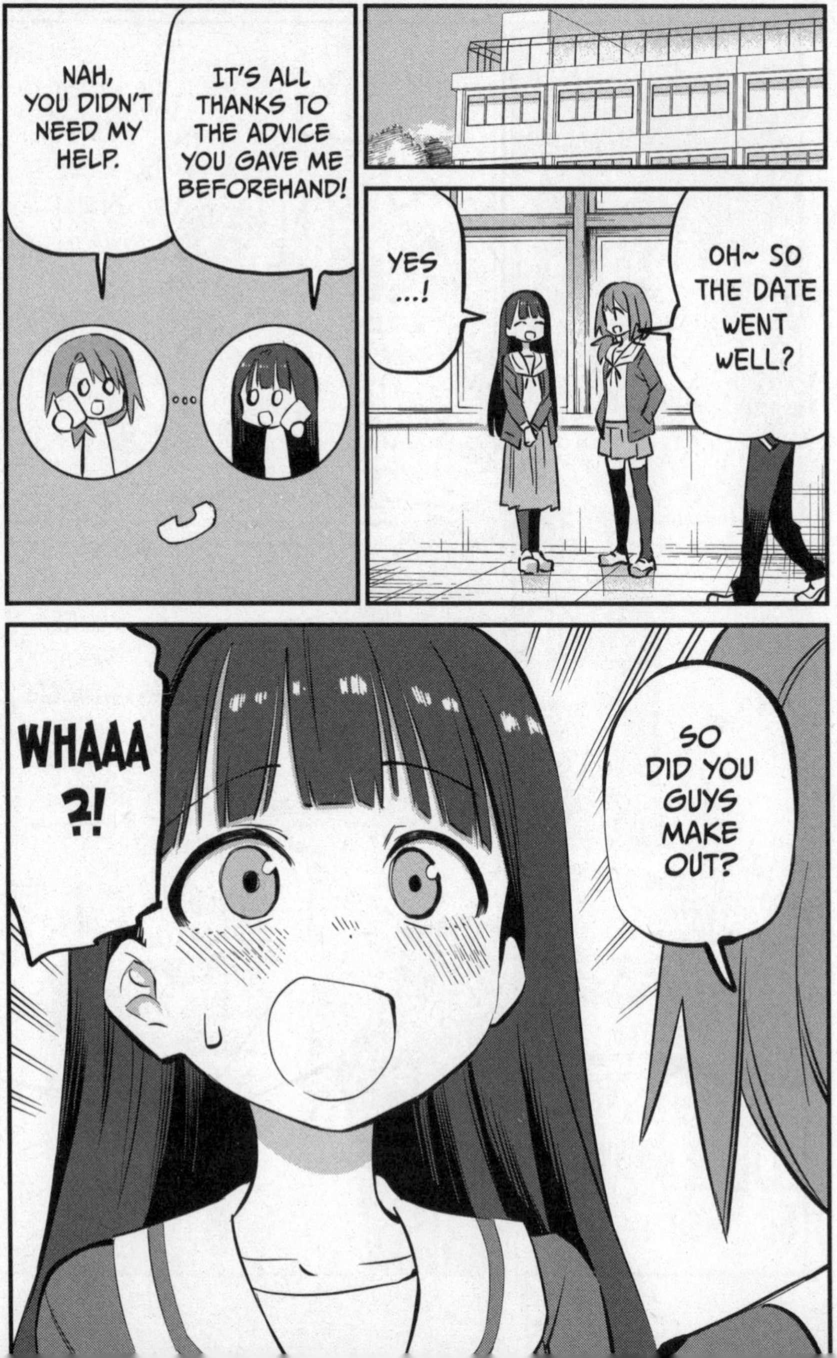
OH~ SO THE DATE WENT WELL?
YES ...!
IT'S ALL THANKS TO THE ADVICE YOU GAVE ME BEFOREHAND!
NAH, YOU DIDN'T NEED MY HELP.
SO DID YOU GUYS MAKE OUT?
WHAAA ?!

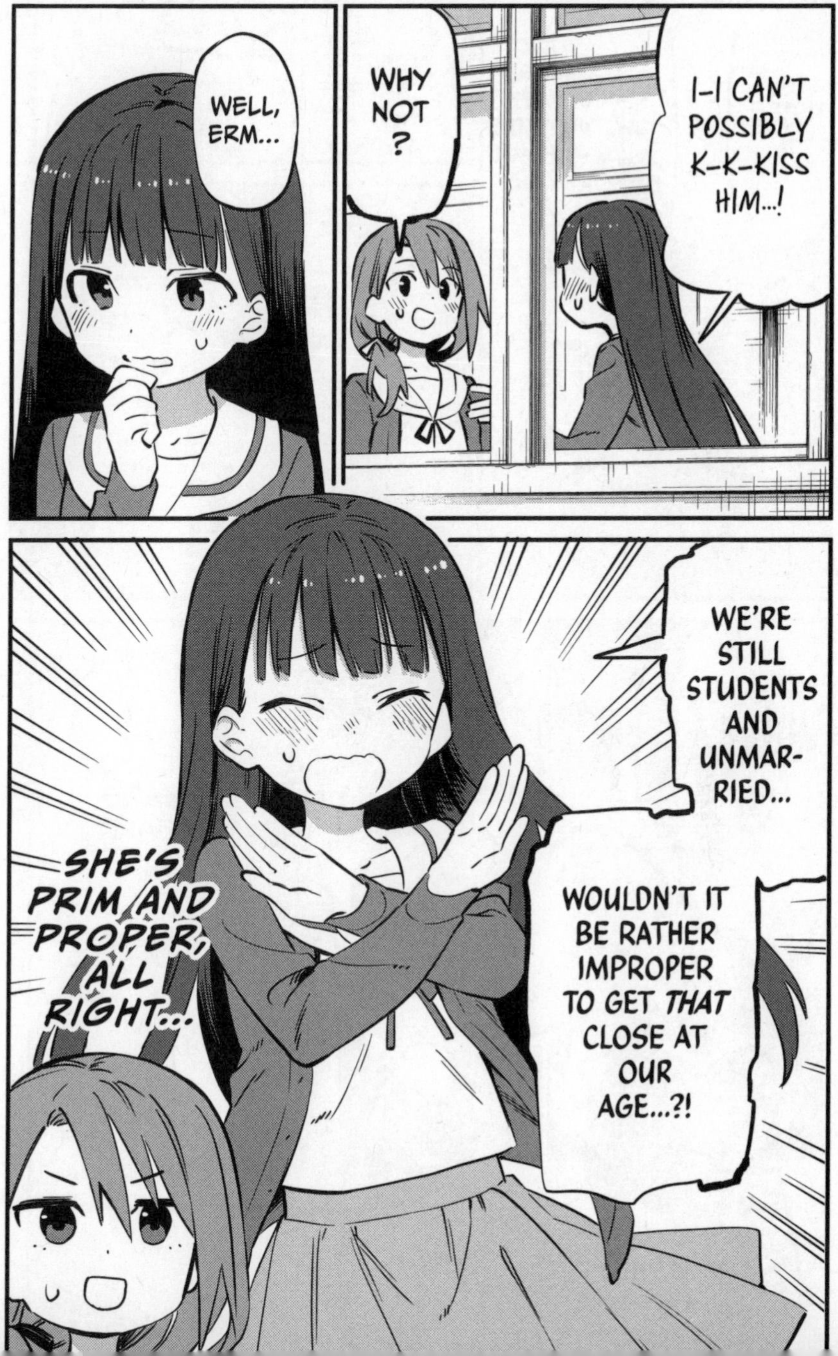
I-I CAN'T POSSIBLY K-K-KISS HIM...!
WHY NOT?
WELL, ERM...
WE'RE STILL STUDENTS AND UNMAR-RIED...
WOULDN'T IT BE RATHER IMPROPER TO GET *THAT* CLOSE AT OUR AGE...?!
SHE'S PRIM AND PROPER, ALL RIGHT...

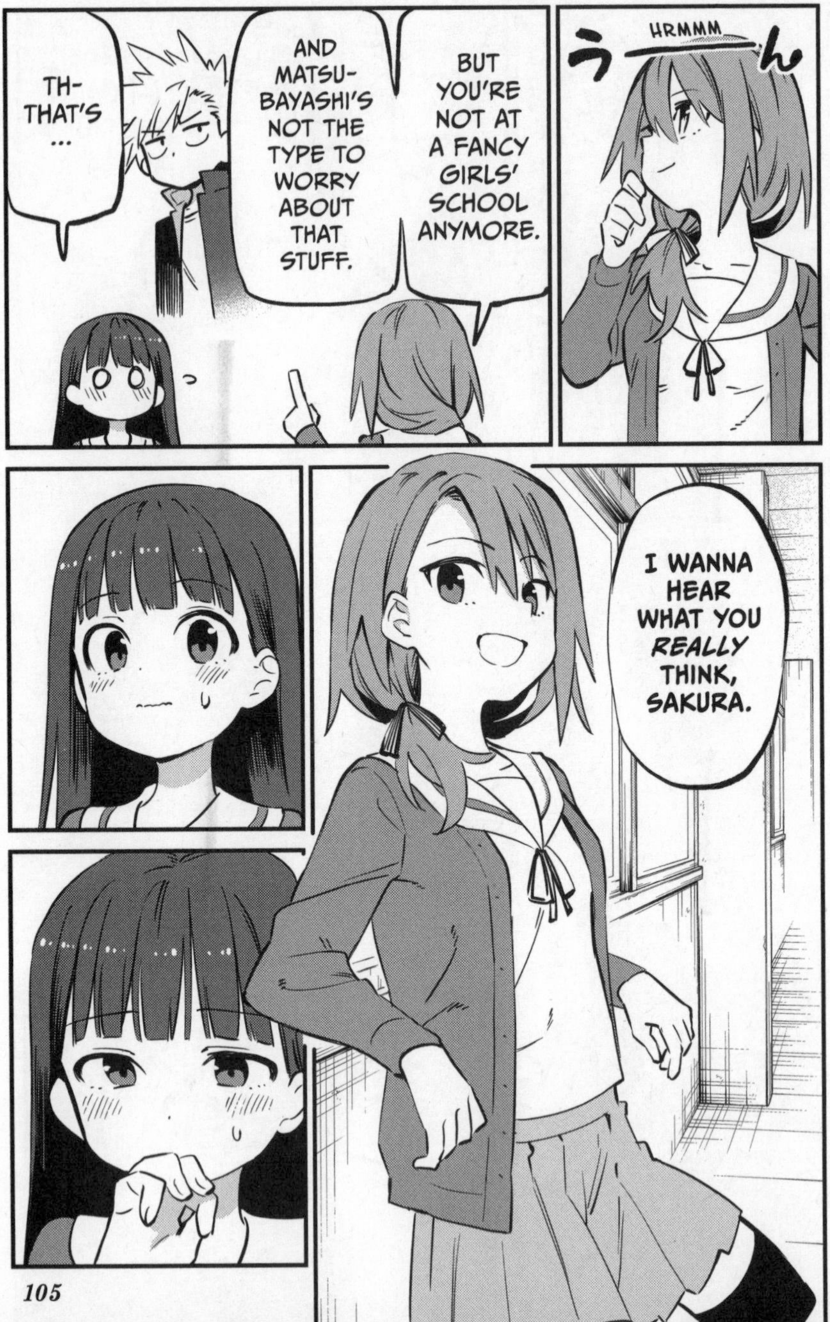
HRMMM
うーん
BUT YOU'RE NOT AT A FANCY GIRLS' SCHOOL ANYMORE.
AND MATSU-BAYASHI'S NOT THE TYPE TO WORRY ABOUT THAT STUFF.
TH-THAT'S...
I WANNA HEAR WHAT YOU *REALLY* THINK, SAKURA.

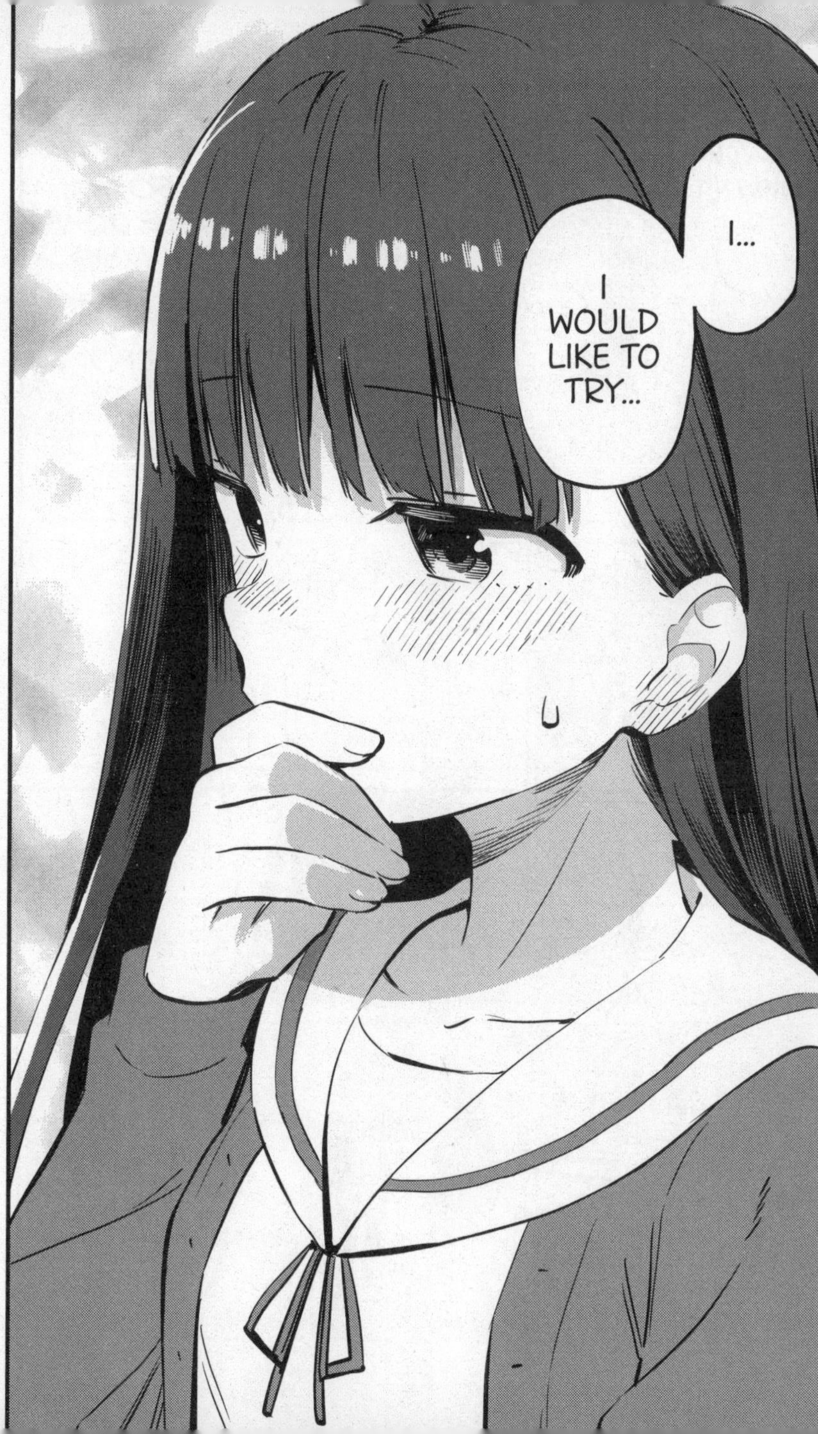
I...
I WOULD LIKE TO TRY...

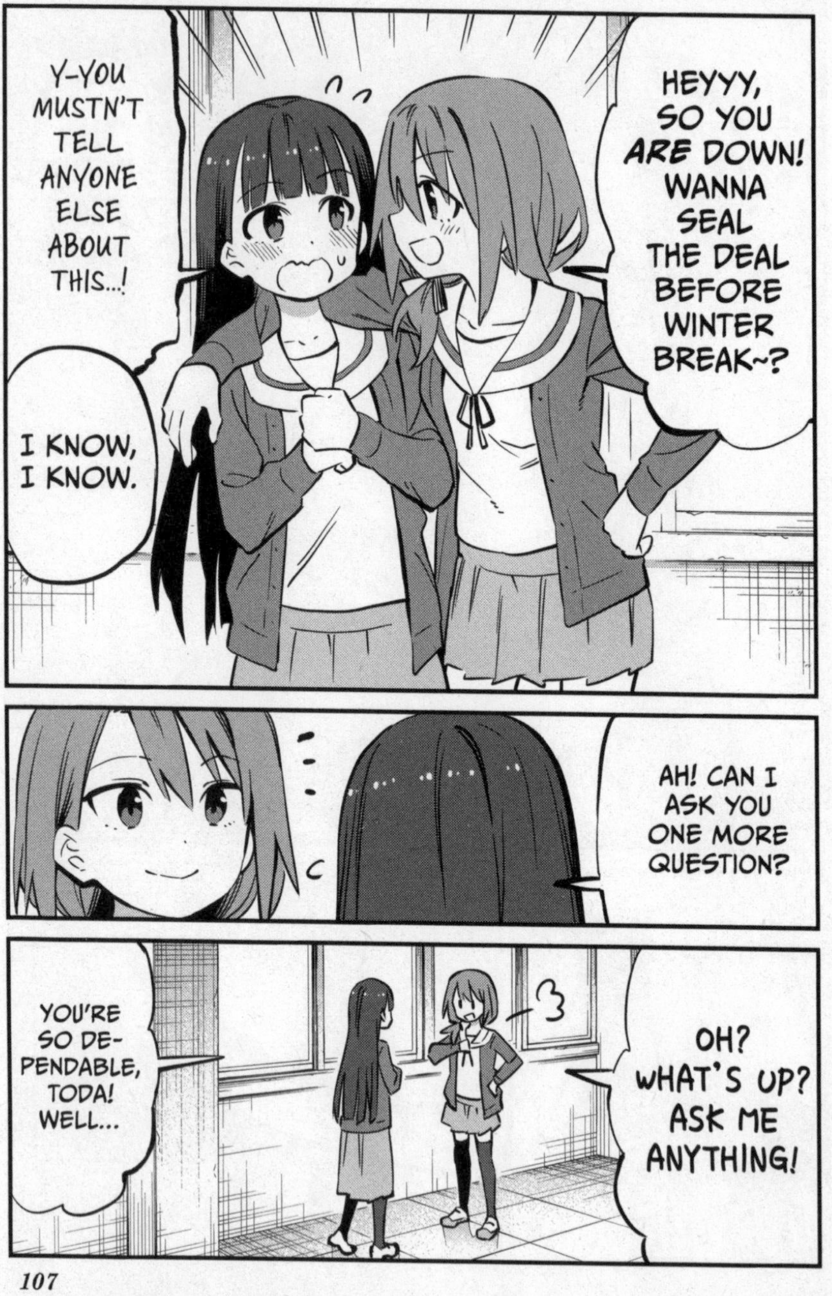
HEYYY, SO YOU ARE DOWN! WANNA SEAL THE DEAL BEFORE WINTER BREAK~?
Y-YOU MUSTN'T TELL ANYONE ELSE ABOUT THIS...!
I KNOW, I KNOW.
AH! CAN I ASK YOU ONE MORE QUESTION?
OH? WHAT'S UP? ASK ME ANYTHING!
YOU'RE SO DE-PENDABLE, TODA! WELL...

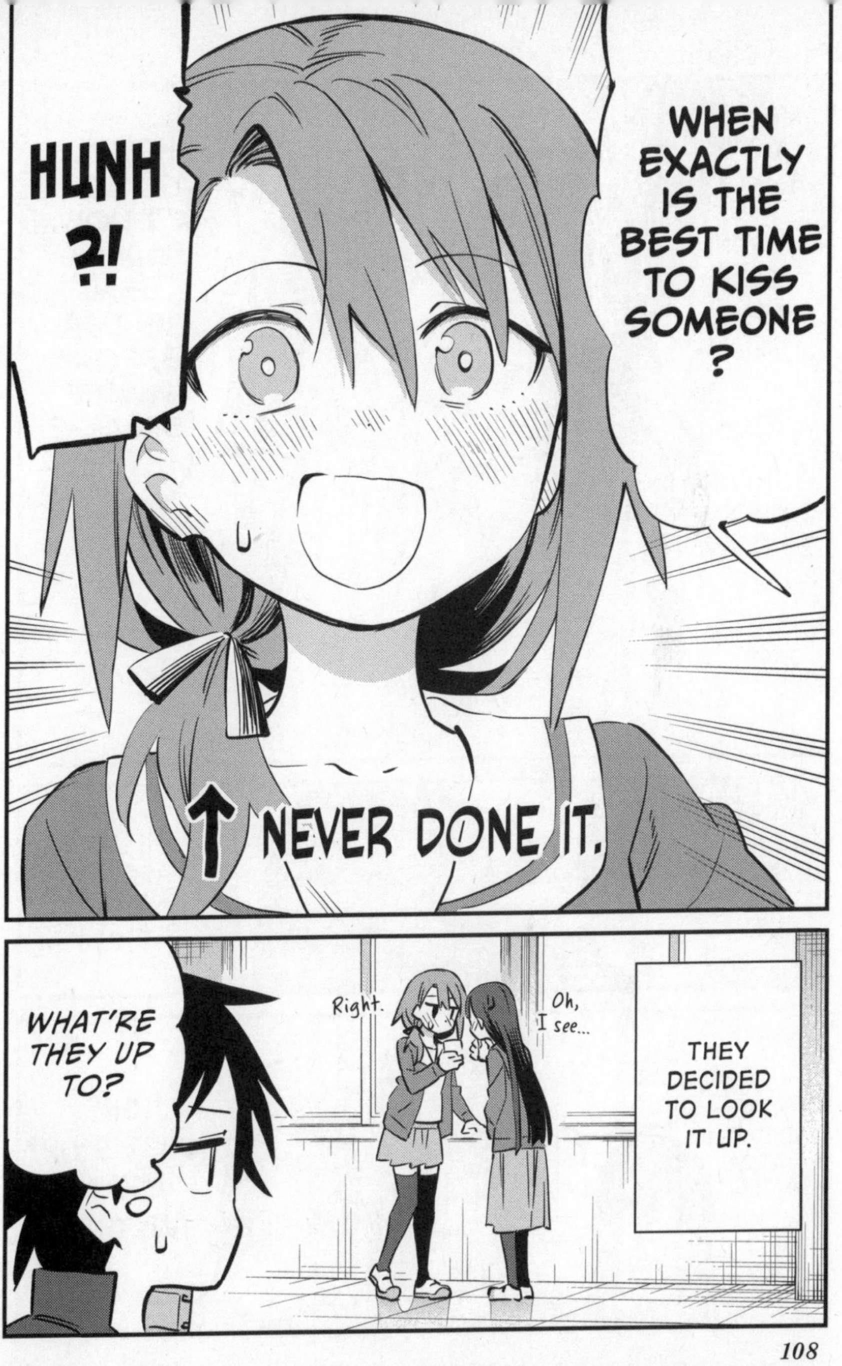
WHEN EXACTLY IS THE BEST TIME TO KISS SOMEONE?
HUNH ?!
↑ NEVER DONE IT.
THEY DECIDED TO LOOK IT UP.
Oh, I see...
Right.
WHAT'RE THEY UP TO?

Final Chapter The Two Who've Gotten Closer

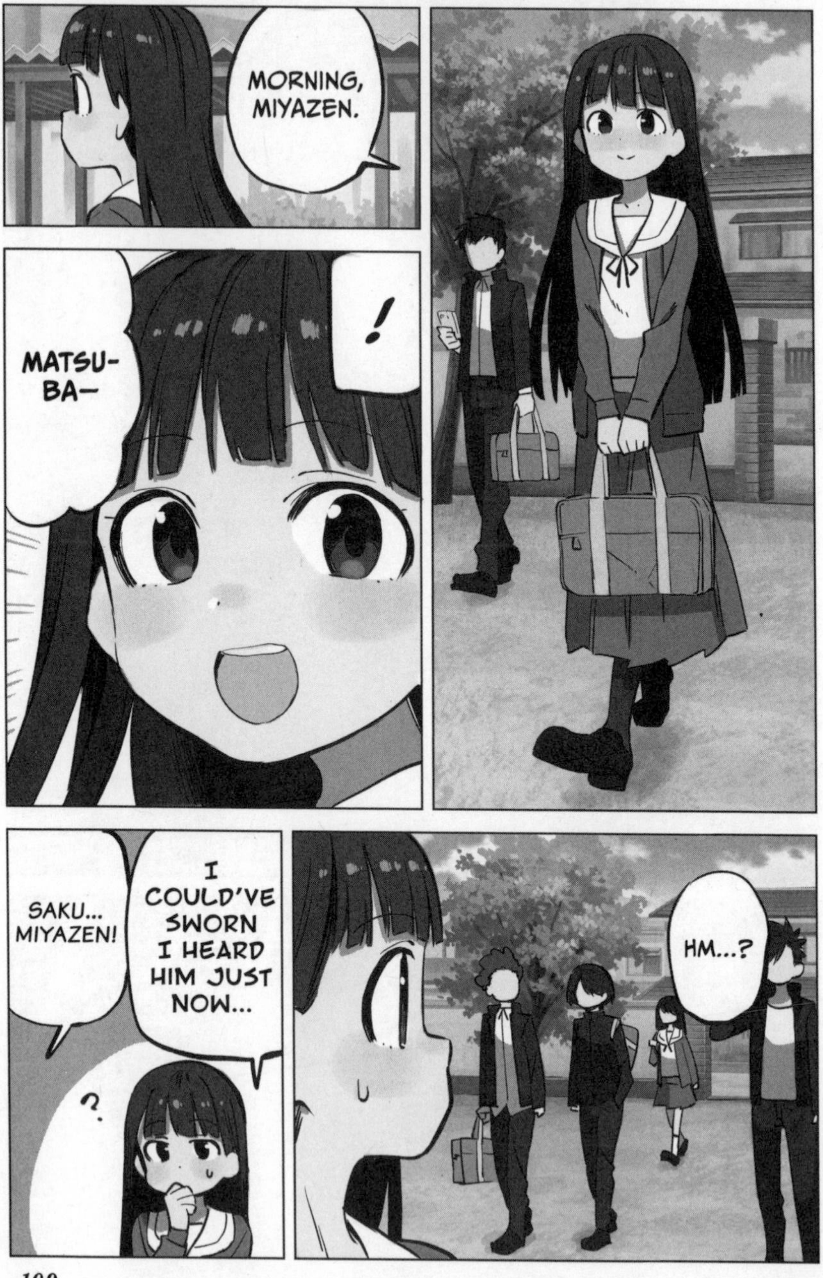
MORNING, MIYAZEN.
!
MATSU-BA—
HM...?
I COULD'VE SWORN I HEARD HIM JUST NOW...
SAKU... MIYAZEN!
?

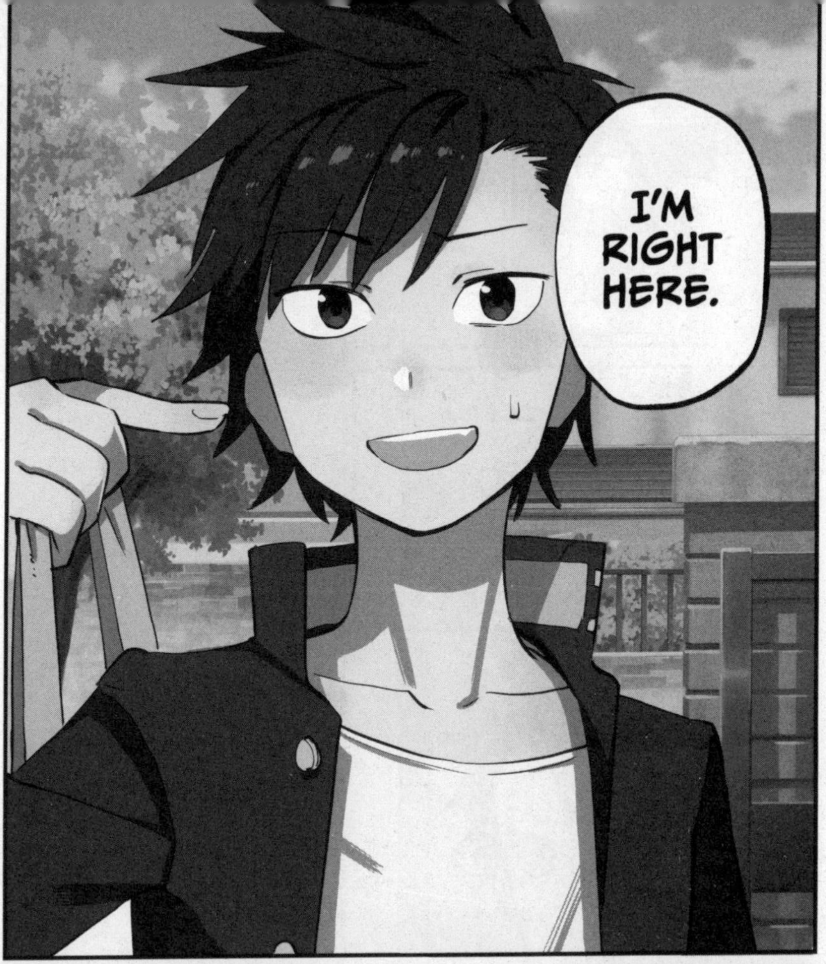
I'M RIGHT HERE.
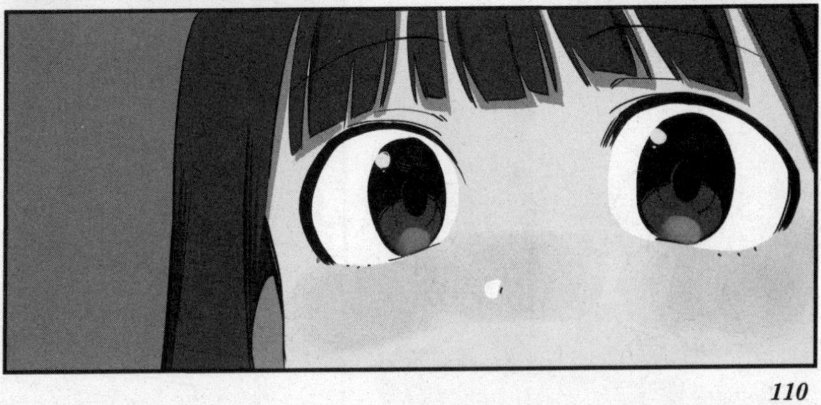

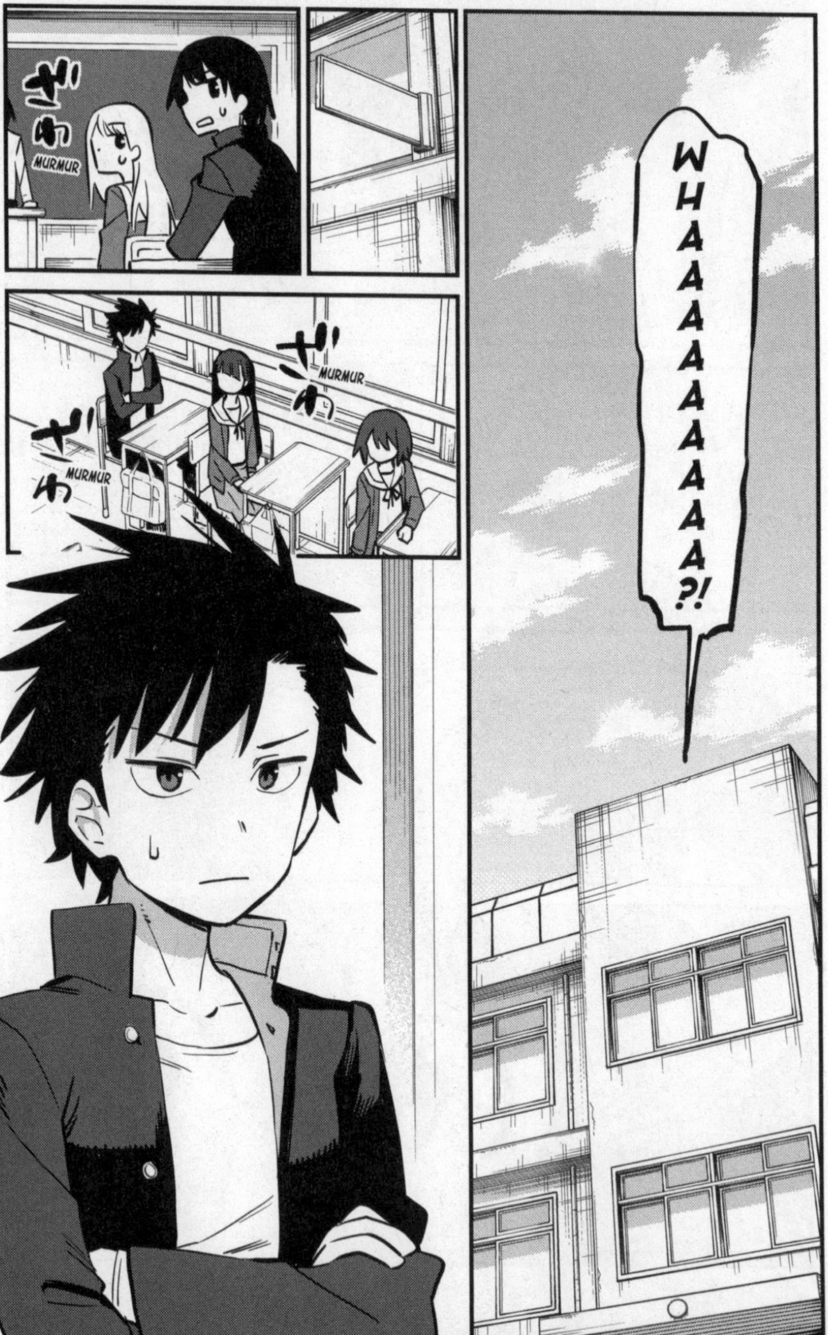
WHAAAAAAAAA?!
ざわ
MURMUR
ざわ
MURMUR
ざわ
MURMUR

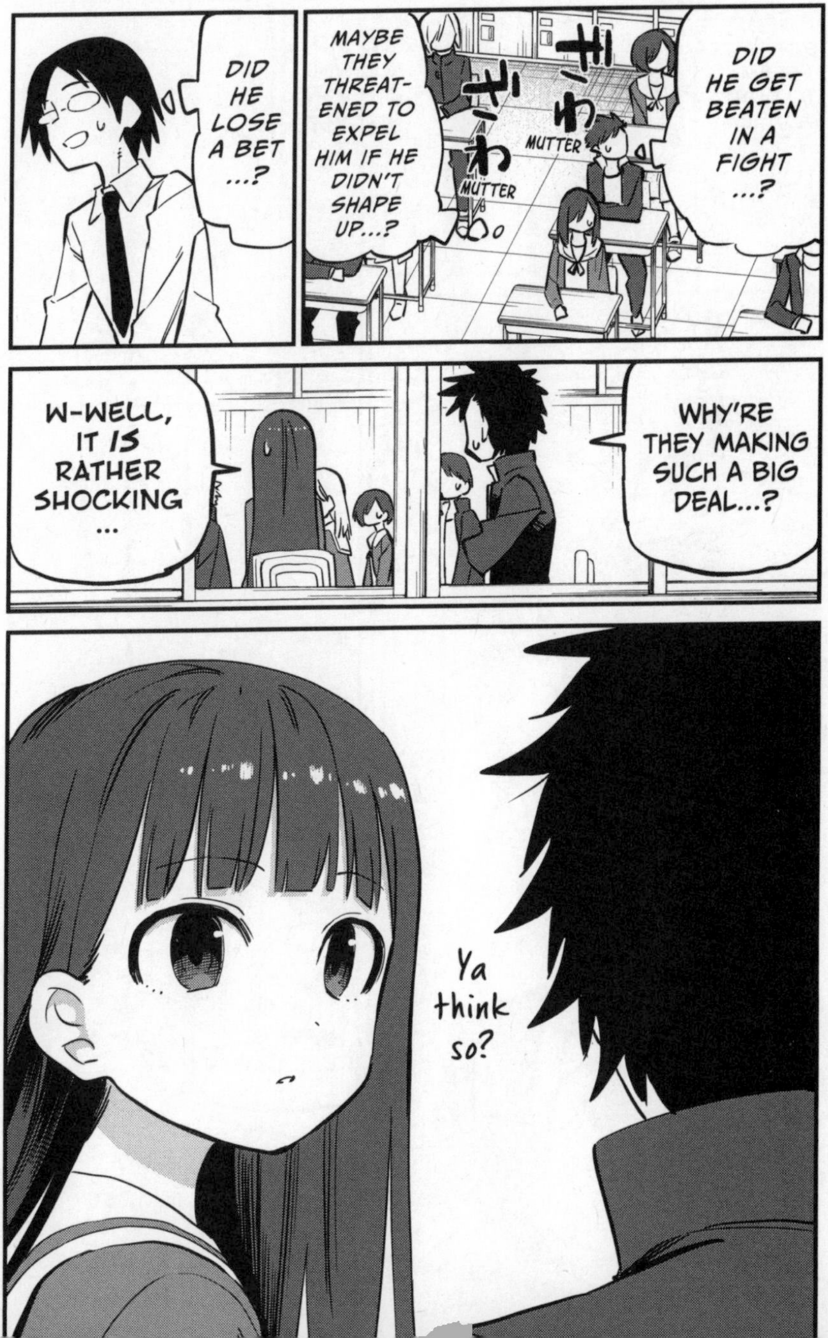
DID HE GET BEATEN IN A FIGHT ...?
ざわ MUTTER
ざわ MUTTER
MAYBE THEY THREAT-ENED TO EXPEL HIM IF HE DIDN'T SHAPE UP...?
DID HE LOSE A BET ...?
WHY'RE THEY MAKING SUCH A BIG DEAL...?
W-WELL, IT IS RATHER SHOCKING ...
Ya think so?

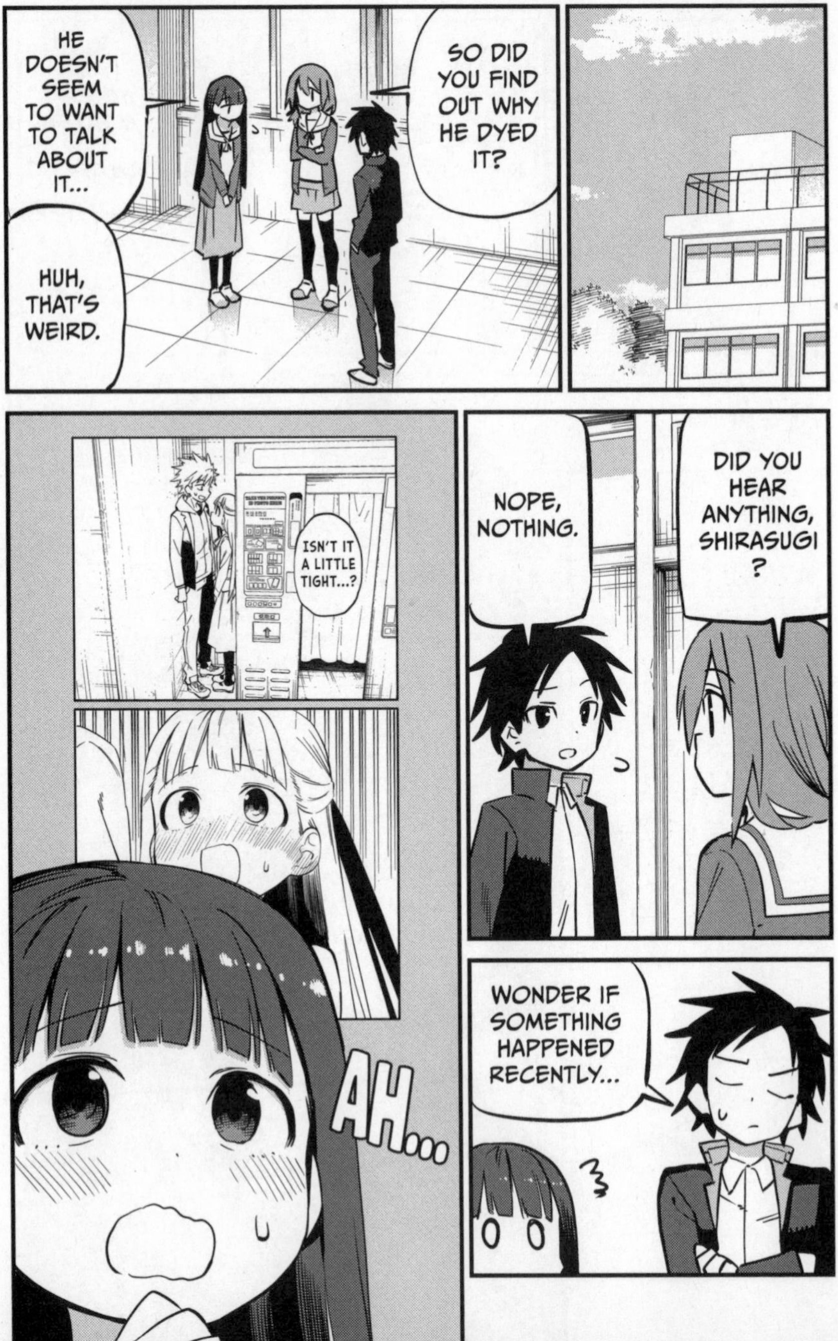
SO DID YOU FIND OUT WHY HE DYED IT?
HE DOESN'T SEEM TO WANT TO TALK ABOUT IT...
HUH, THAT'S WEIRD.
DID YOU HEAR ANYTHING, SHIRASUGI?
NOPE, NOTHING.
WONDER IF SOMETHING HAPPENED RECENTLY...
ISN'T IT A LITTLE TIGHT...?
AH...

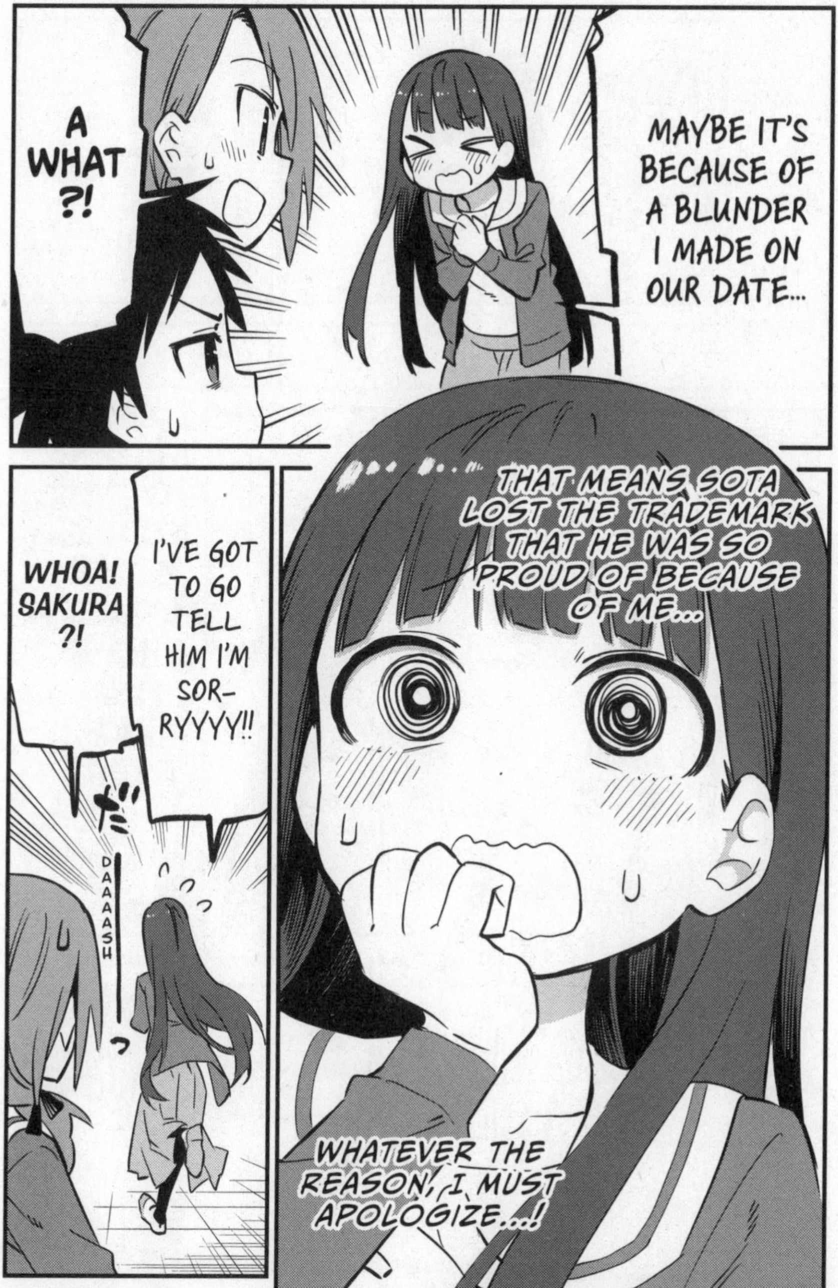
MAYBE IT'S BECAUSE OF A BLUNDER I MADE ON OUR DATE...
A WHAT?!
THAT MEANS SOTA LOST THE TRADEMARK THAT HE WAS SO PROUD OF BECAUSE OF ME...
WHATEVER THE REASON, I MUST APOLOGIZE...!
I'VE GOT TO GO TELL HIM I'M SOR-RYYYY!!
WHOA! SAKURA?!
DAAAAASH

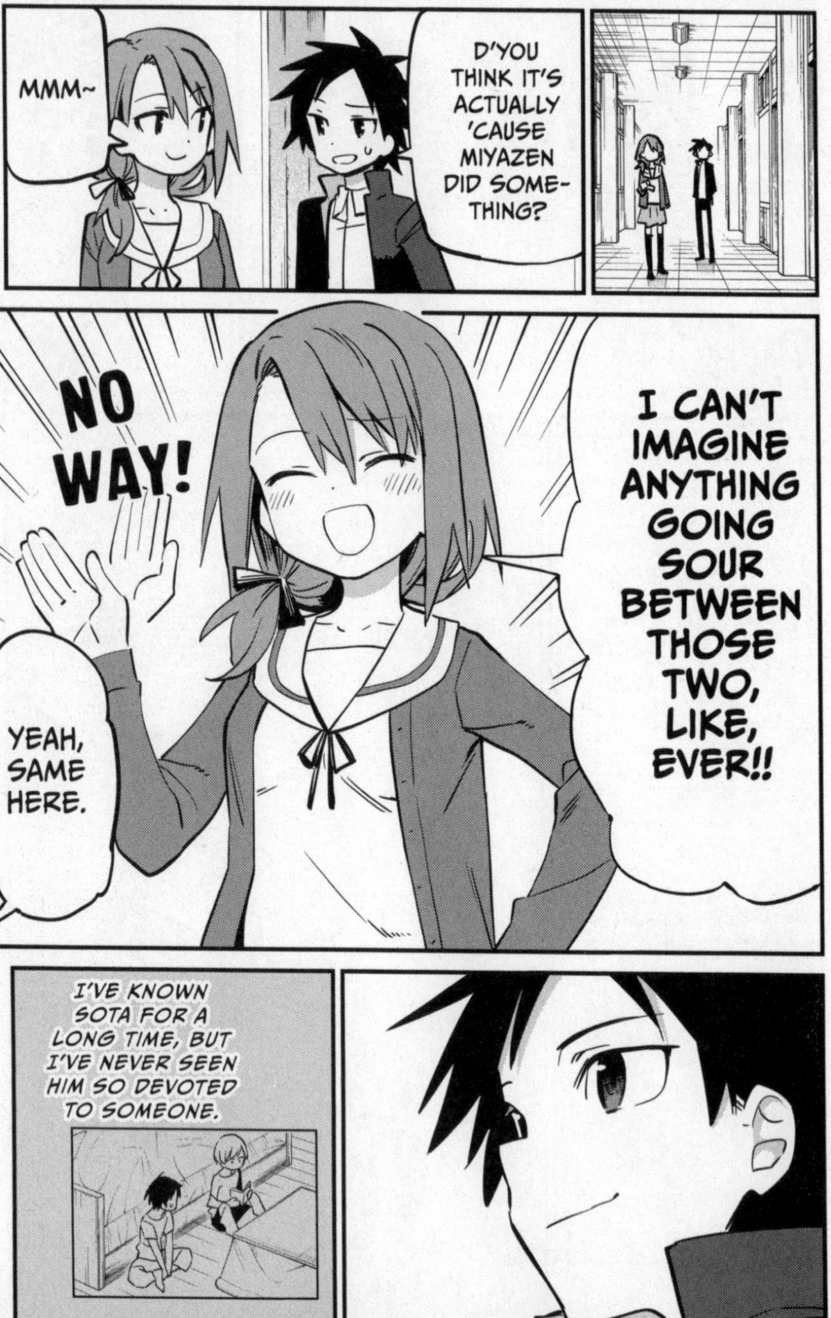
D'YOU THINK IT'S ACTUALLY 'CAUSE MIYAZEN DID SOME-THING?
MMM~
I CAN'T IMAGINE ANYTHING GOING SOUR BETWEEN THOSE TWO, LIKE, EVER!!
NO WAY!
YEAH, SAME HERE.
I'VE KNOWN SOTA FOR A LONG TIME, BUT I'VE NEVER SEEN HIM SO DEVOTED TO SOMEONE.

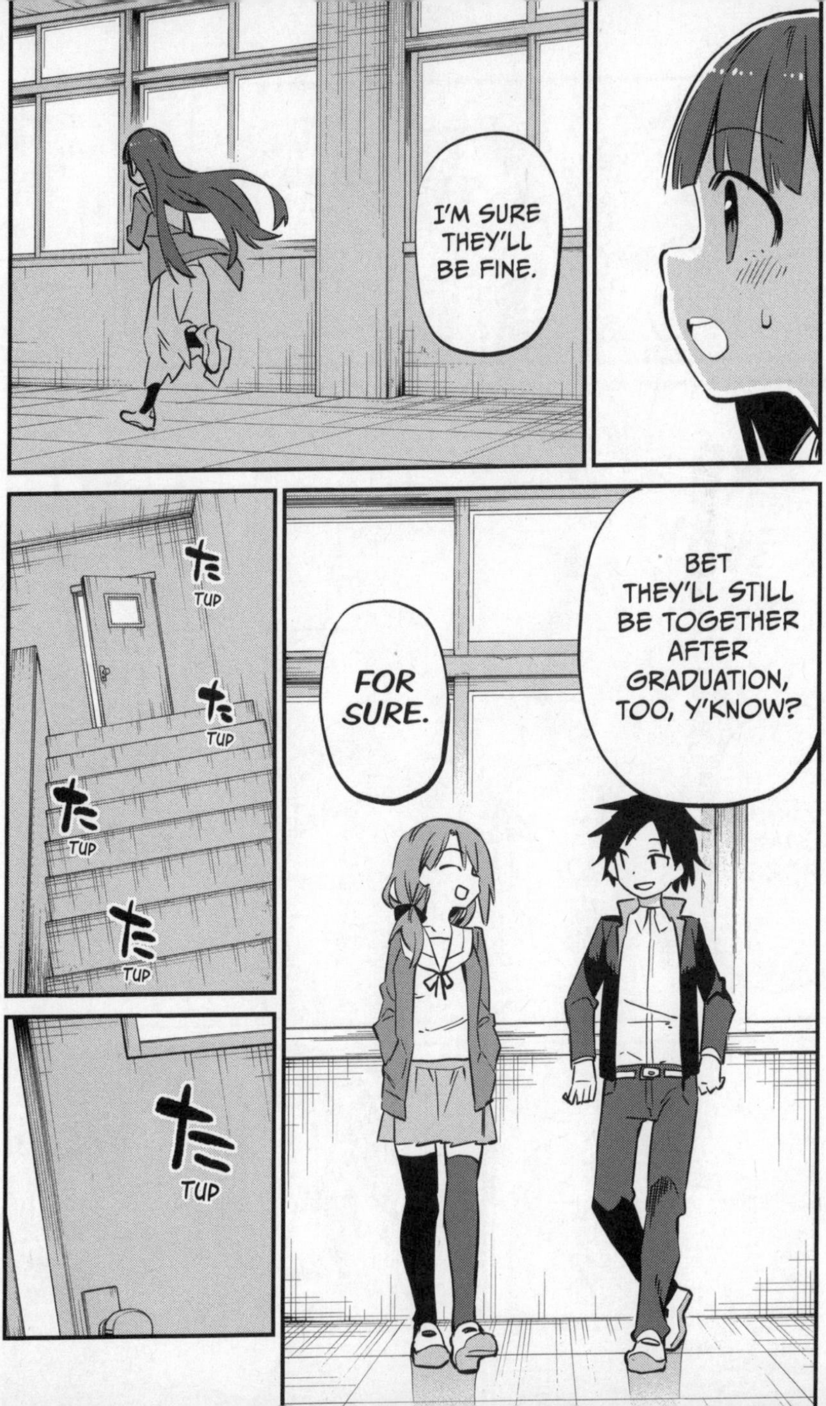
I'M SURE THEY'LL BE FINE.
BET THEY'LL STILL BE TOGETHER AFTER GRADUATION, TOO, Y'KNOW?
FOR SURE.
た TUP
た TUP
た TUP
た TUP
た TUP

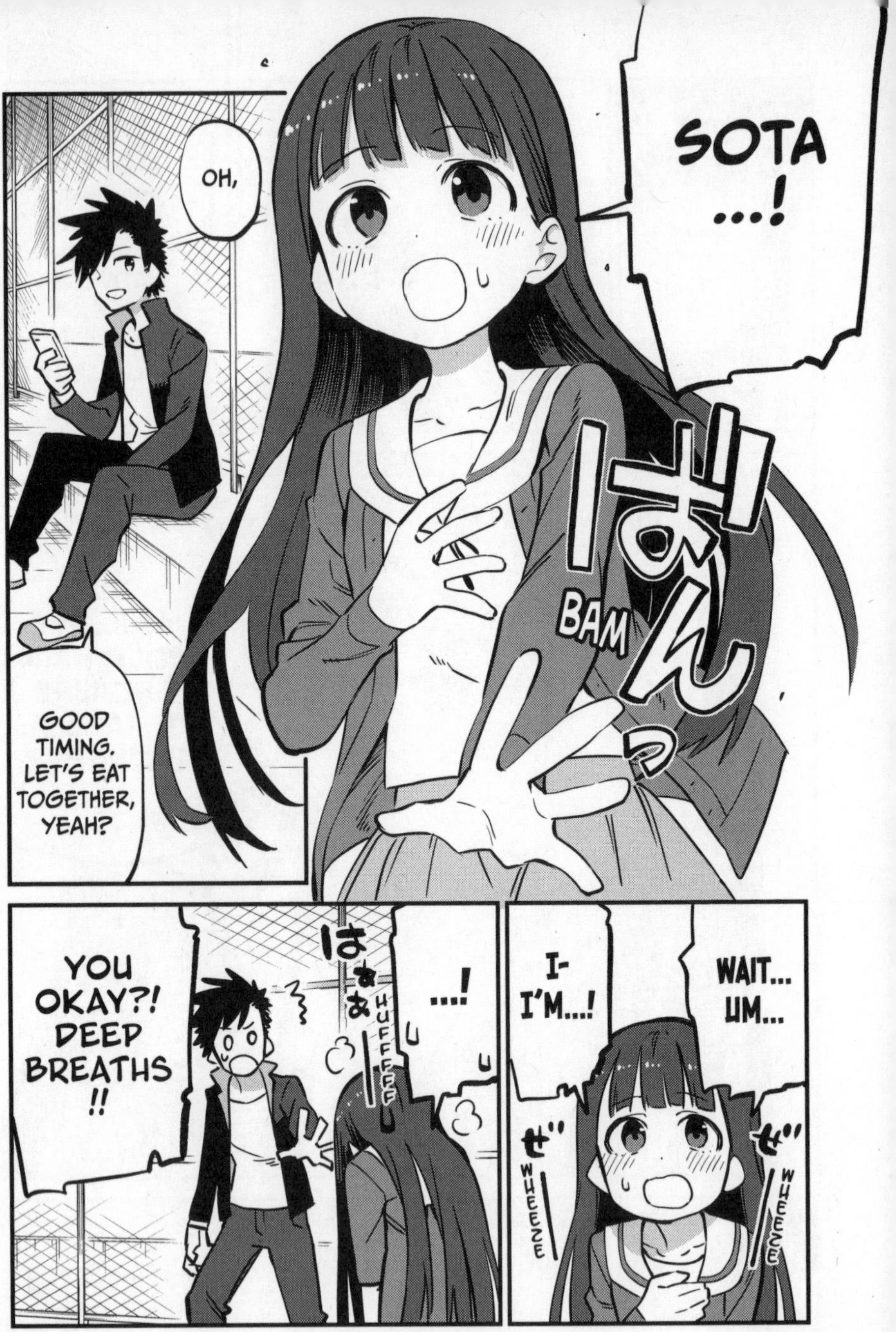
SOTA ...!
ばんっ
BAM
OH,
GOOD TIMING. LET'S EAT TOGETHER, YEAH?
WAIT... UM...
I- I'M...!
ぜ
WHEEZE
ぜ
WHEEZE
...!
はぁぁ
HUFFFFFF
YOU OKAY?! DEEP BREATHS !!

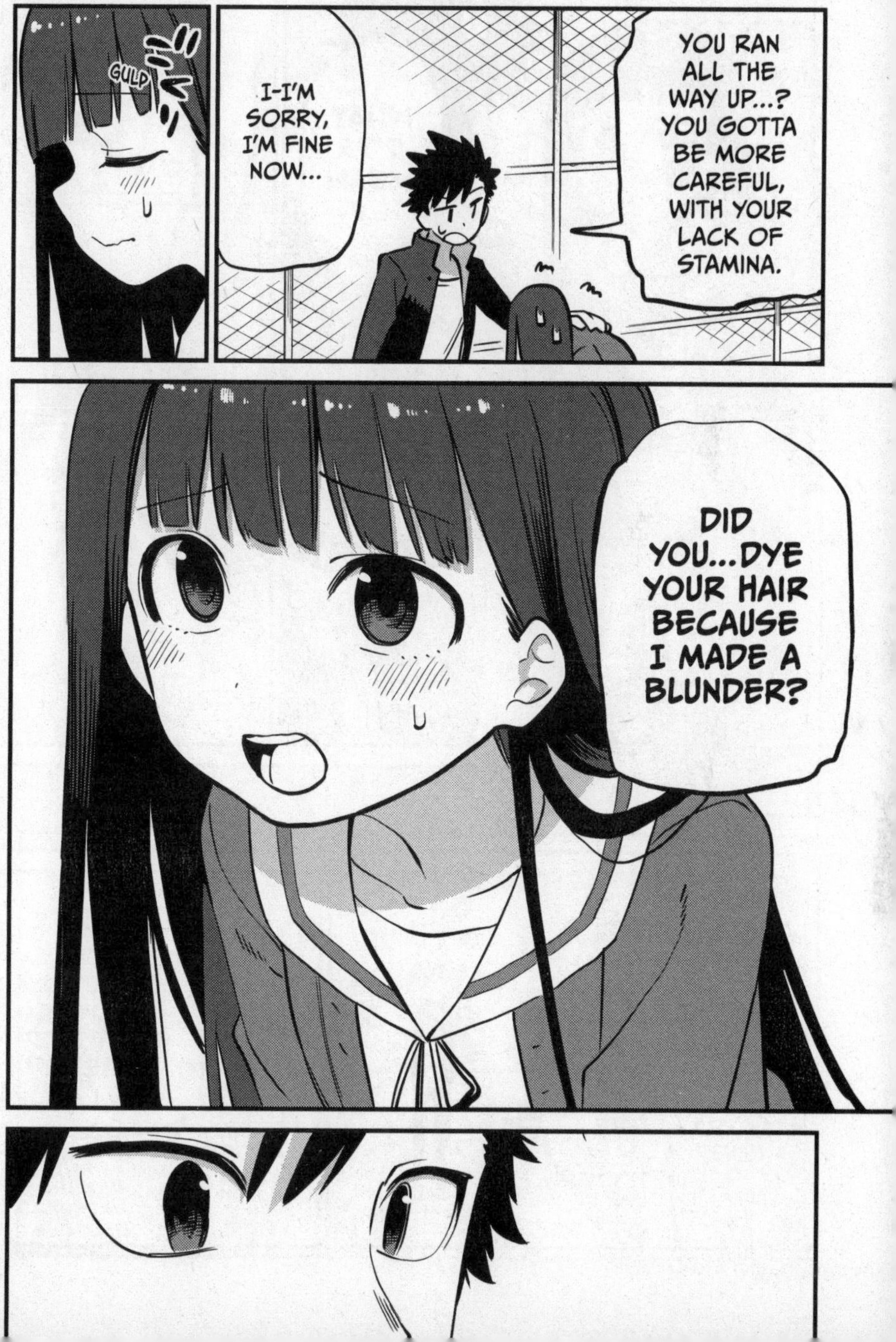
YOU RAN ALL THE WAY UP...? YOU GOTTA BE MORE CAREFUL, WITH YOUR LACK OF STAMINA.
I-I'M SORRY, I'M FINE NOW...
GULP
DID YOU...DYE YOUR HAIR BECAUSE I MADE A BLUNDER?

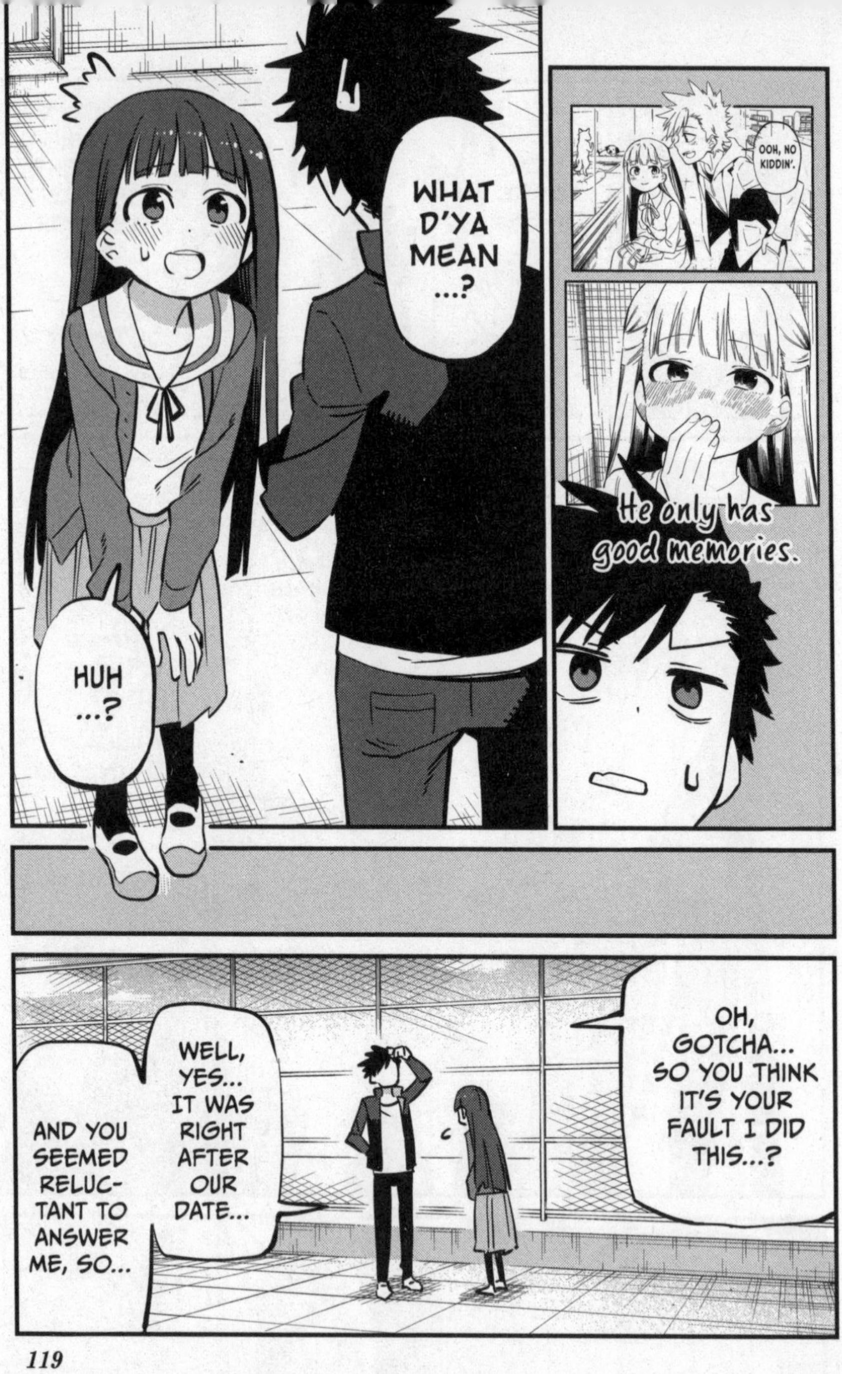
OOH, NO KIDDIN'.
He only has good memories.
WHAT D'YA MEAN ...?
HUH ...?
OH, GOTCHA... SO YOU THINK IT'S YOUR FAULT I DID THIS...?
WELL, YES... IT WAS RIGHT AFTER OUR DATE...
AND YOU SEEMED RELUC-TANT TO ANSWER ME, SO...

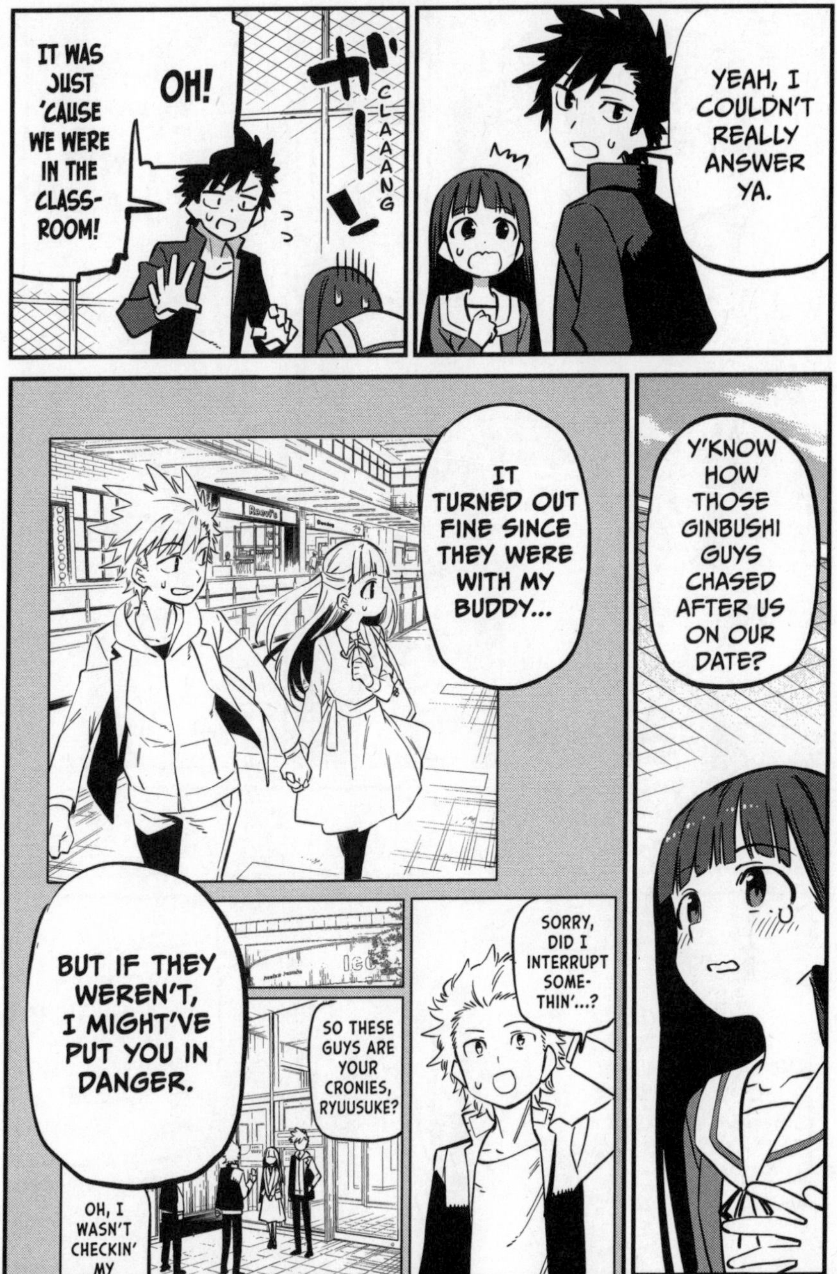
YEAH, I COULDN'T REALLY ANSWER YA.
CLAAAANG
OH!
IT WAS JUST 'CAUSE WE WERE IN THE CLASS-ROOM!
Y'KNOW HOW THOSE GINBUSHI GUYS CHASED AFTER US ON OUR DATE?
IT TURNED OUT FINE SINCE THEY WERE WITH MY BUDDY...
SORRY, DID I INTERRUPT SOME-THIN'...?
BUT IF THEY WEREN'T, I MIGHT'VE PUT YOU IN DANGER.
SO THESE GUYS ARE YOUR CRONIES, RYUUSUKE?
OH, I WASN'T CHECKIN' MY PHONE.

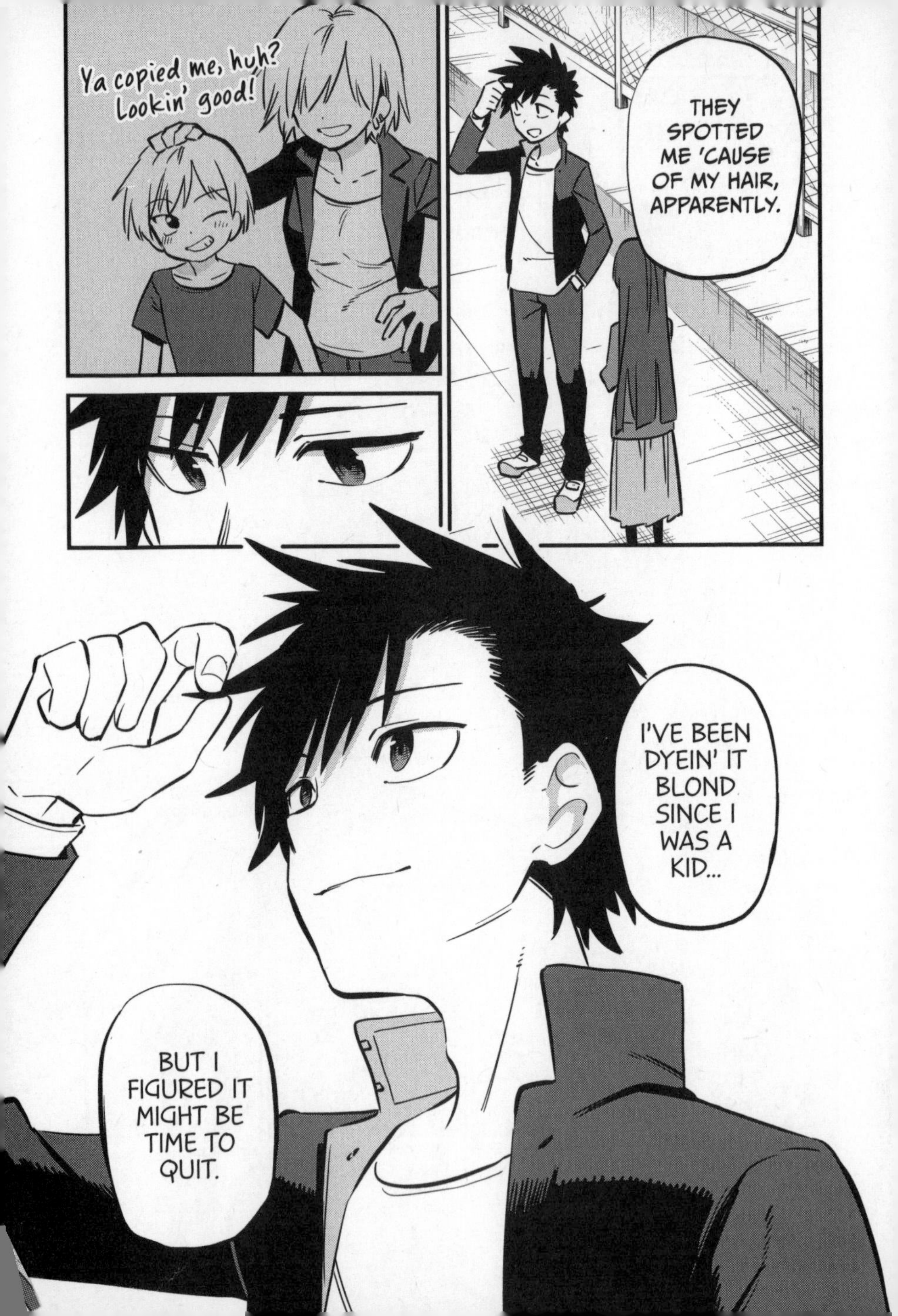
THEY SPOTTED ME 'CAUSE OF MY HAIR, APPARENTLY.
Ya copied me, huh? Lookin' good!
I'VE BEEN DYEIN' IT BLOND SINCE I WAS A KID...
BUT I FIGURED IT MIGHT BE TIME TO QUIT.

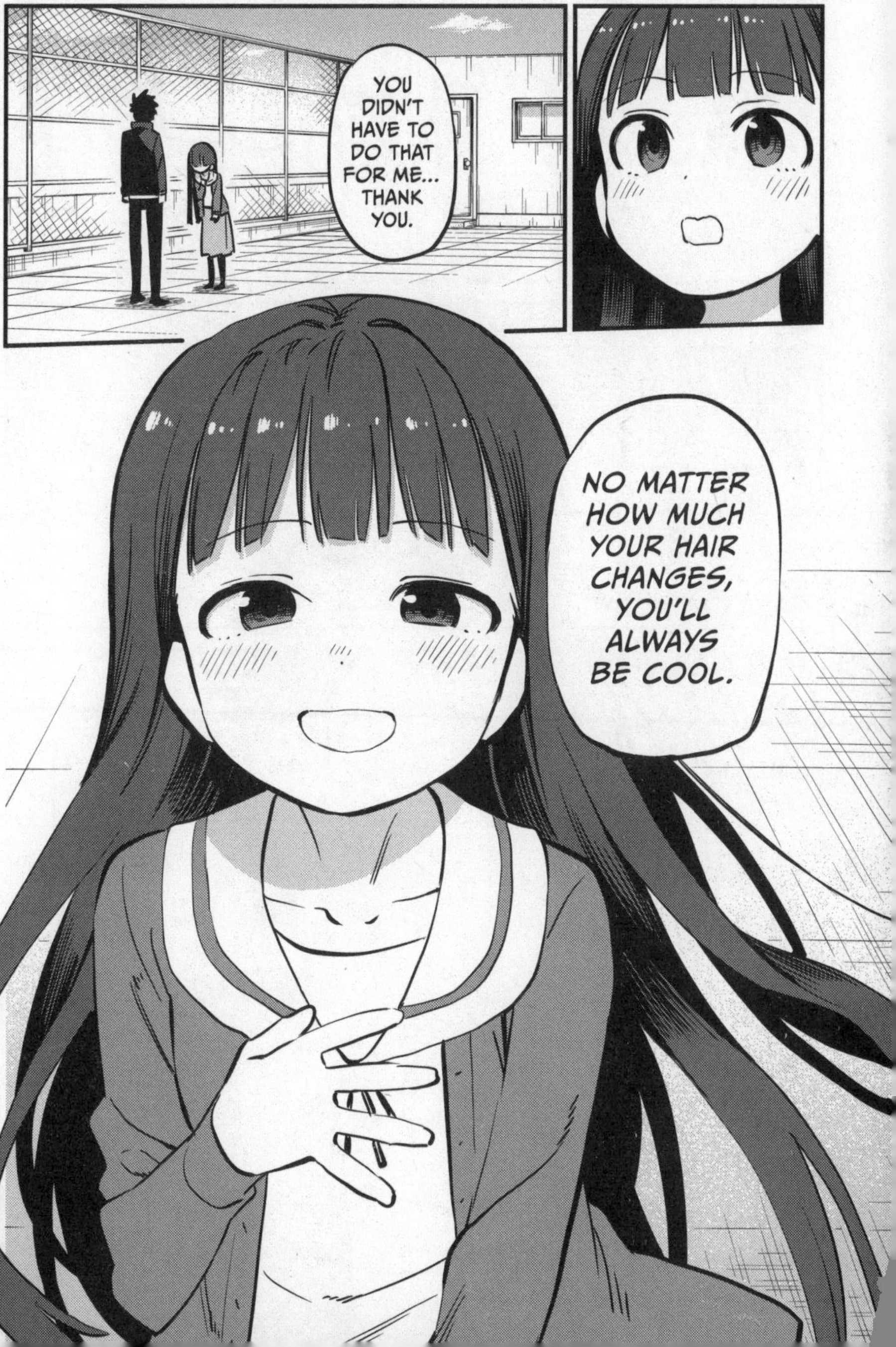
YOU DIDN'T HAVE TO DO THAT FOR ME... THANK YOU.
NO MATTER HOW MUCH YOUR HAIR CHANGES, YOU'LL ALWAYS BE COOL.

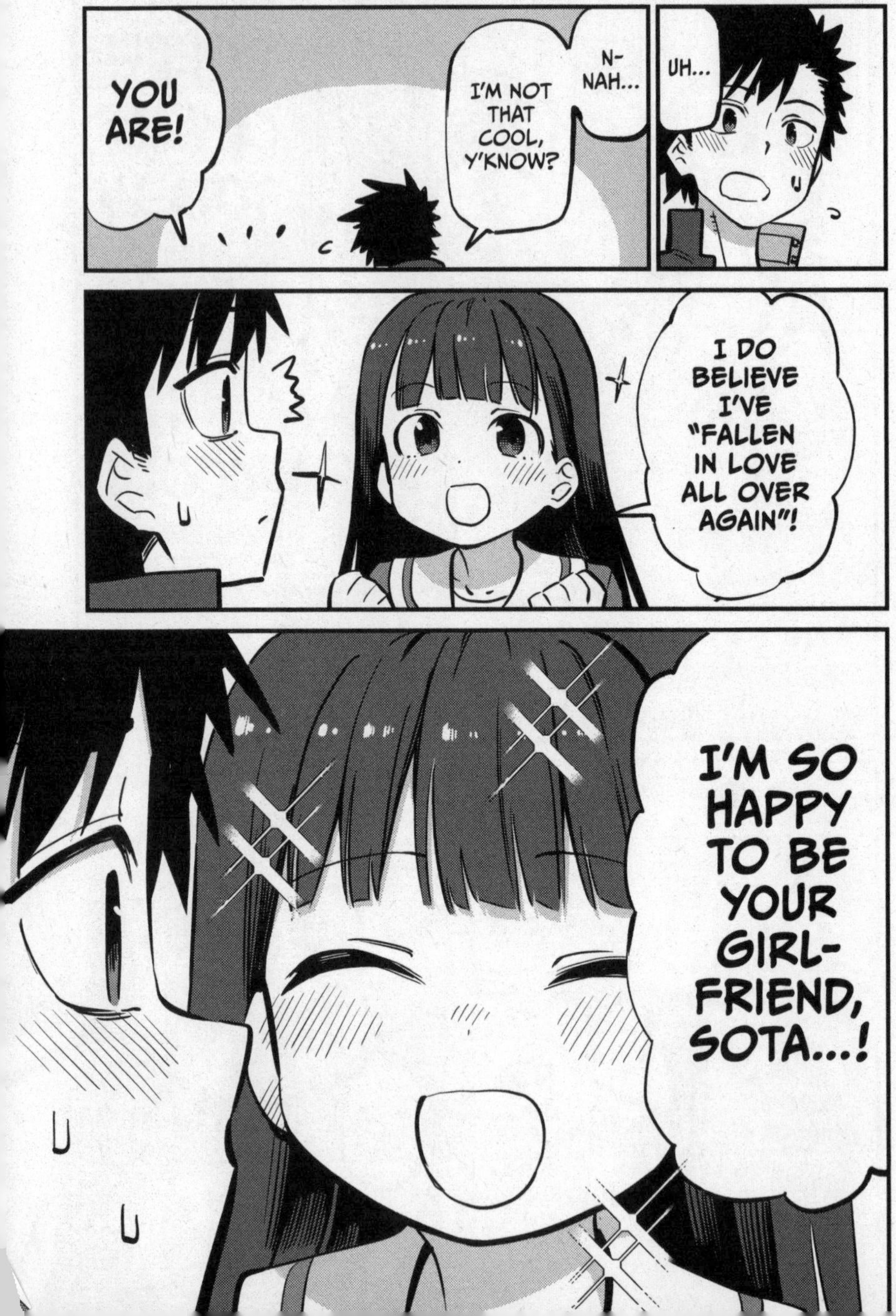
UH...
N-NAH...
I'M NOT THAT COOL, Y'KNOW?
YOU ARE!
I DO BELIEVE I'VE "FALLEN IN LOVE ALL OVER AGAIN"!
I'M SO HAPPY TO BE YOUR GIRL-FRIEND, SOTA...!

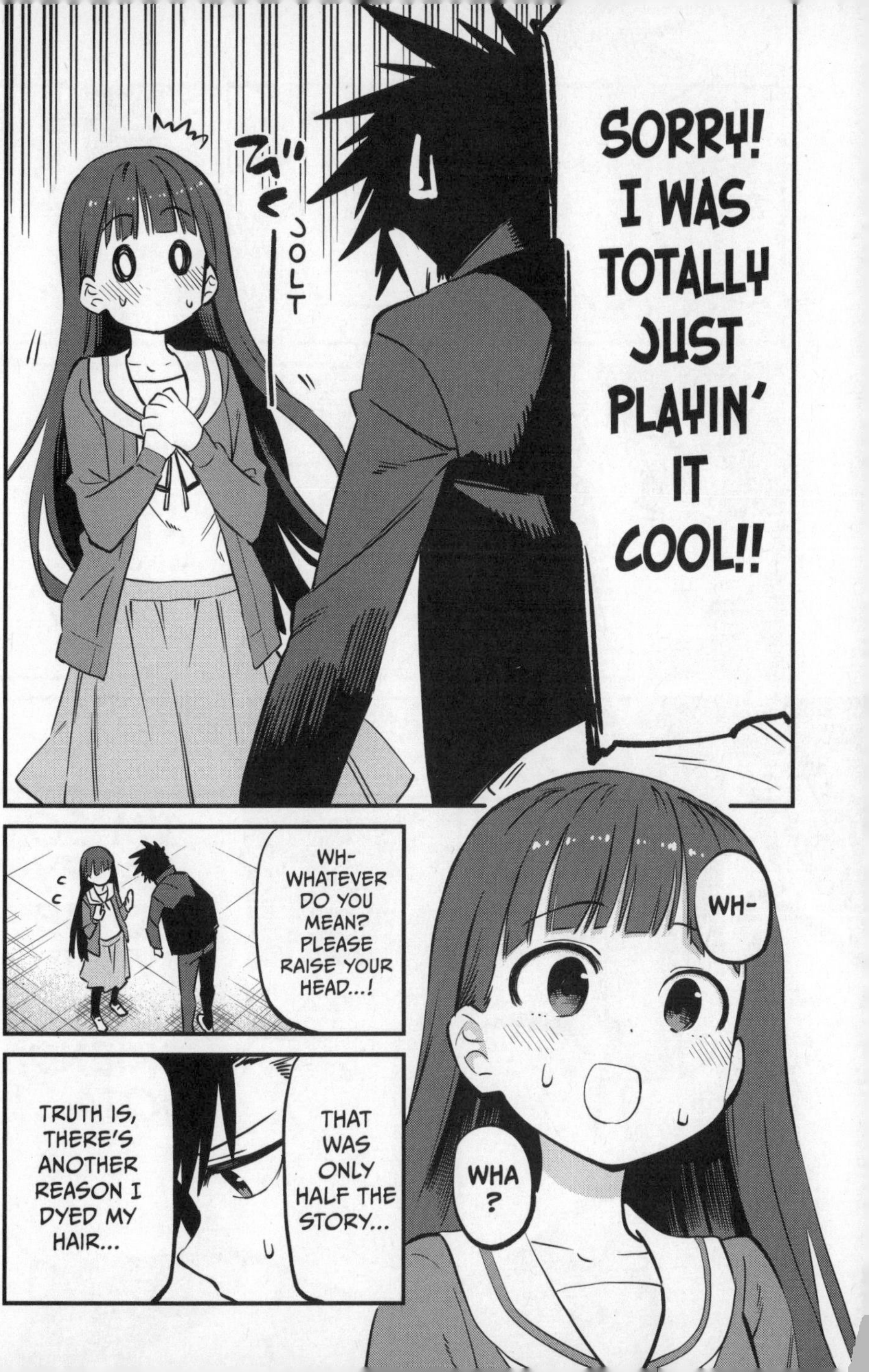
SORRY! I WAS TOTALLY JUST PLAYIN' IT COOL!!
JOLT
WH-
WHA?
WH- WHATEVER DO YOU MEAN? PLEASE RAISE YOUR HEAD...!
THAT WAS ONLY HALF THE STORY...
TRUTH IS, THERE'S ANOTHER REASON I DYED MY HAIR...

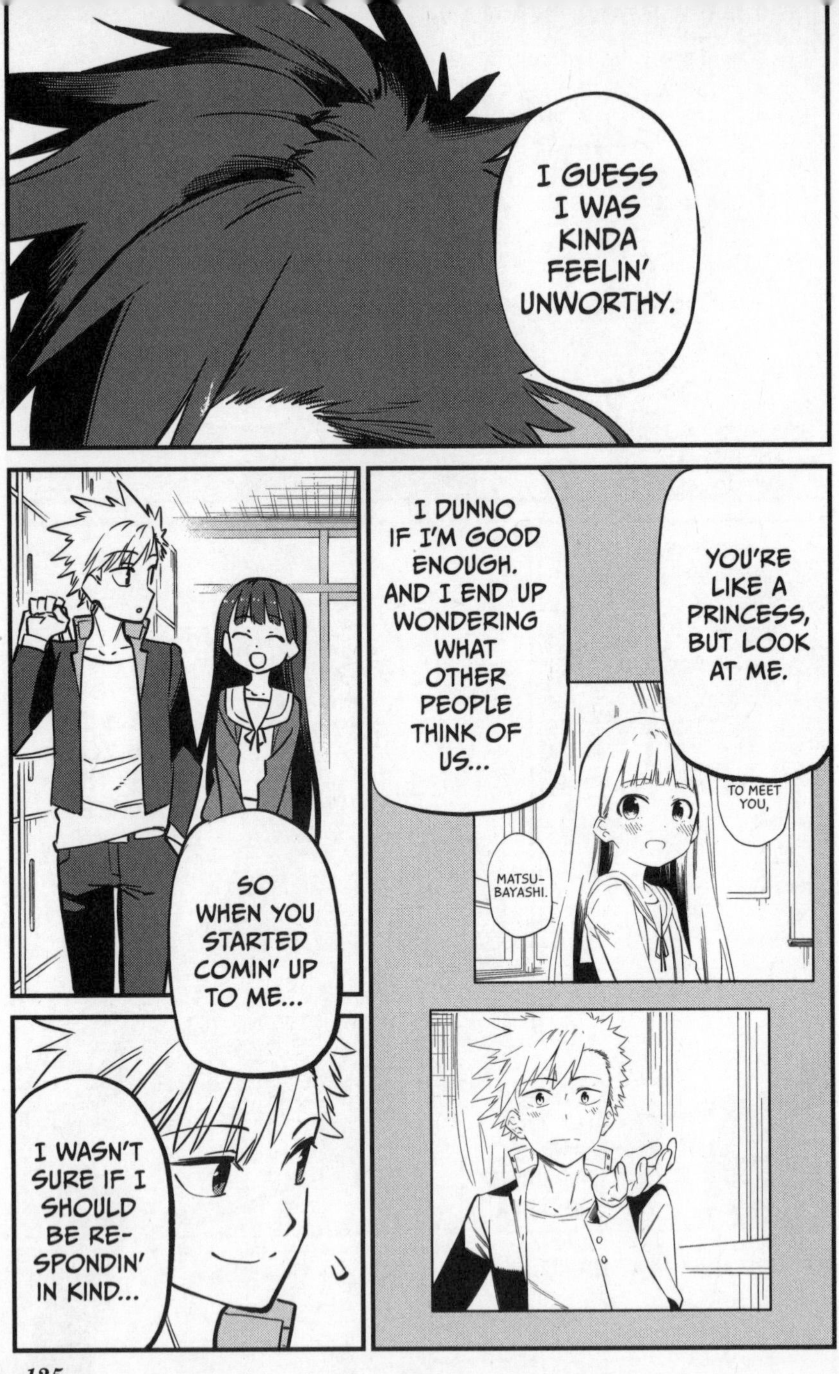
I GUESS I WAS KINDA FEELIN' UNWORTHY.
YOU'RE LIKE A PRINCESS, BUT LOOK AT ME.
I DUNNO IF I'M GOOD ENOUGH. AND I END UP WONDERING WHAT OTHER PEOPLE THINK OF US...
TO MEET YOU,
MATSU-BAYASHI.
SO WHEN YOU STARTED COMIN' UP TO ME...
I WASN'T SURE IF I SHOULD BE RE-SPONDIN' IN KIND...

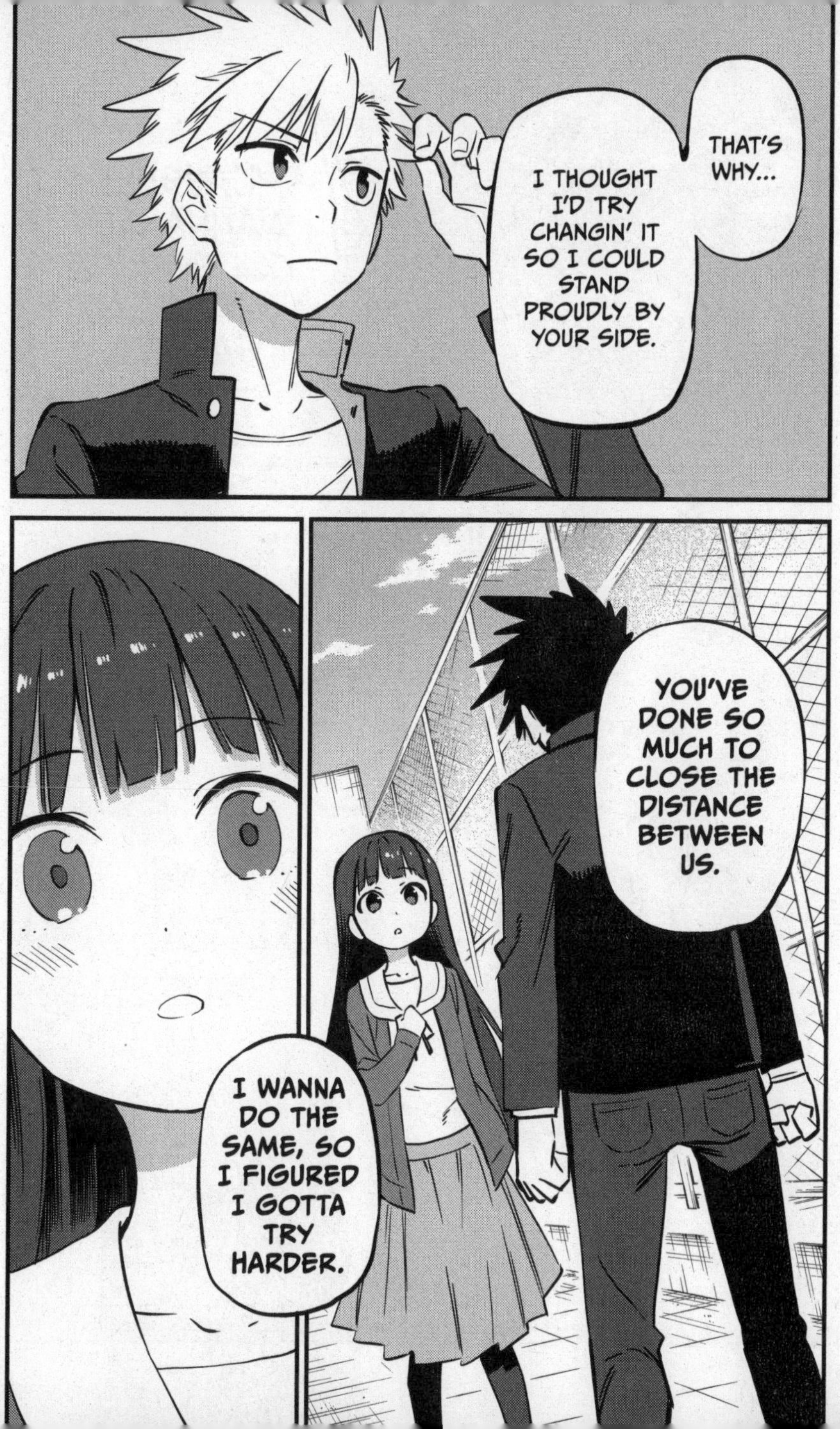
THAT'S WHY...
I THOUGHT I'D TRY CHANGIN' IT SO I COULD STAND PROUDLY BY YOUR SIDE.
YOU'VE DONE SO MUCH TO CLOSE THE DISTANCE BETWEEN US.
I WANNA DO THE SAME, SO I FIGURED I GOTTA TRY HARDER.

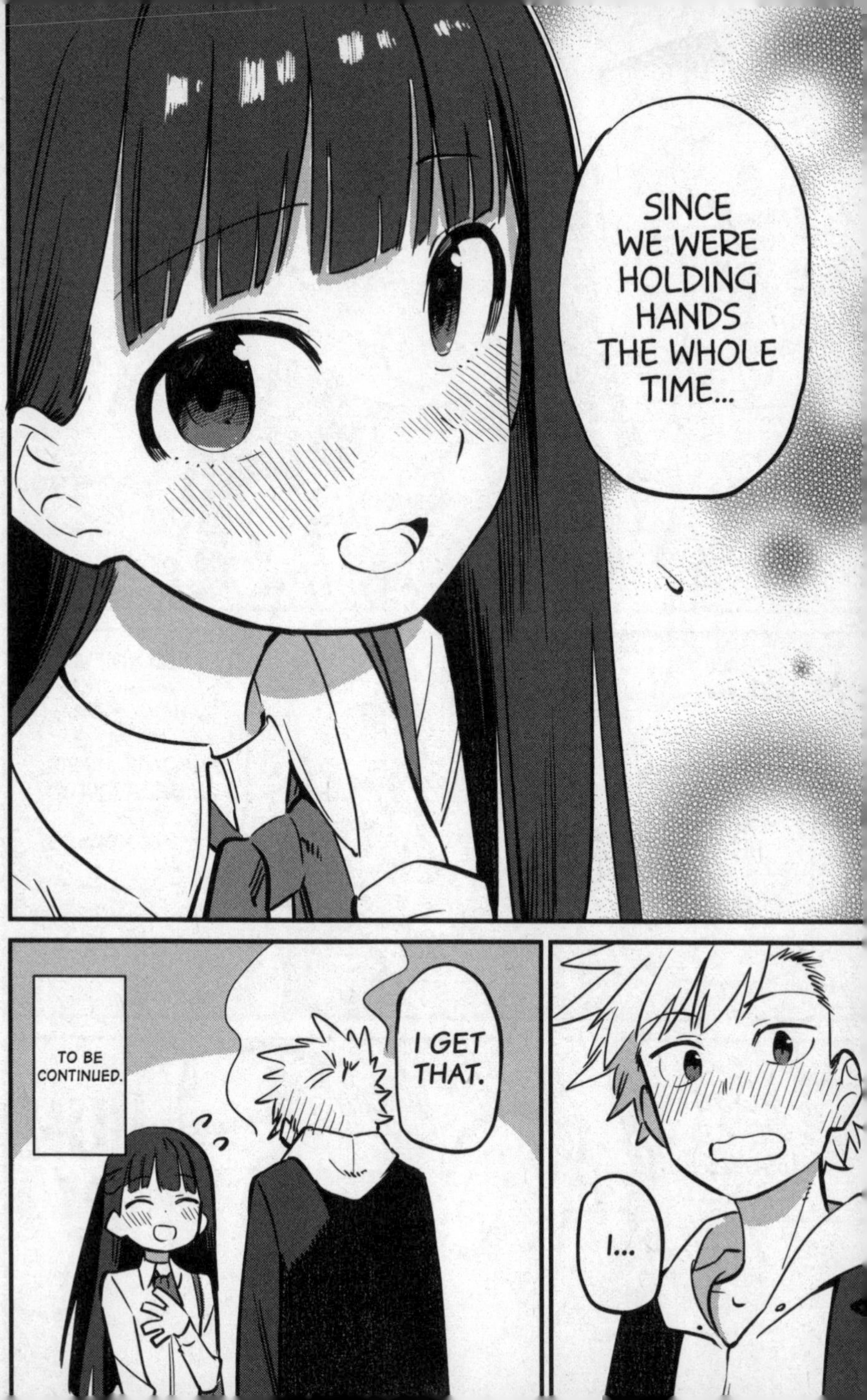
SINCE WE WERE HOLDING HANDS THE WHOLE TIME...
I...
I GET THAT.
TO BE CONTINUED.

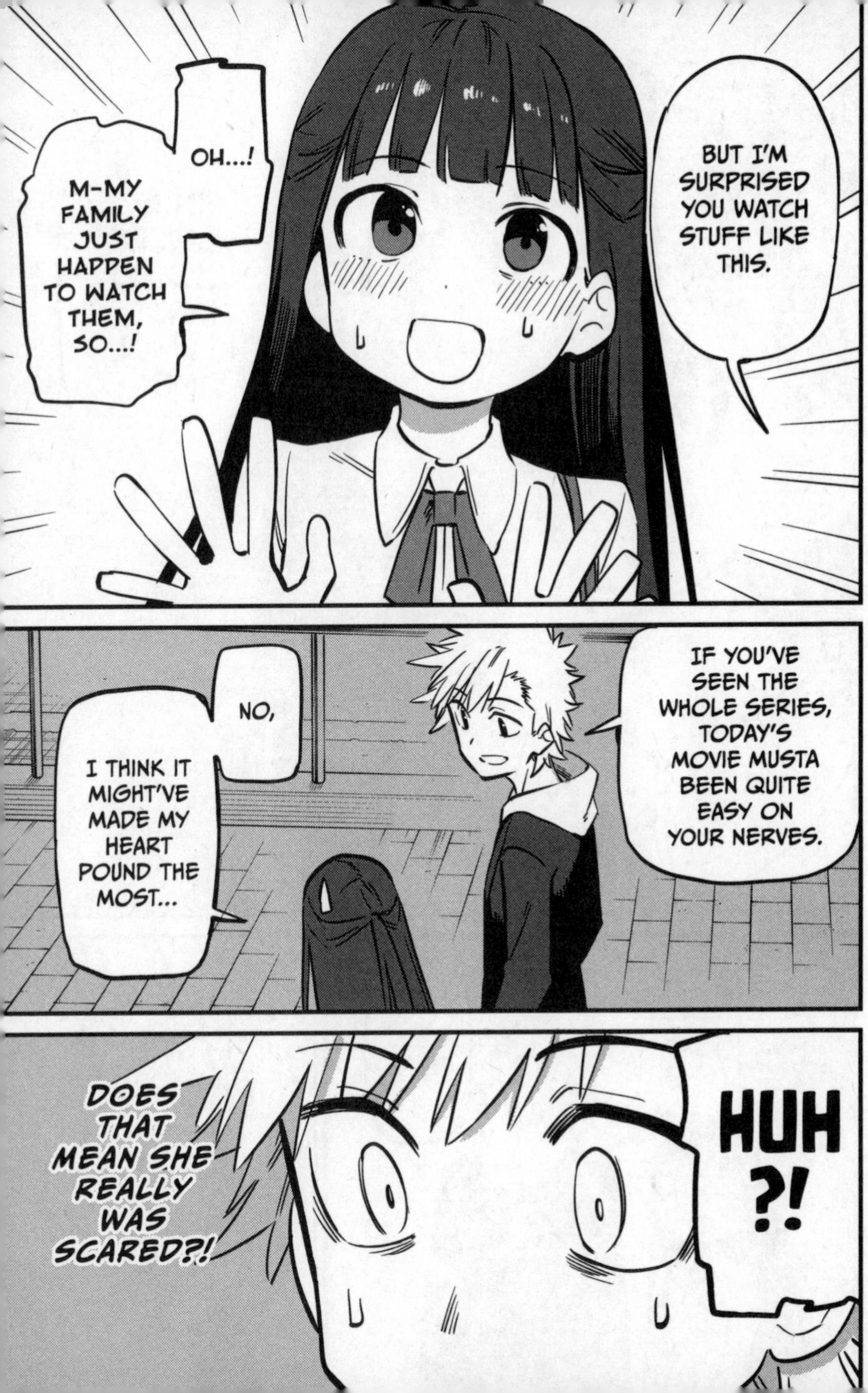
BUT I'M SURPRISED YOU WATCH STUFF LIKE THIS.
OH...!
M-MY FAMILY JUST HAPPEN TO WATCH THEM, SO...!
IF YOU'VE SEEN THE WHOLE SERIES, TODAY'S MOVIE MUSTA BEEN QUITE EASY ON YOUR NERVES.
NO,
I THINK IT MIGHT'VE MADE MY HEART POUND THE MOST...
HUH ?!
DOES THAT MEAN SHE REALLY WAS SCARED?!

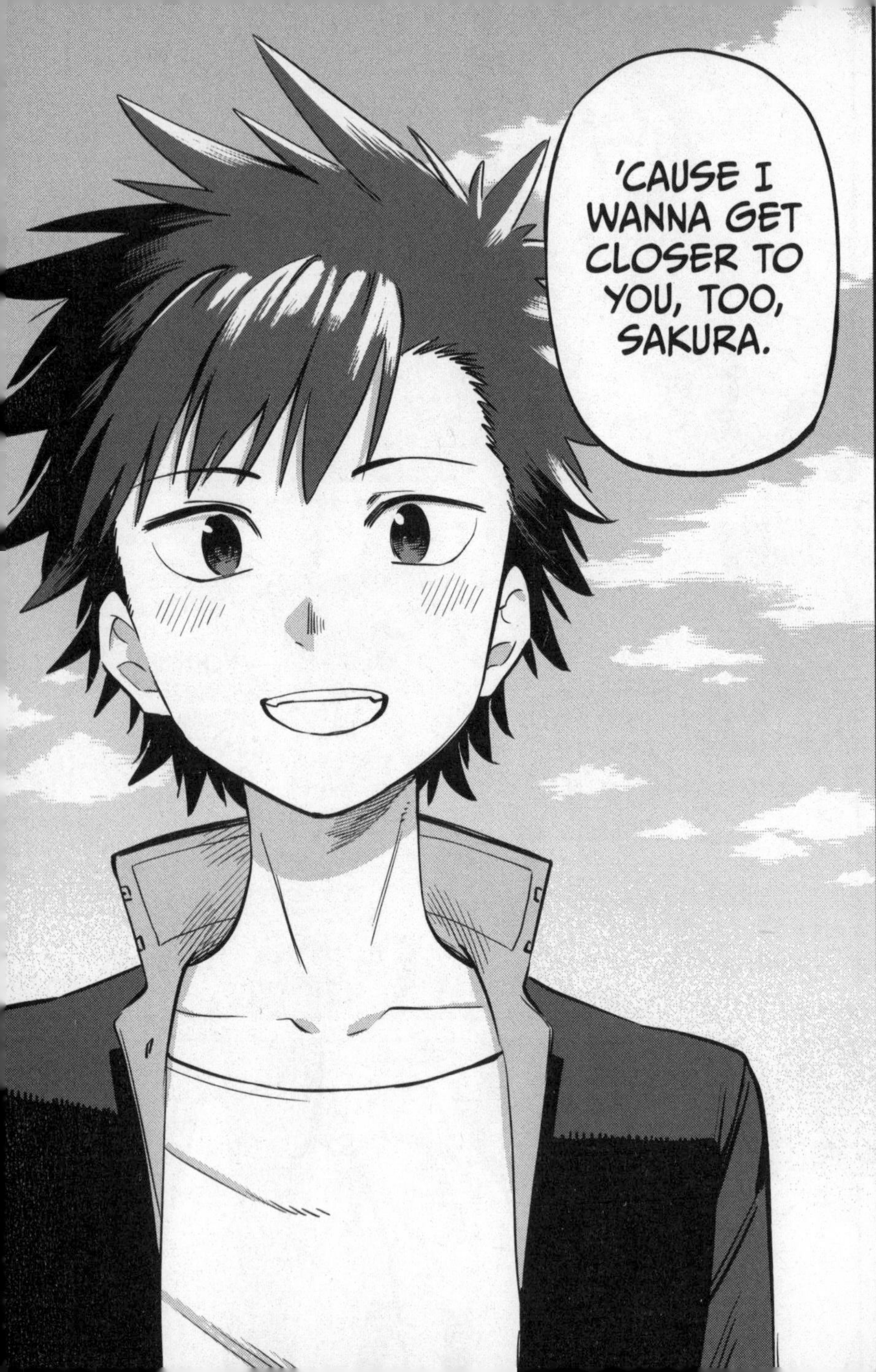
'CAUSE I WANNA GET CLOSER TO YOU, TOO, SAKURA.

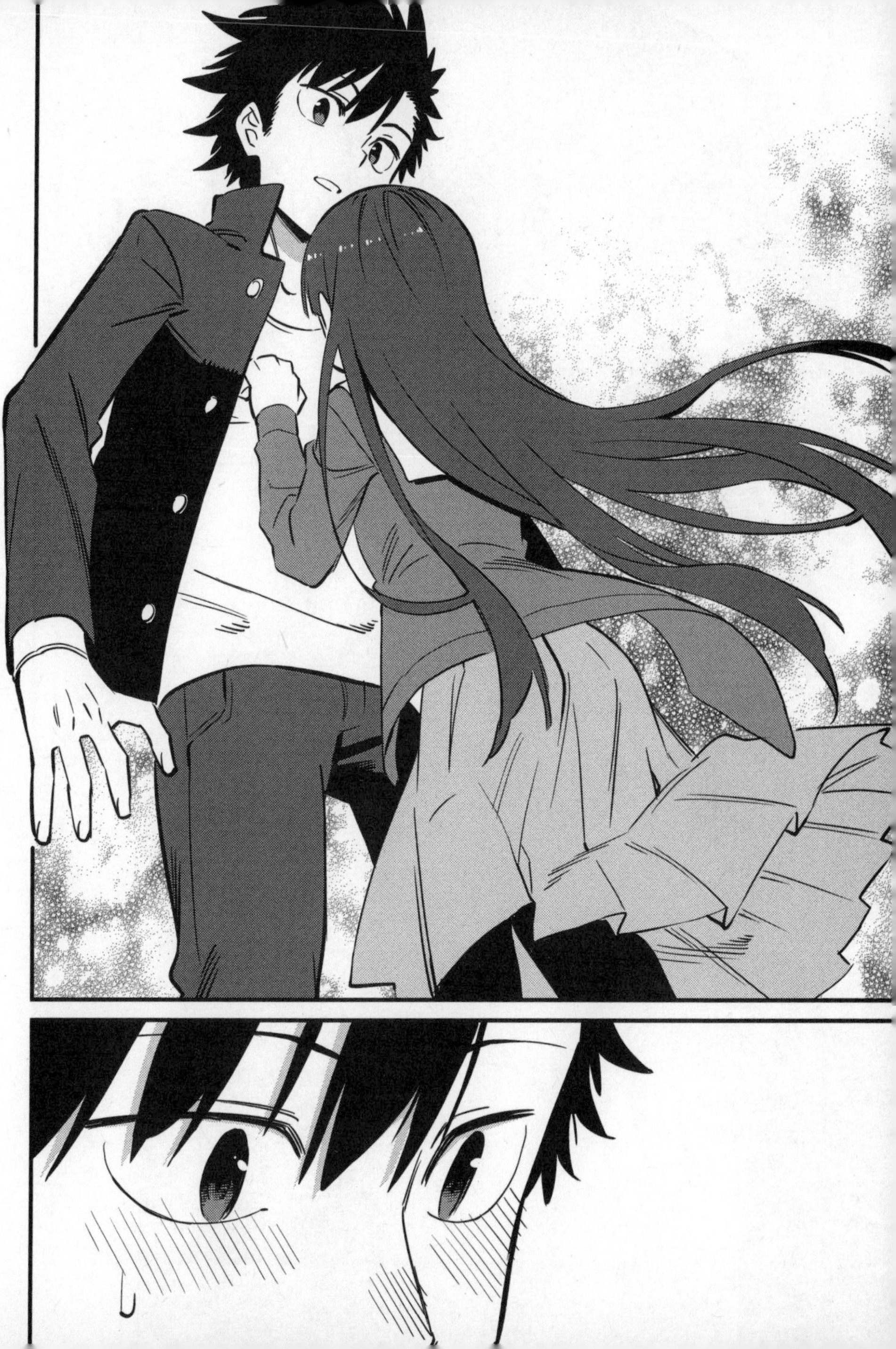

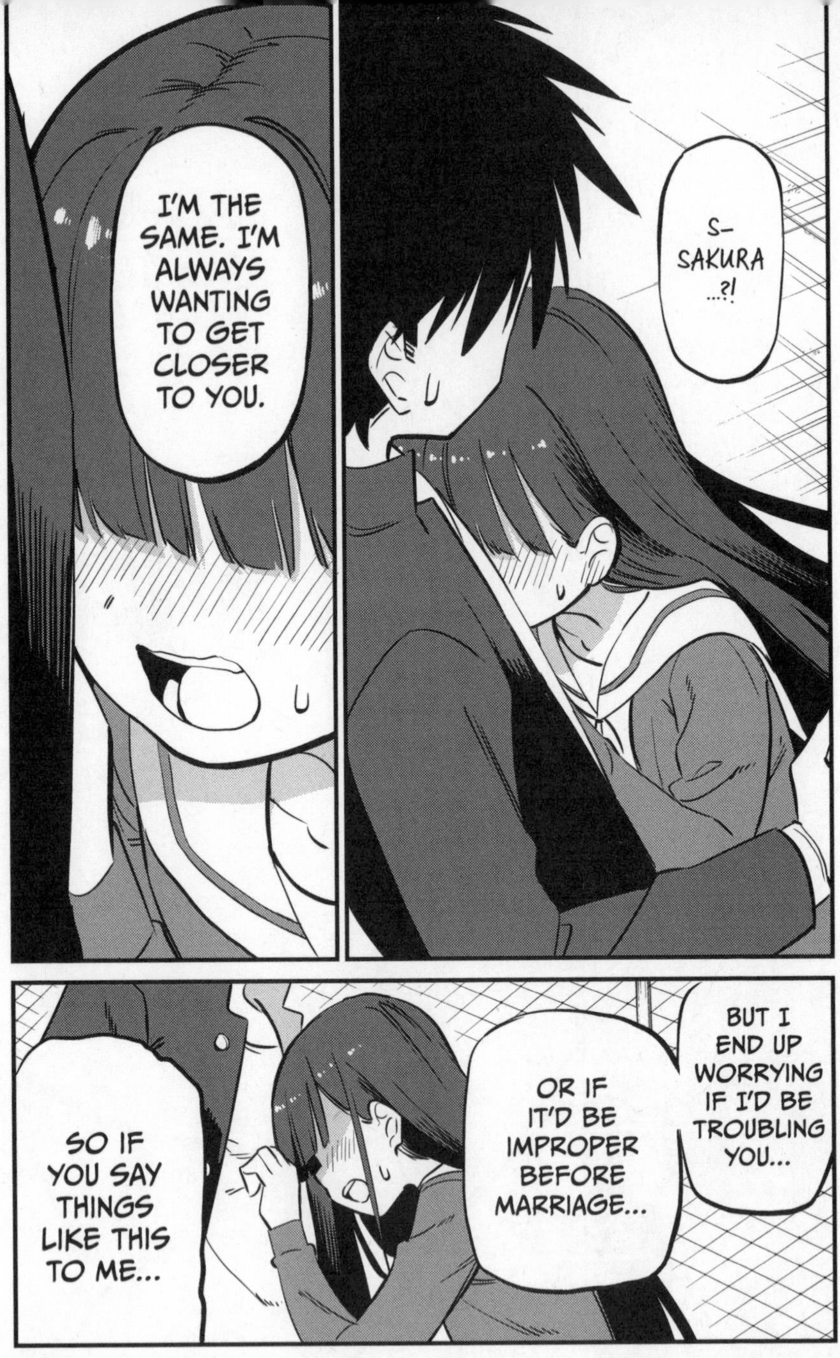
S-SAKURA ...?!
I'M THE SAME. I'M ALWAYS WANTING TO GET CLOSER TO YOU.
BUT I END UP WORRYING IF I'D BE TROUBLING YOU...
OR IF IT'D BE IMPROPER BEFORE MARRIAGE...
SO IF YOU SAY THINGS LIKE THIS TO ME...

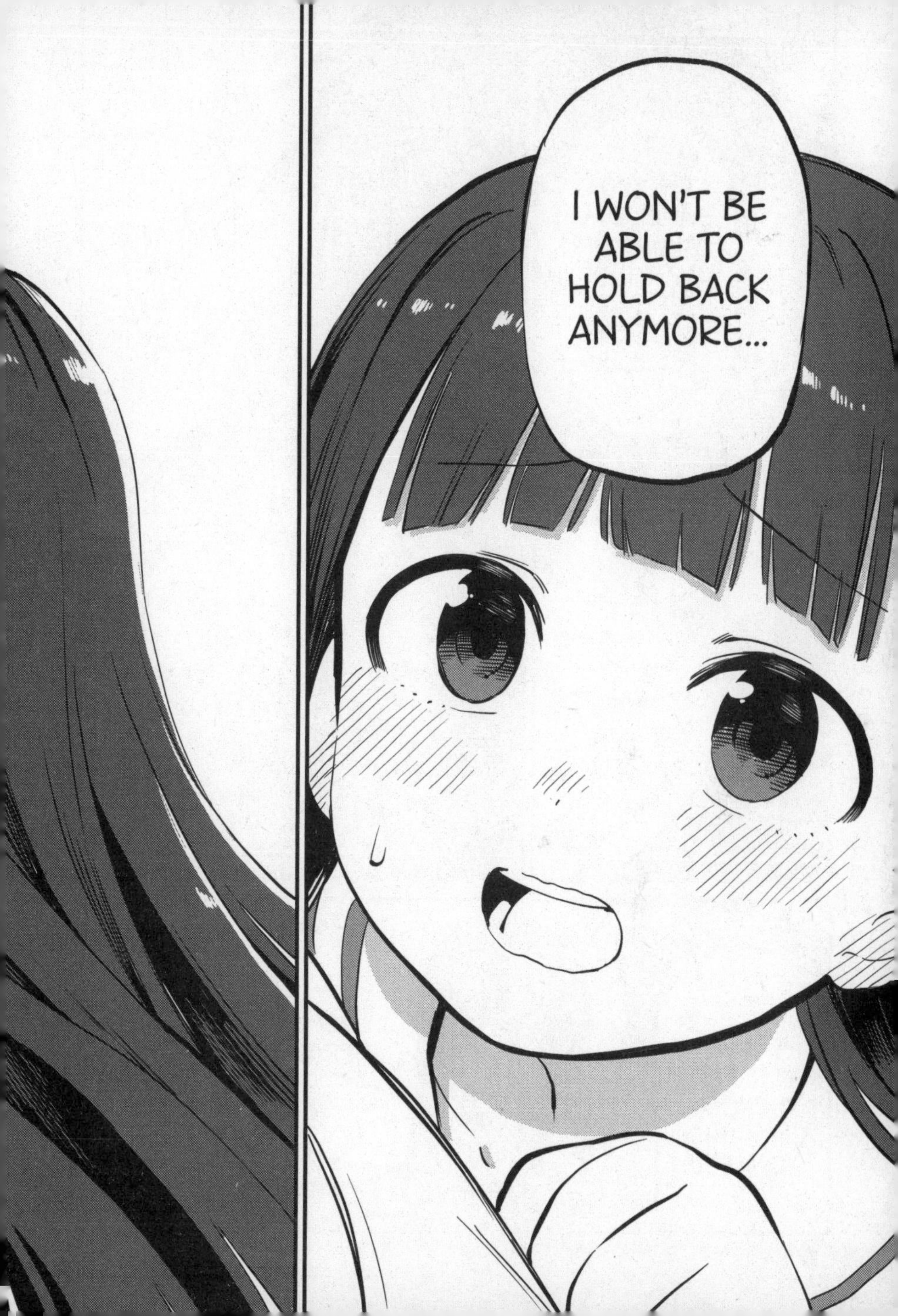
I WON'T BE ABLE TO HOLD BACK ANYMORE...

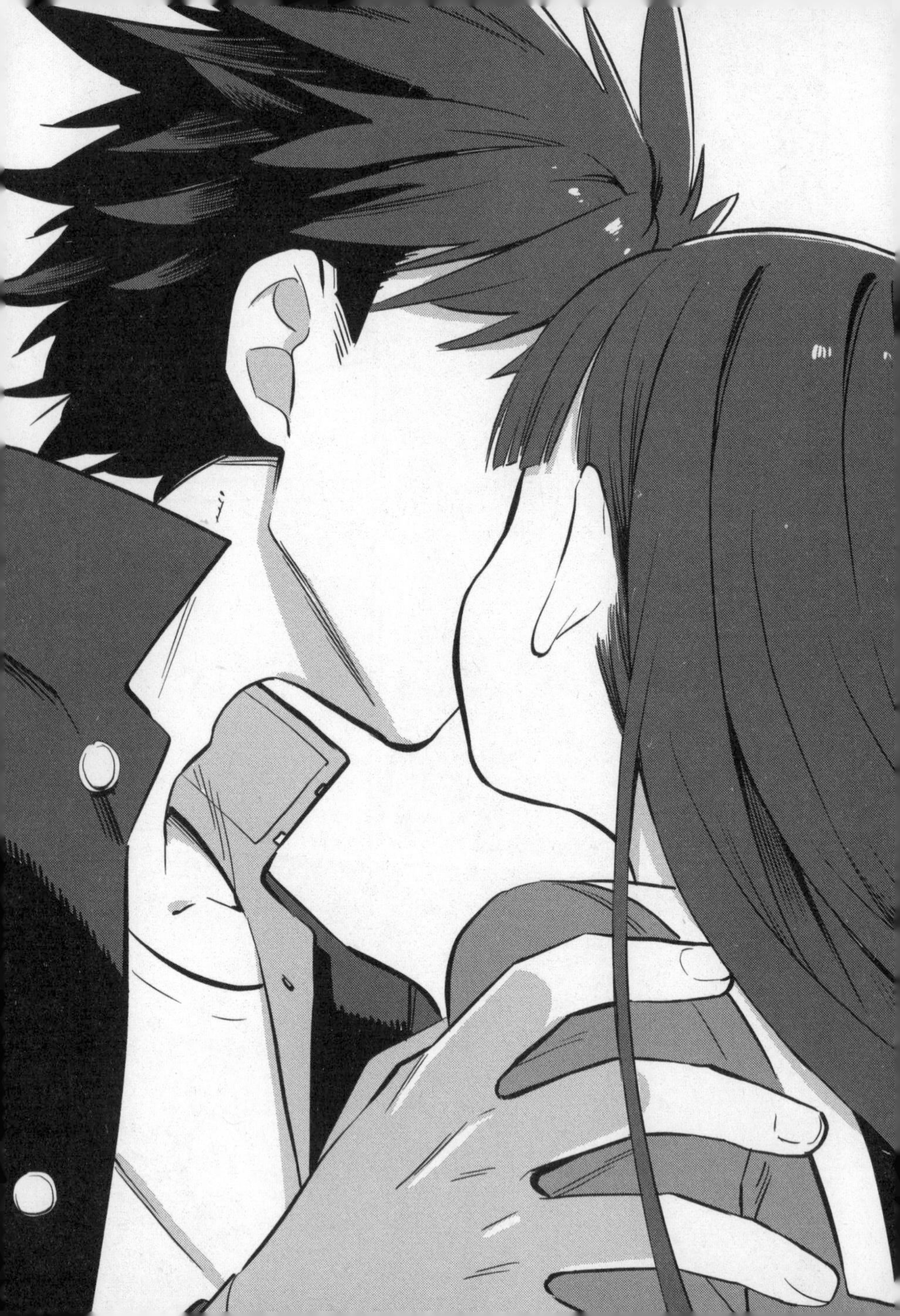

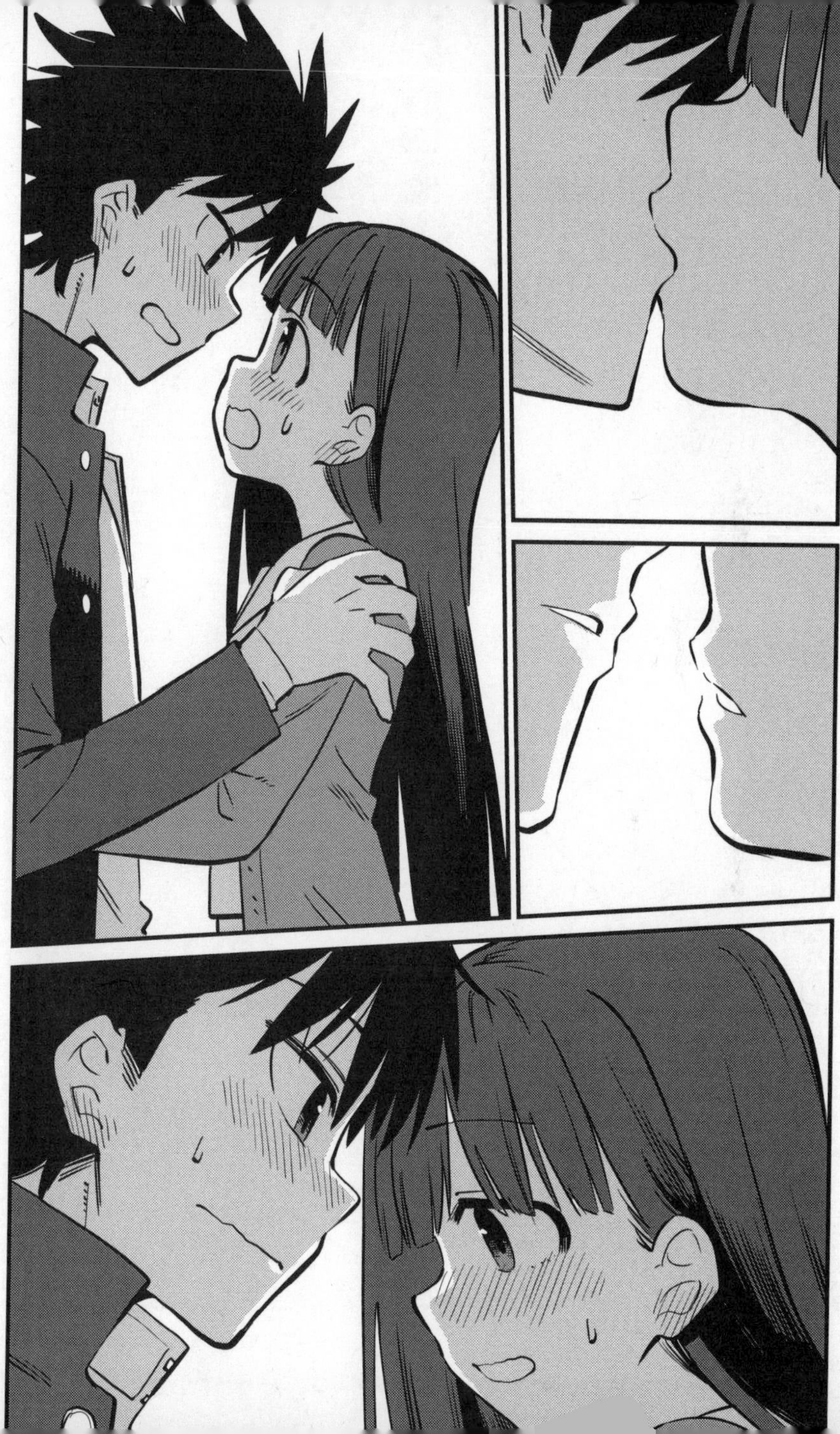

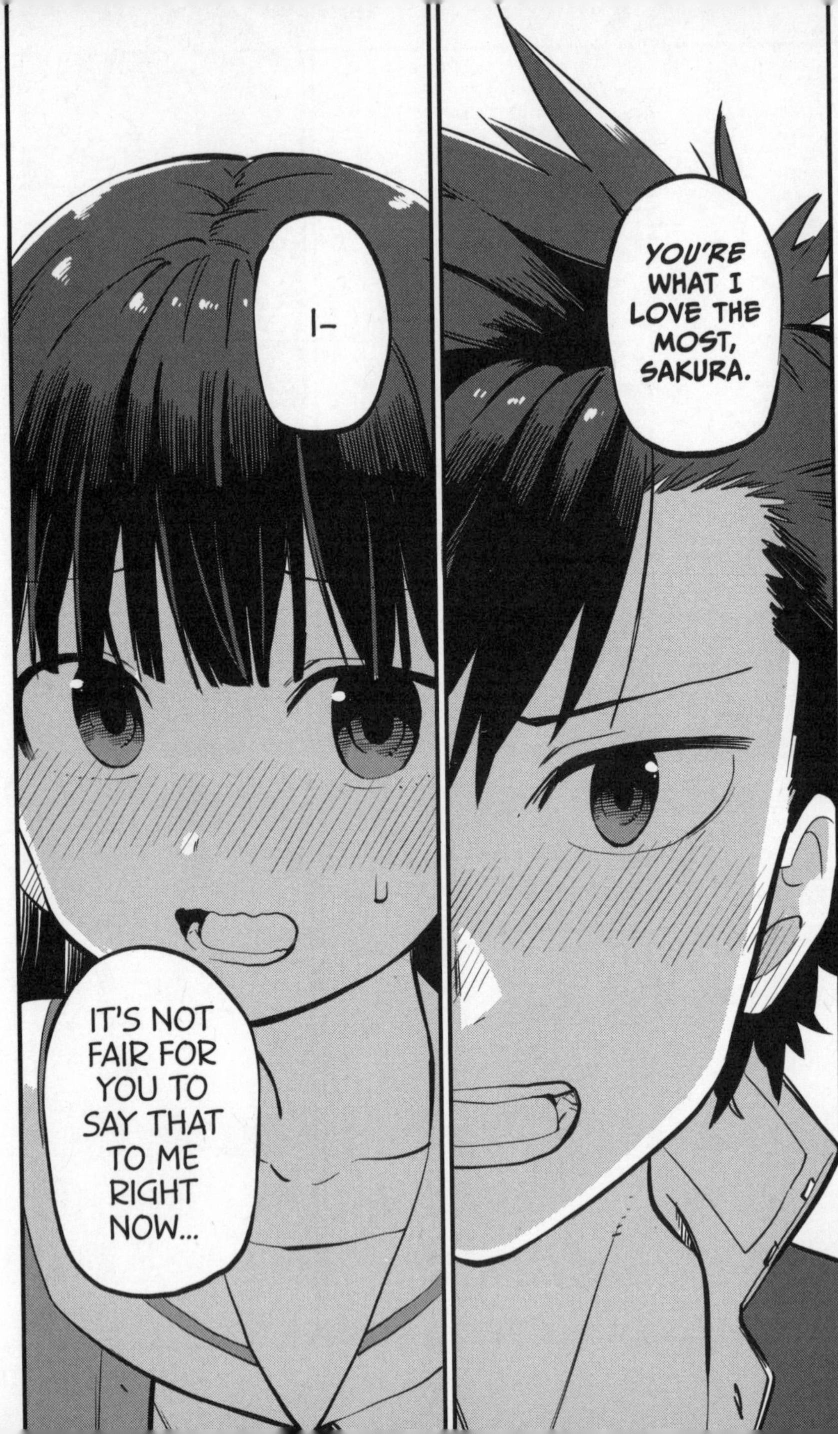
YOU'RE WHAT I LOVE THE MOST, SAKURA.
I—
IT'S NOT FAIR FOR YOU TO SAY THAT TO ME RIGHT NOW...

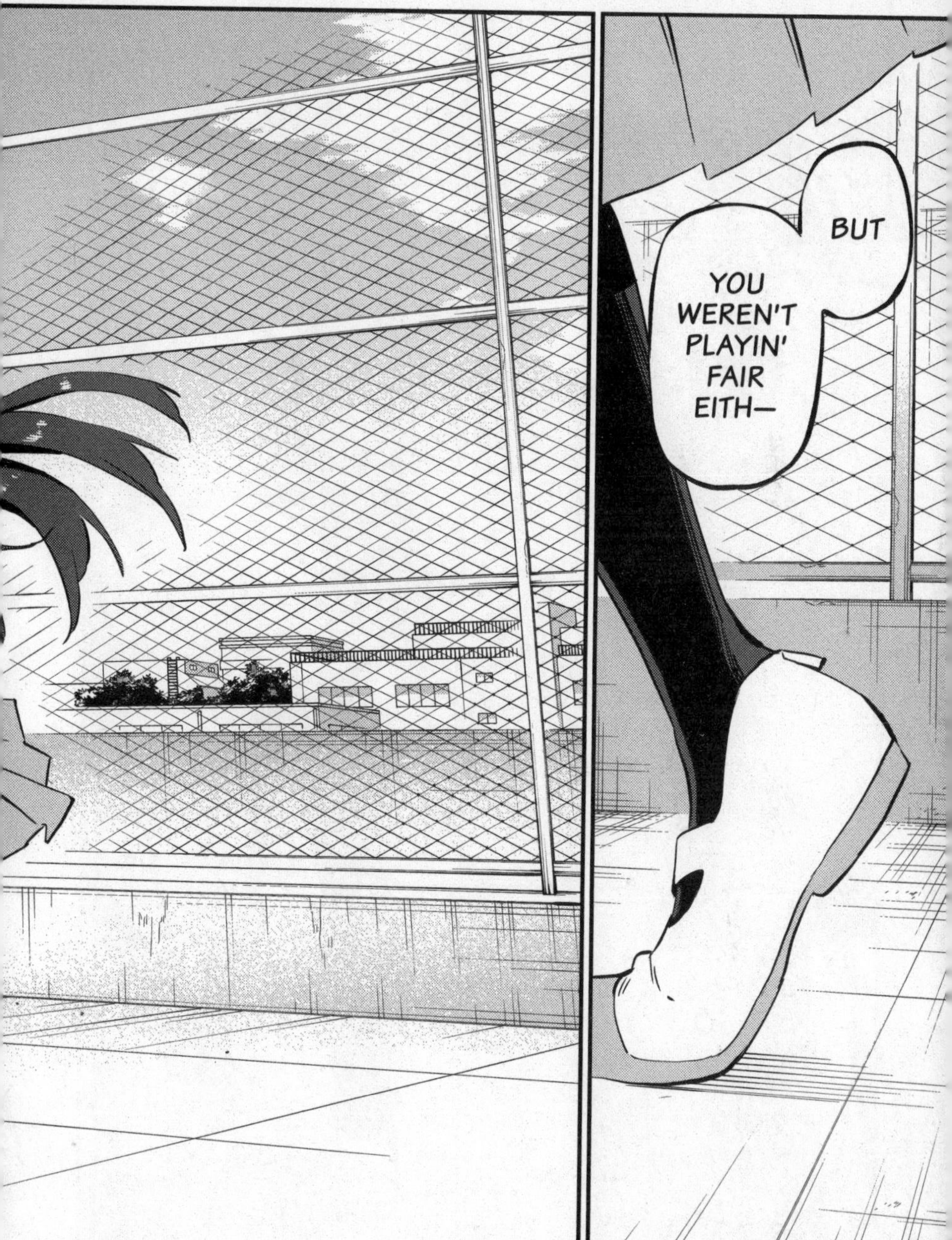
BUT
YOU WEREN'T PLAYIN' FAIR EITH—

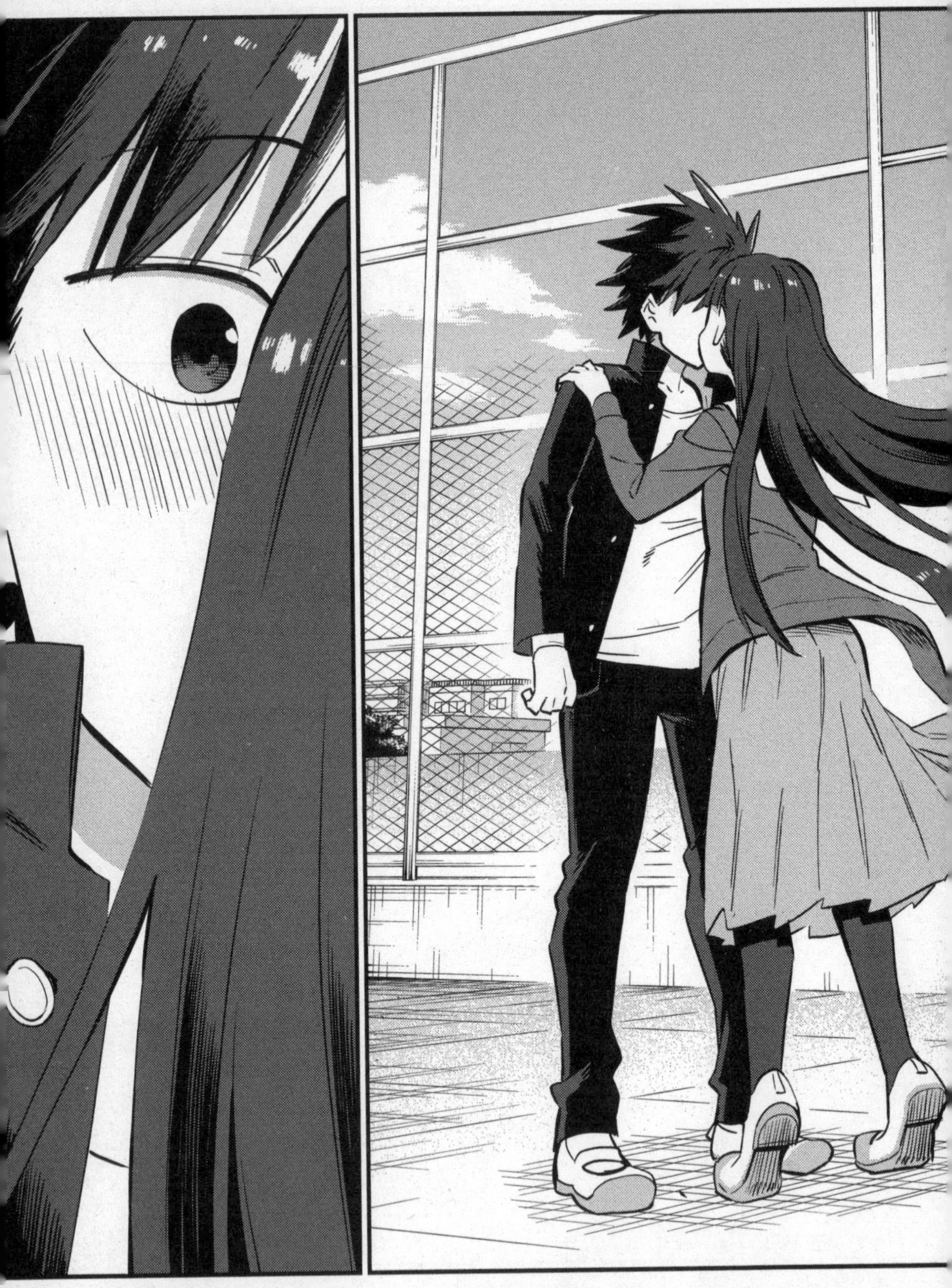

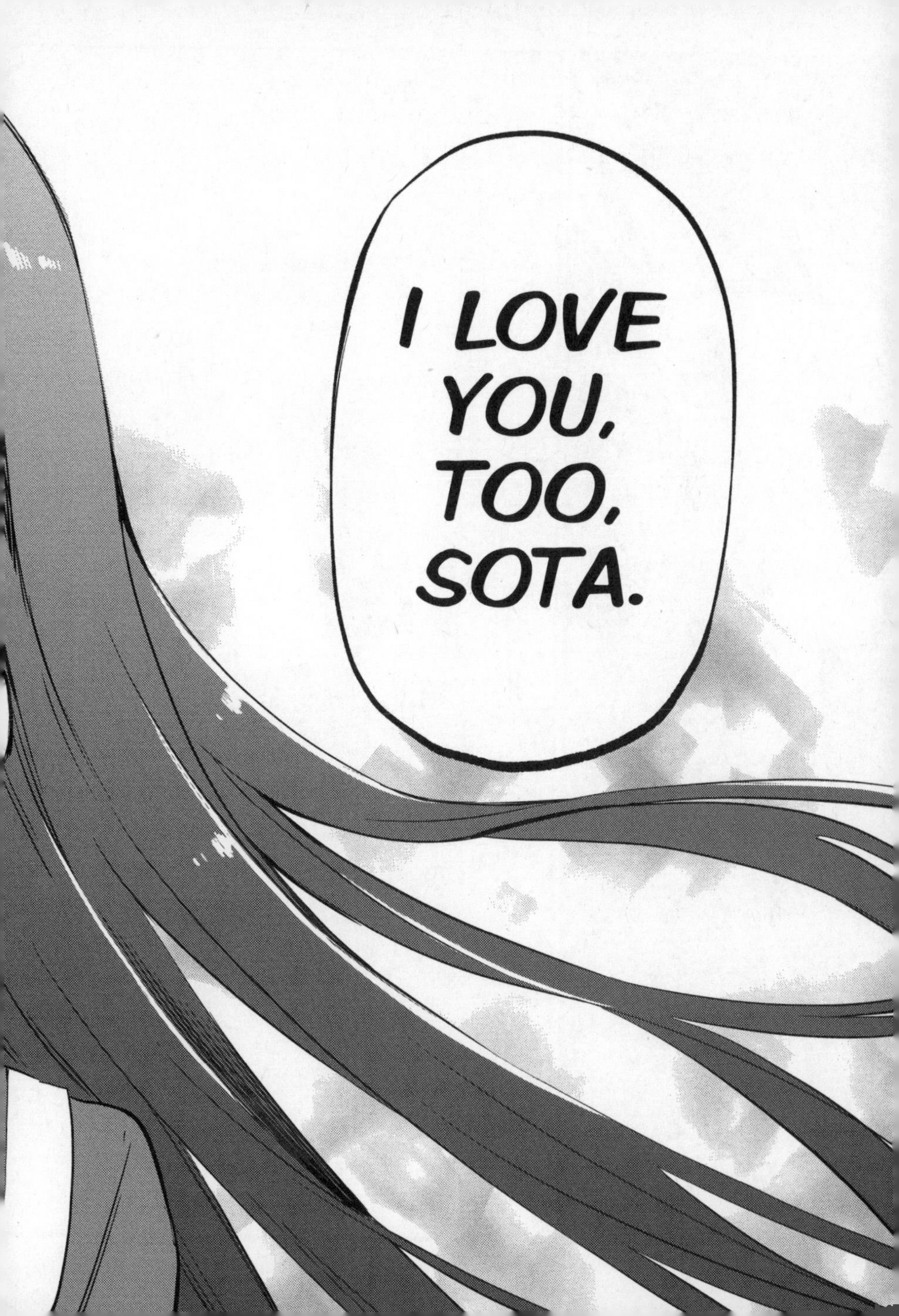
I LOVE YOU, TOO, SOTA.

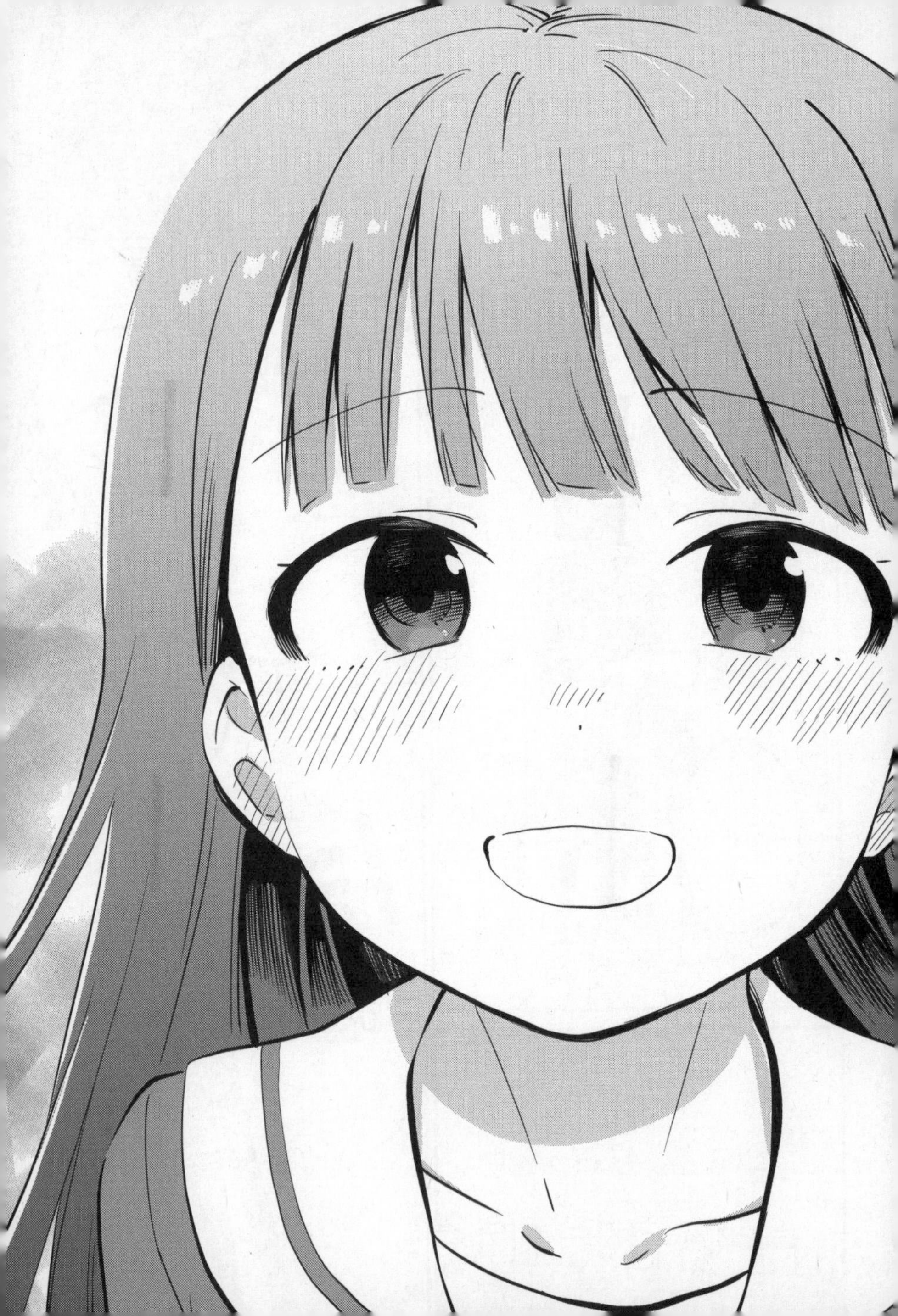

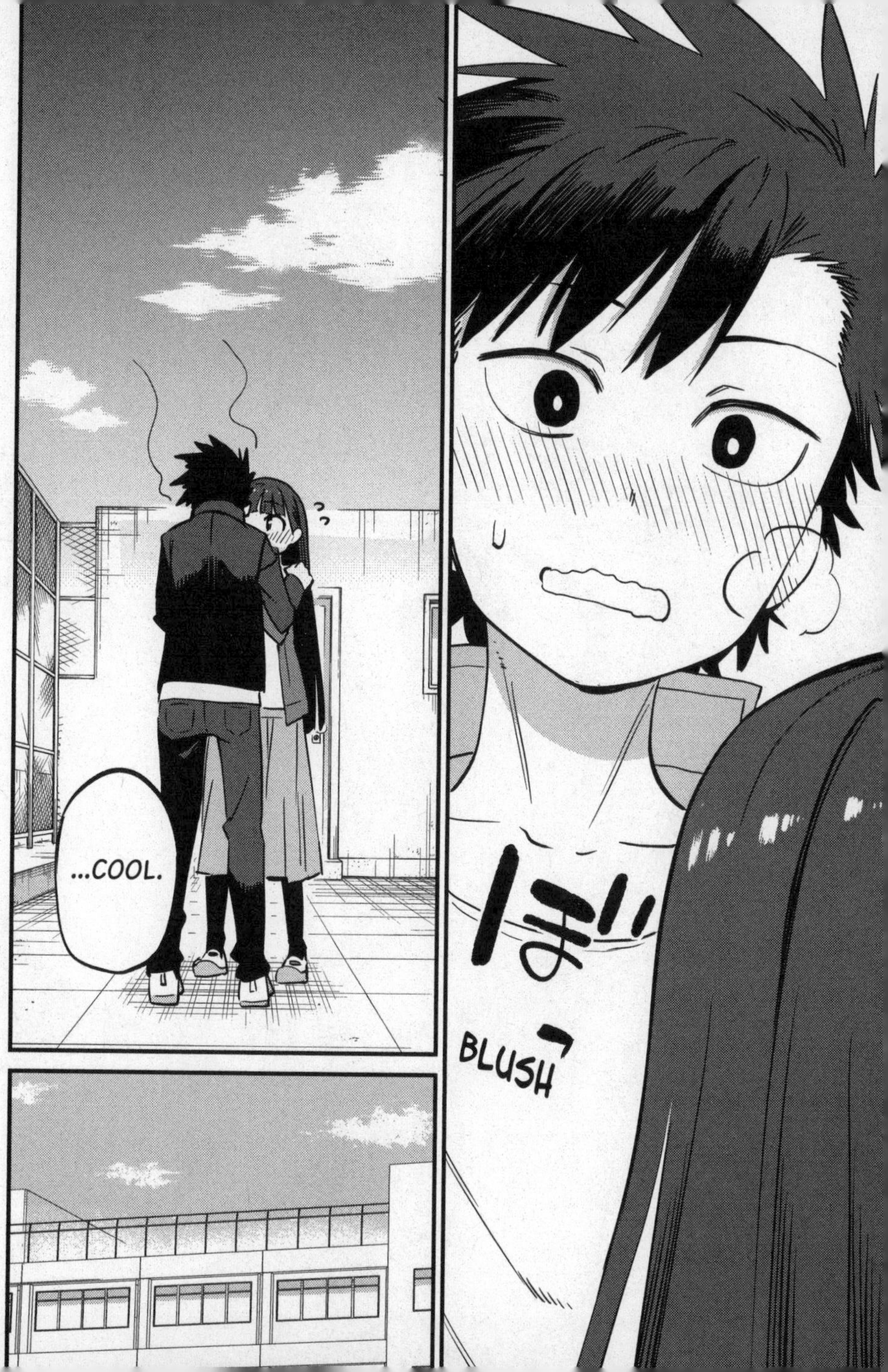
ぼっ
BLUSH
...COOL.

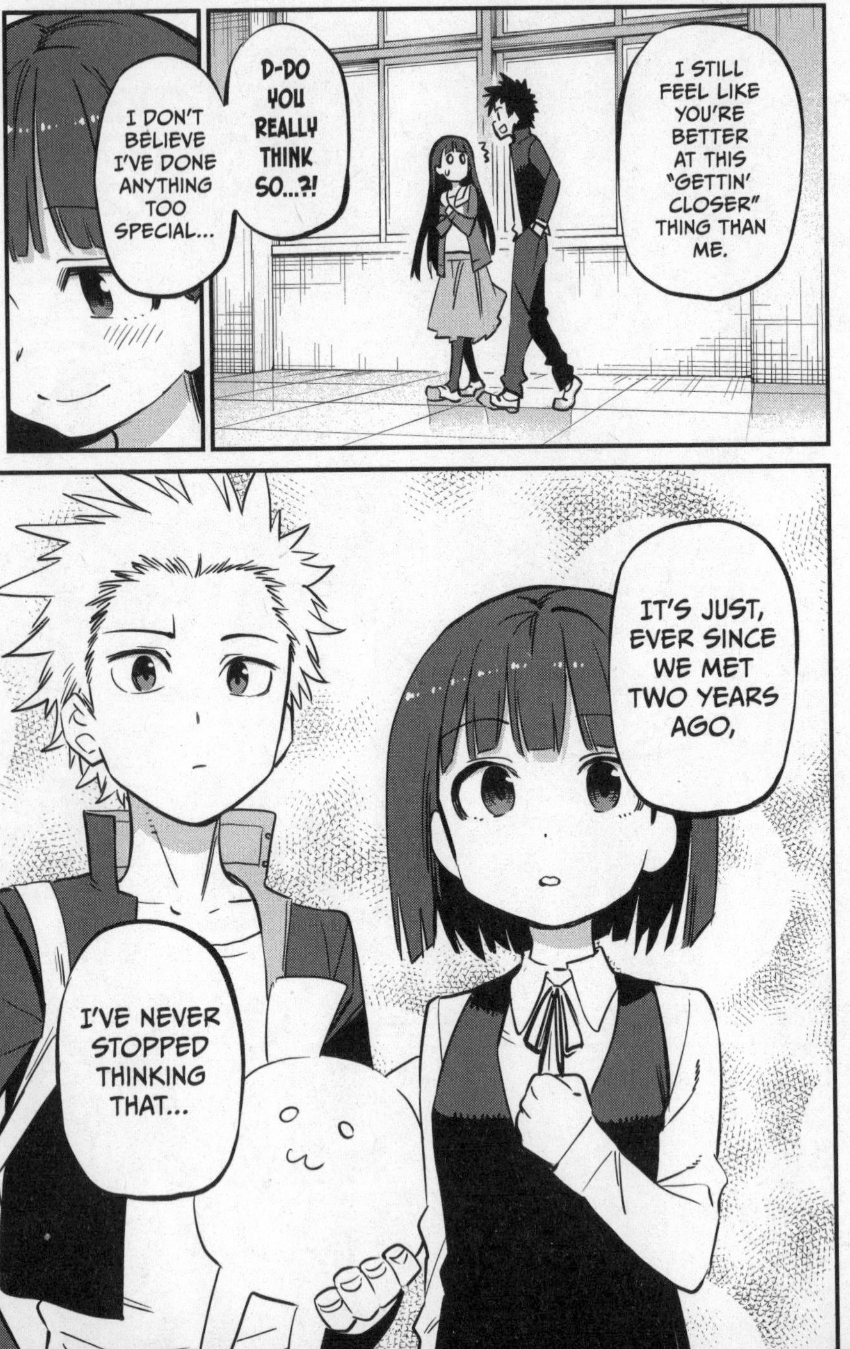
I STILL FEEL LIKE YOU'RE BETTER AT THIS "GETTIN' CLOSER" THING THAN ME.
D-DO YOU REALLY THINK SO...?!
I DON'T BELIEVE I'VE DONE ANYTHING TOO SPECIAL...
IT'S JUST, EVER SINCE WE MET TWO YEARS AGO,
I'VE NEVER STOPPED THINKING THAT...

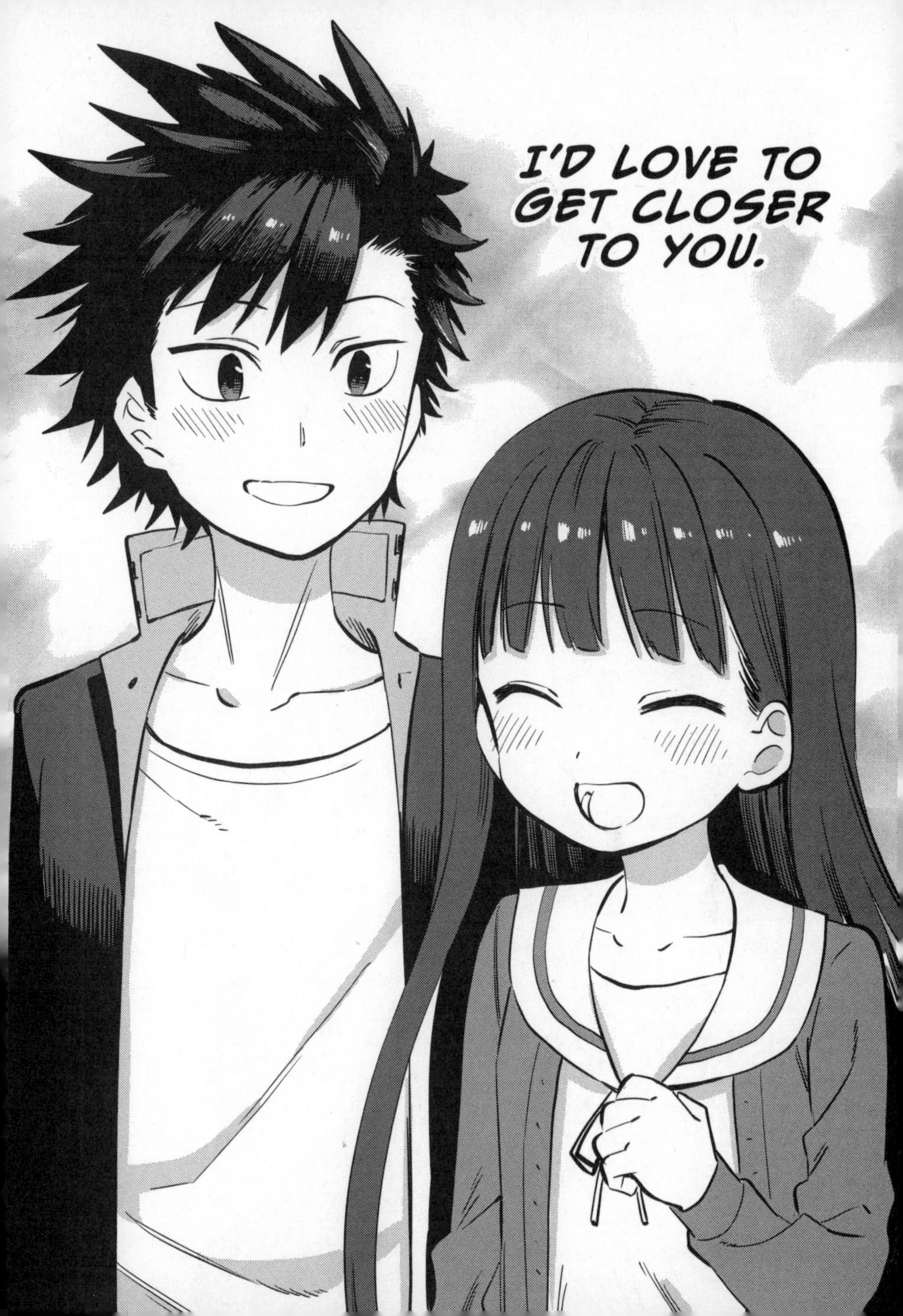
I'D LOVE TO GET CLOSER TO YOU.

Bonus Chapter Getting Even Closer

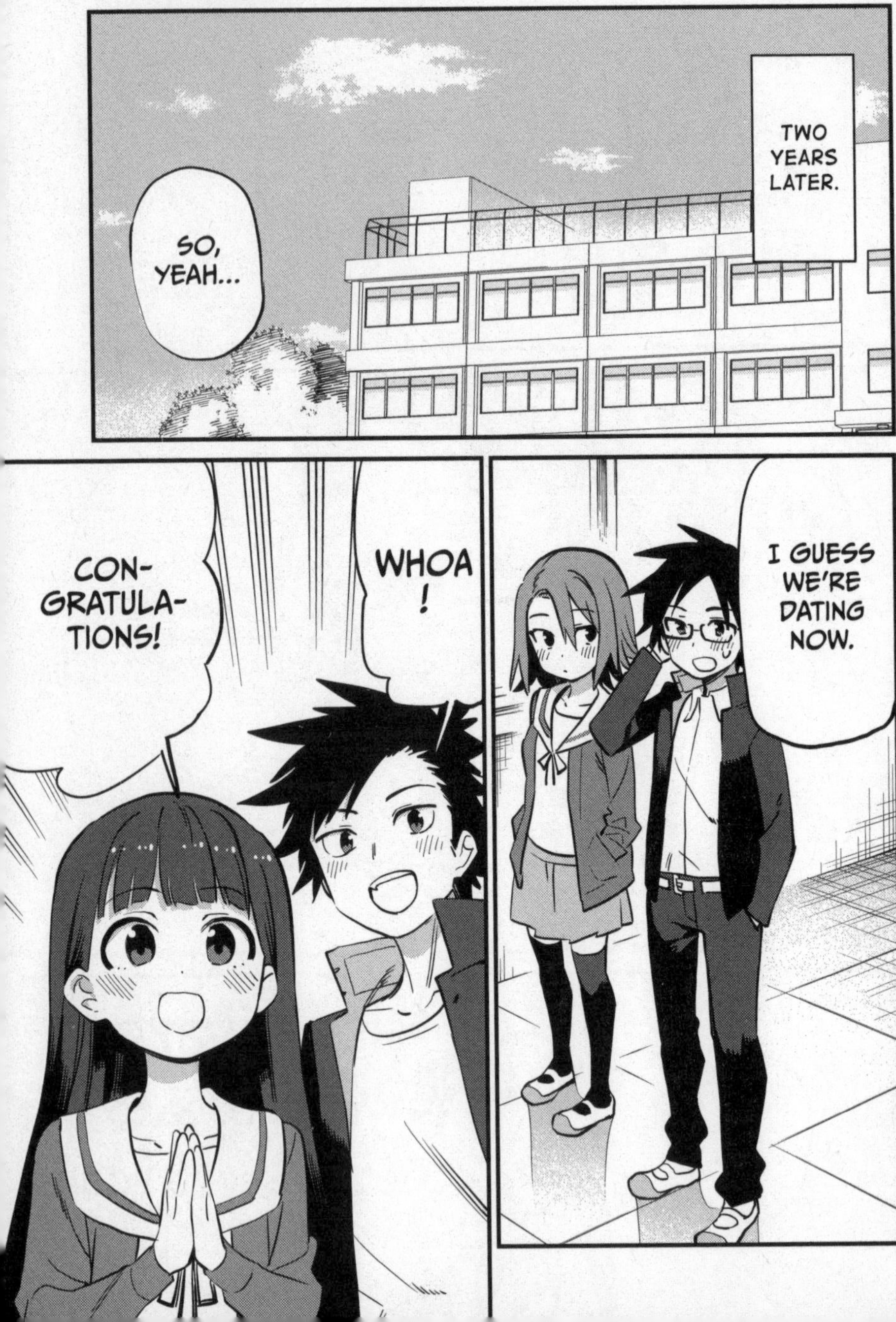
TWO YEARS LATER.
SO, YEAH...
I GUESS WE'RE DATING NOW.
WHOA!
CONGRATULATIONS!

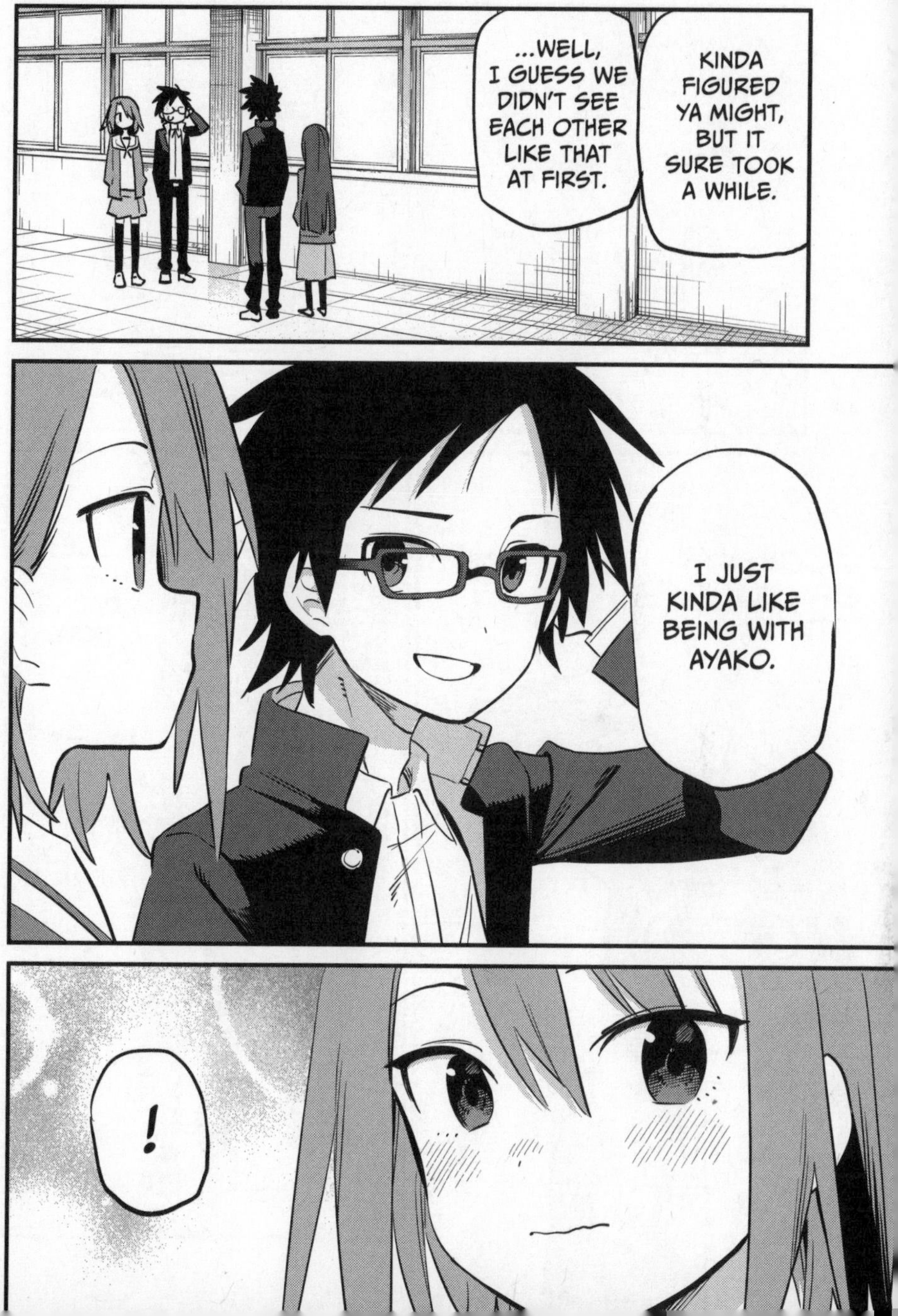
KINDA FIGURED YA MIGHT, BUT IT SURE TOOK A WHILE.
...WELL, I GUESS WE DIDN'T SEE EACH OTHER LIKE THAT AT FIRST.
I JUST KINDA LIKE BEING WITH AYAKO.
!

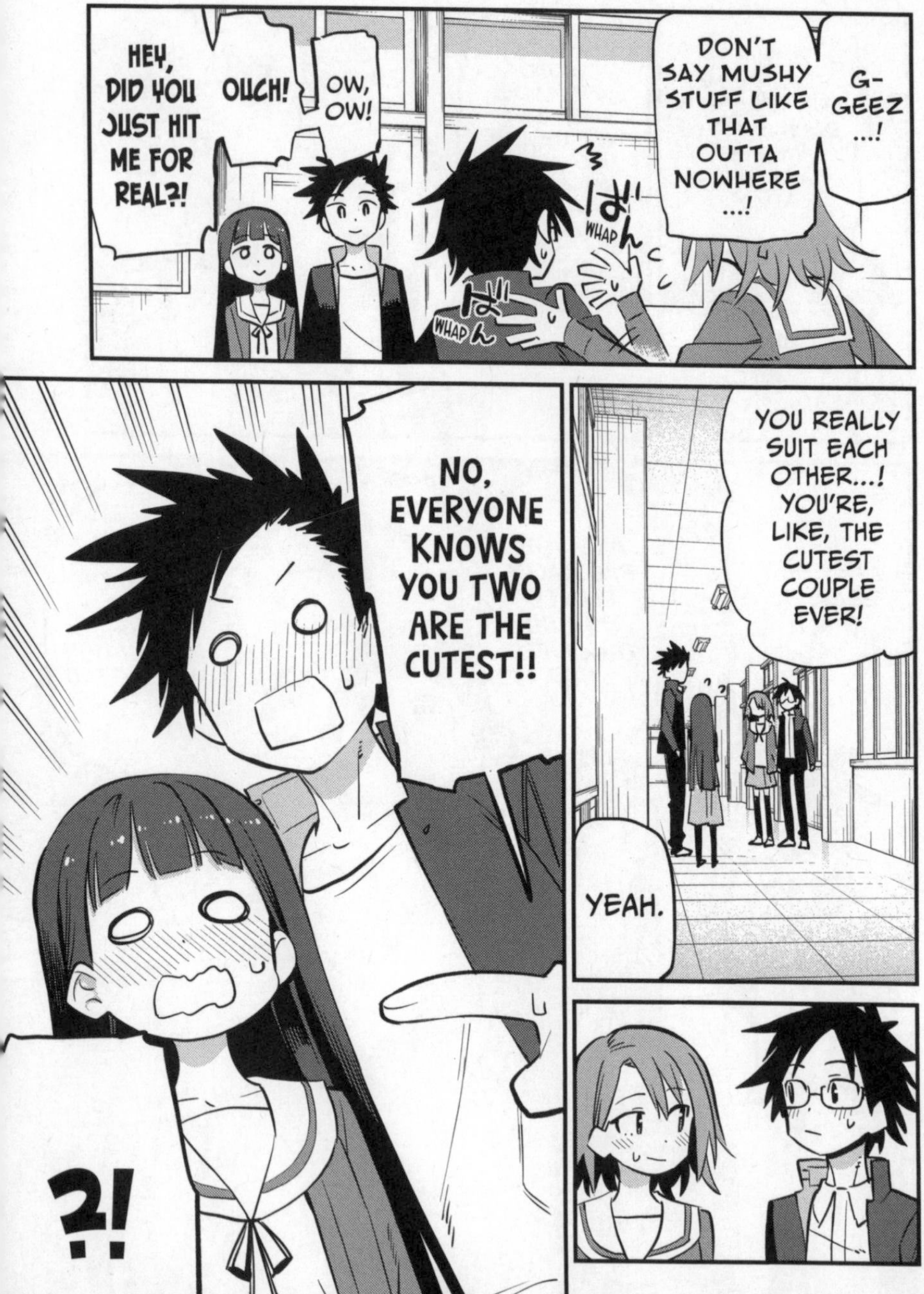
G-GEEZ ...!
DON'T SAY MUSHY STUFF LIKE THAT OUTTA NOWHERE ...!
ばん WHAP
OW, OW!
OUCH!
HEY, DID YOU JUST HIT ME FOR REAL?!
ばん WHAP
YOU REALLY SUIT EACH OTHER...! YOU'RE, LIKE, THE CUTEST COUPLE EVER!
YEAH.
NO, EVERYONE KNOWS YOU TWO ARE THE CUTEST!!
?!

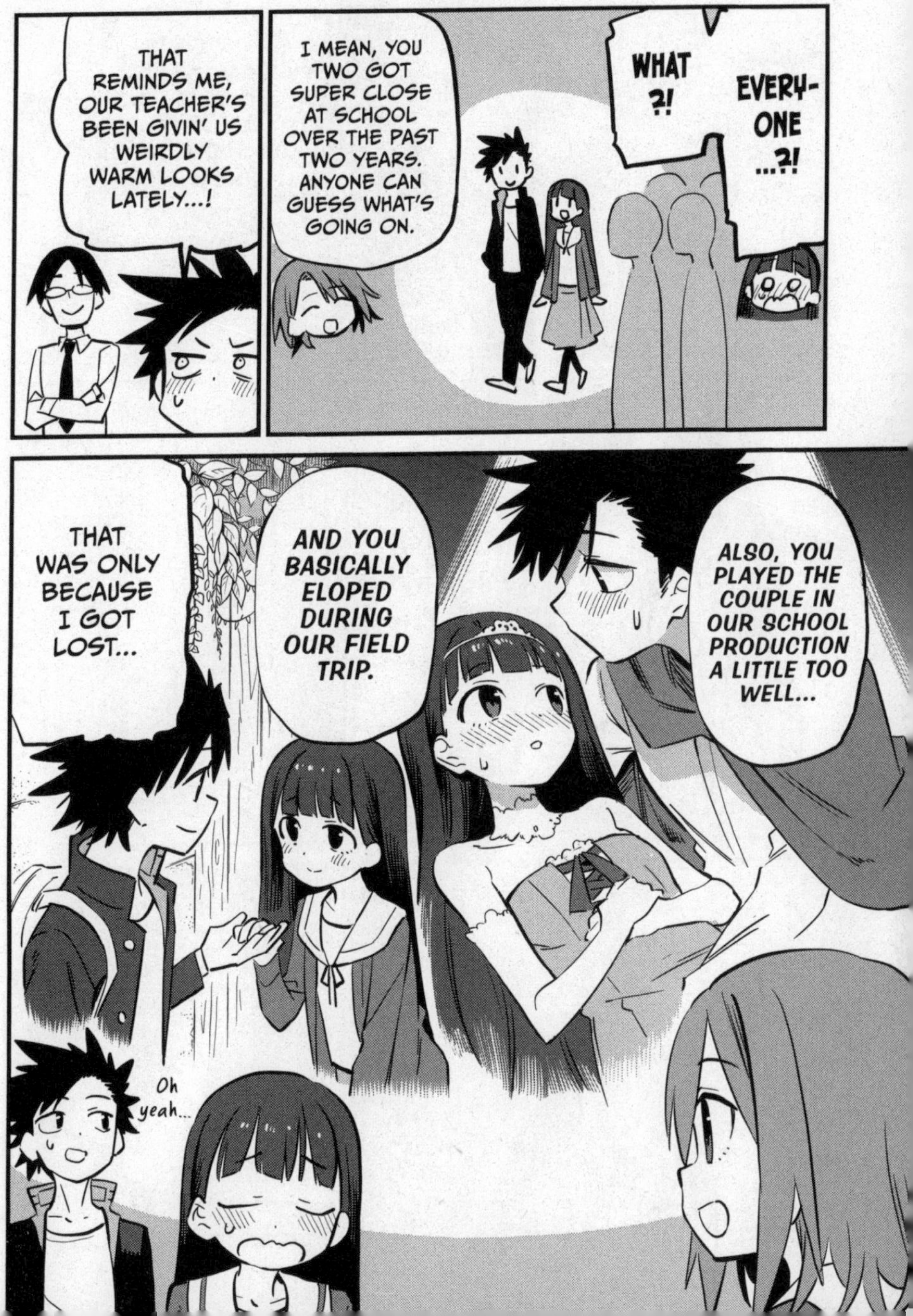
EVERY-ONE ...?! WHAT ?!
I MEAN, YOU TWO GOT SUPER CLOSE AT SCHOOL OVER THE PAST TWO YEARS. ANYONE CAN GUESS WHAT'S GOING ON.
THAT REMINDS ME, OUR TEACHER'S BEEN GIVIN' US WEIRDLY WARM LOOKS LATELY...!
ALSO, YOU PLAYED THE COUPLE IN OUR SCHOOL PRODUCTION A LITTLE TOO WELL...
AND YOU BASICALLY ELOPED DURING OUR FIELD TRIP.
THAT WAS ONLY BECAUSE I GOT LOST...
Oh yeah...

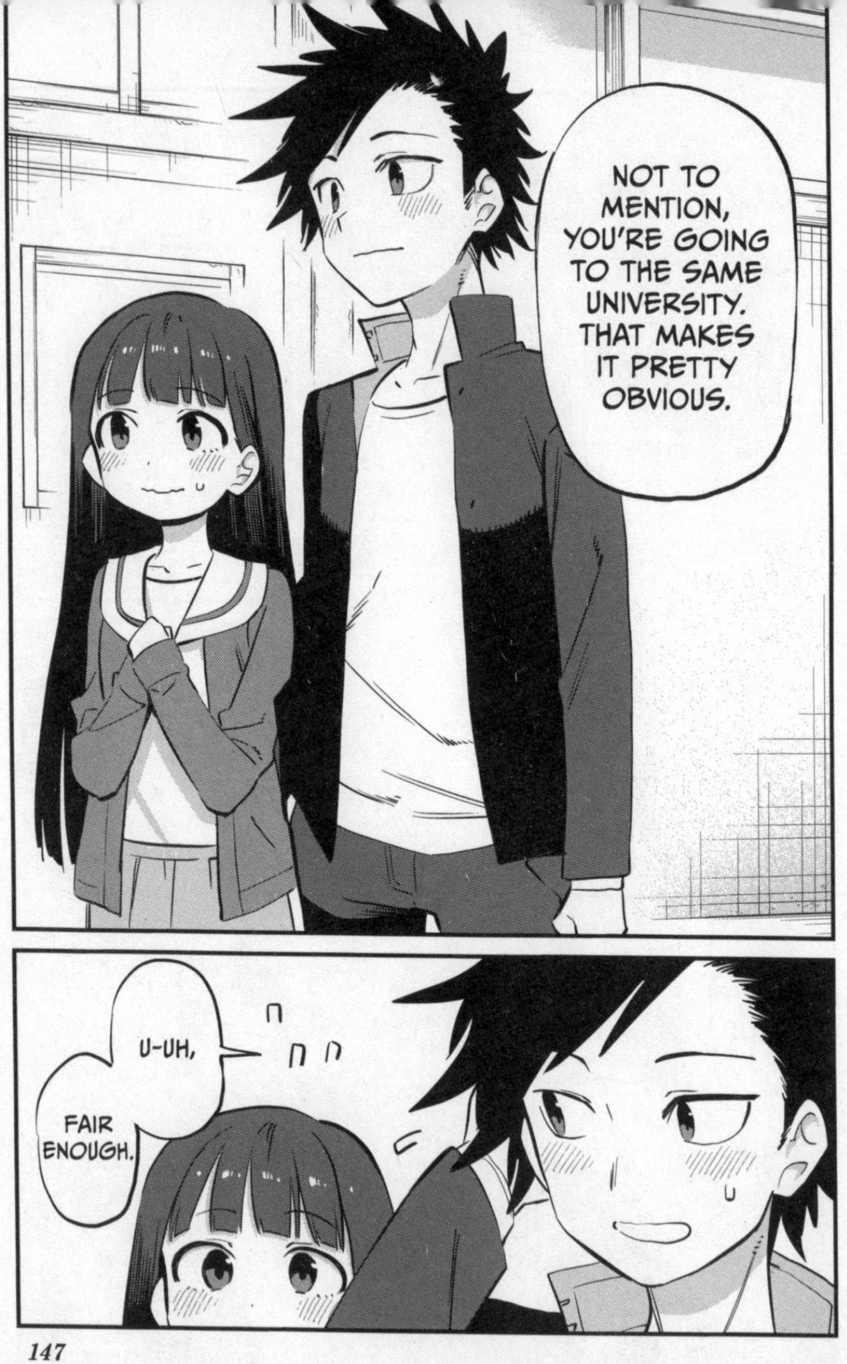
NOT TO MENTION, YOU'RE GOING TO THE SAME UNIVERSITY. THAT MAKES IT PRETTY OBVIOUS.
U-UH,
FAIR ENOUGH.

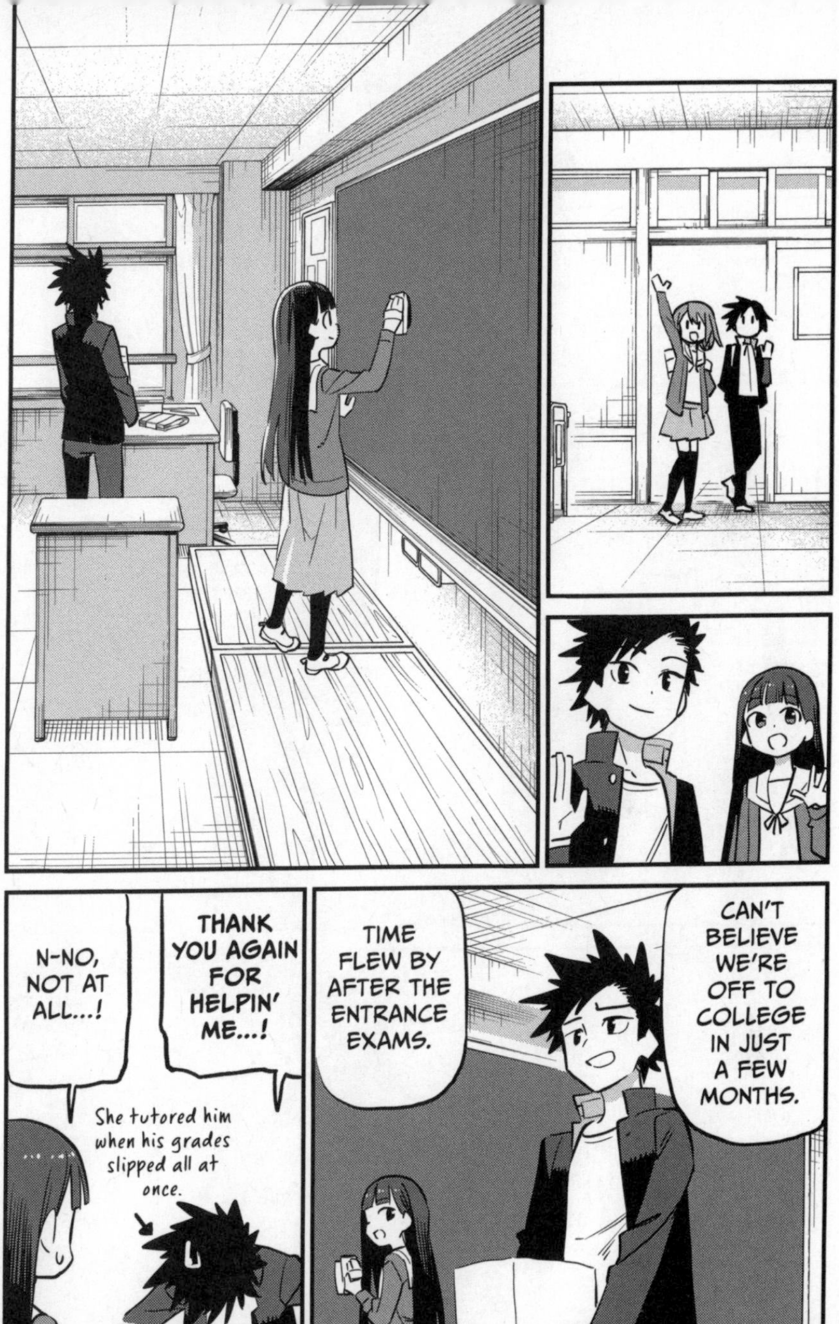
CAN'T BELIEVE WE'RE OFF TO COLLEGE IN JUST A FEW MONTHS.
TIME FLEW BY AFTER THE ENTRANCE EXAMS.
THANK YOU AGAIN FOR HELPIN' ME...!
N-NO, NOT AT ALL...!
She tutored him when his grades slipped all at once.

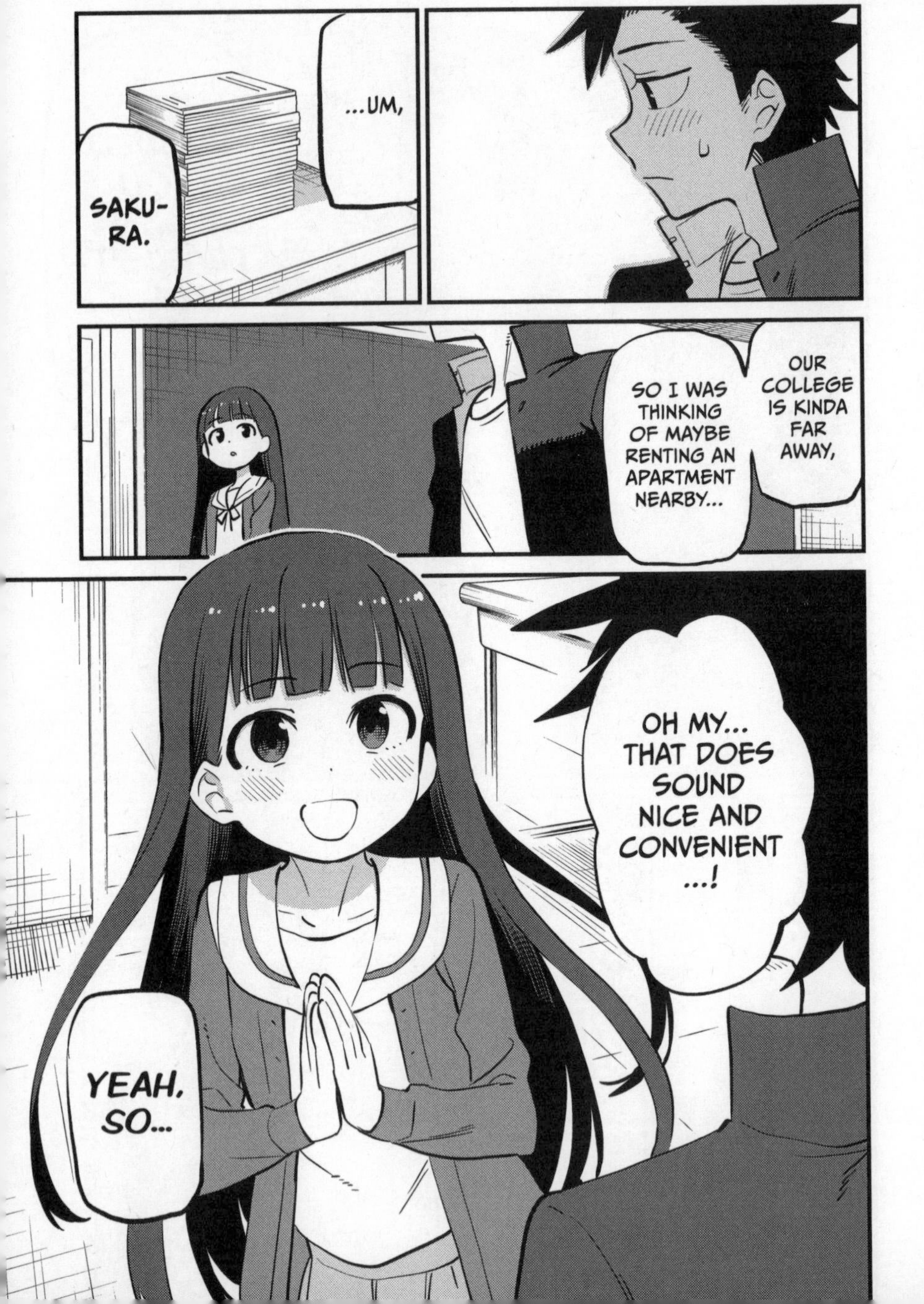
...UM,
SAKU-RA.
OUR COLLEGE IS KINDA FAR AWAY,
SO I WAS THINKING OF MAYBE RENTING AN APARTMENT NEARBY...
OH MY... THAT DOES SOUND NICE AND CONVENIENT ...!
YEAH. SO...

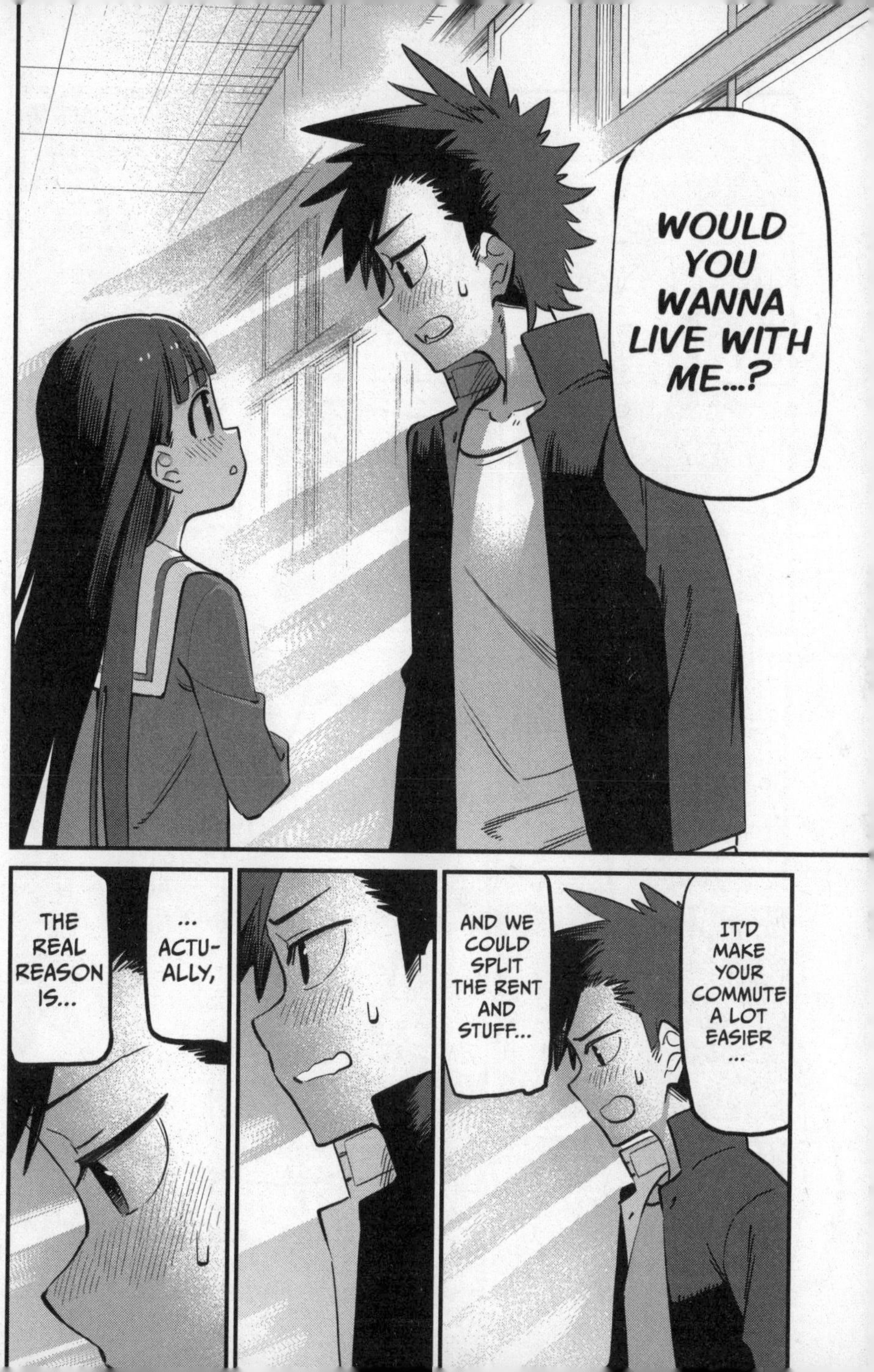
WOULD YOU WANNA LIVE WITH ME...?
IT'D MAKE YOUR COMMUTE A LOT EASIER ...
AND WE COULD SPLIT THE RENT AND STUFF...
... ACTU-ALLY,
THE REAL REASON IS...

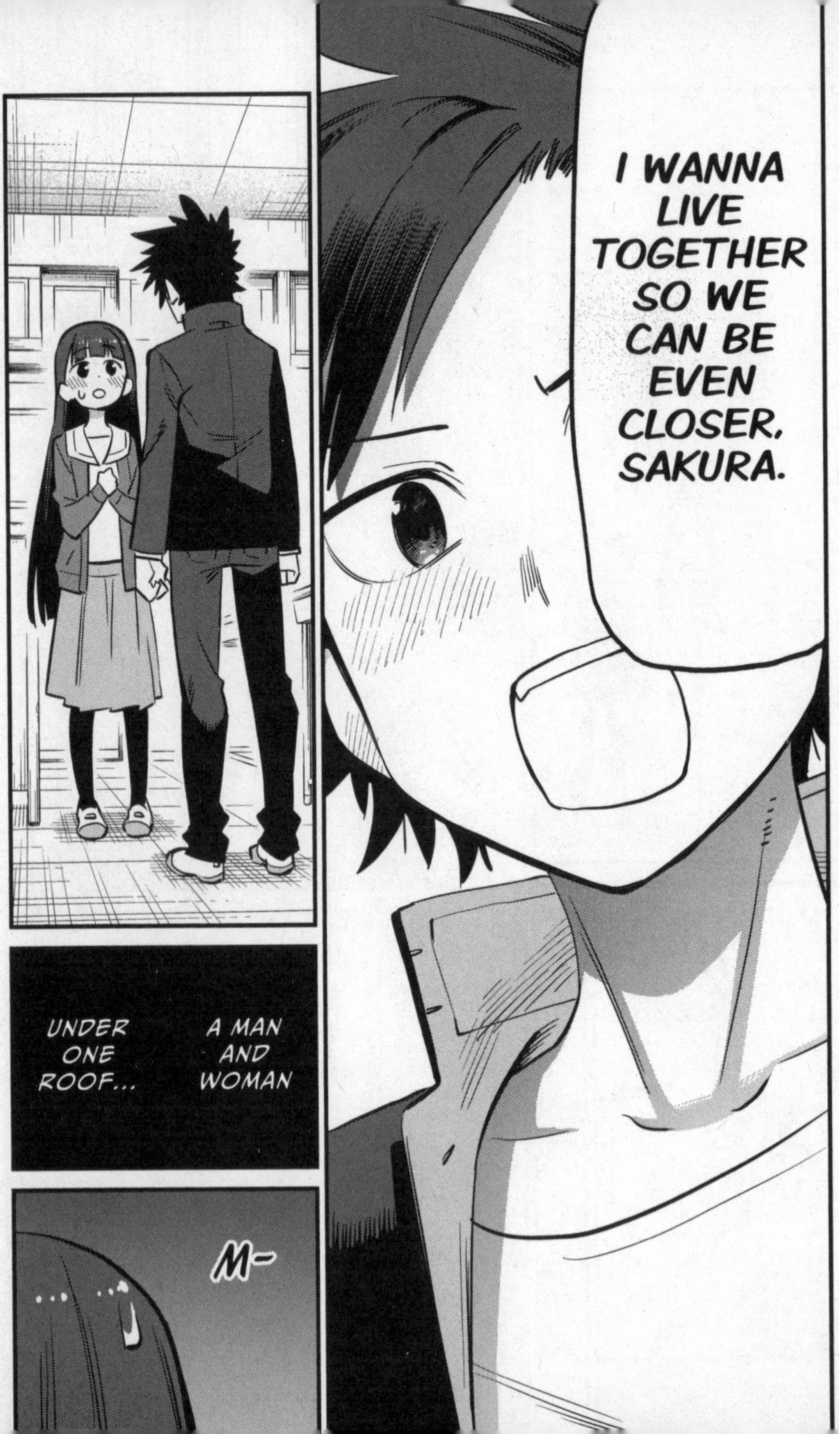
I WANNA LIVE TOGETHER SO WE CAN BE EVEN CLOSER, SAKURA.
A MAN AND WOMAN
UNDER ONE ROOF...
M-
... ...

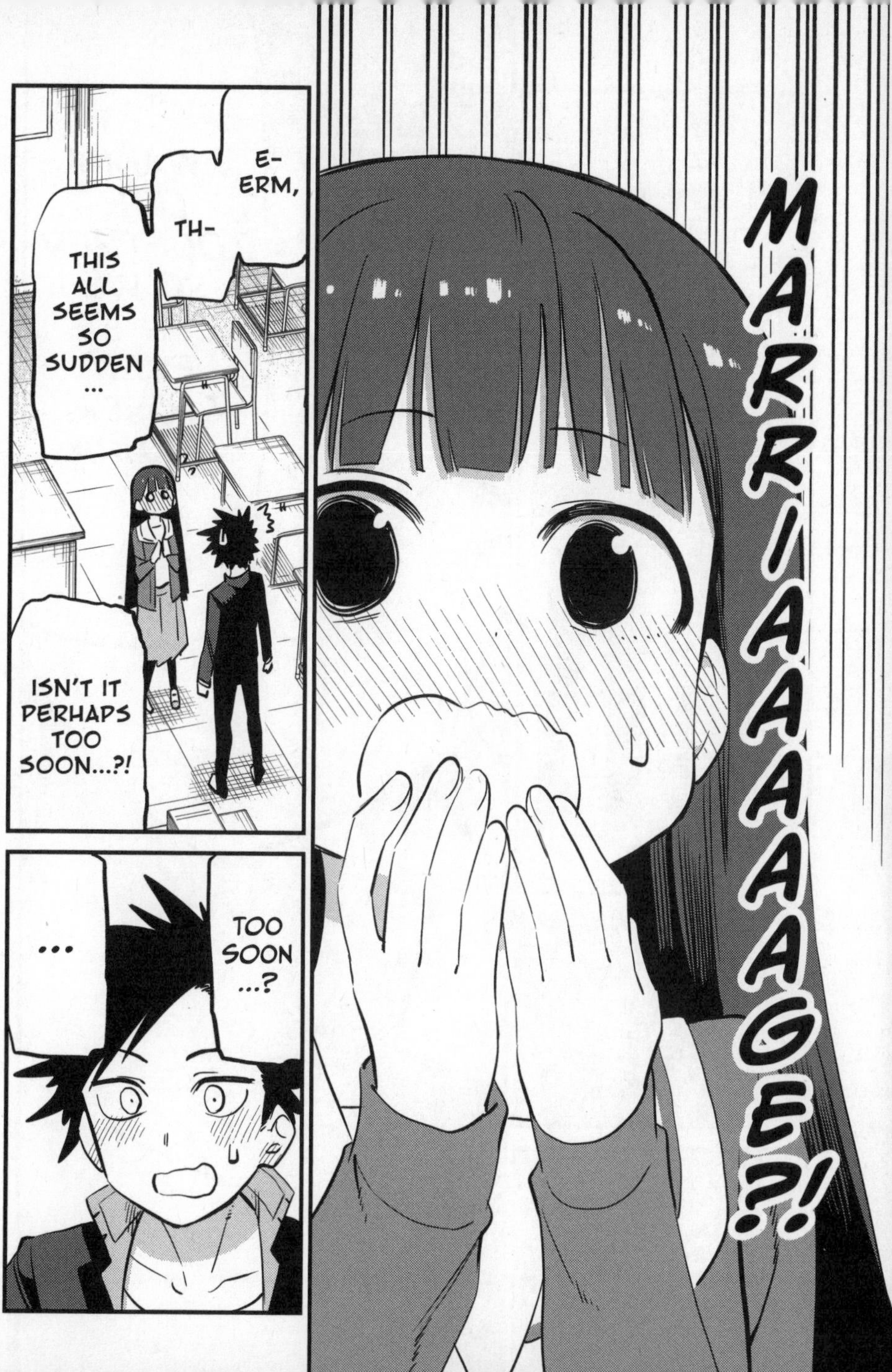
MARRIAAAAGE?!
E-ERM,
TH-
THIS ALL SEEMS SO SUDDEN ...
ISN'T IT PERHAPS TOO SOON...?!
TOO SOON ...?
...

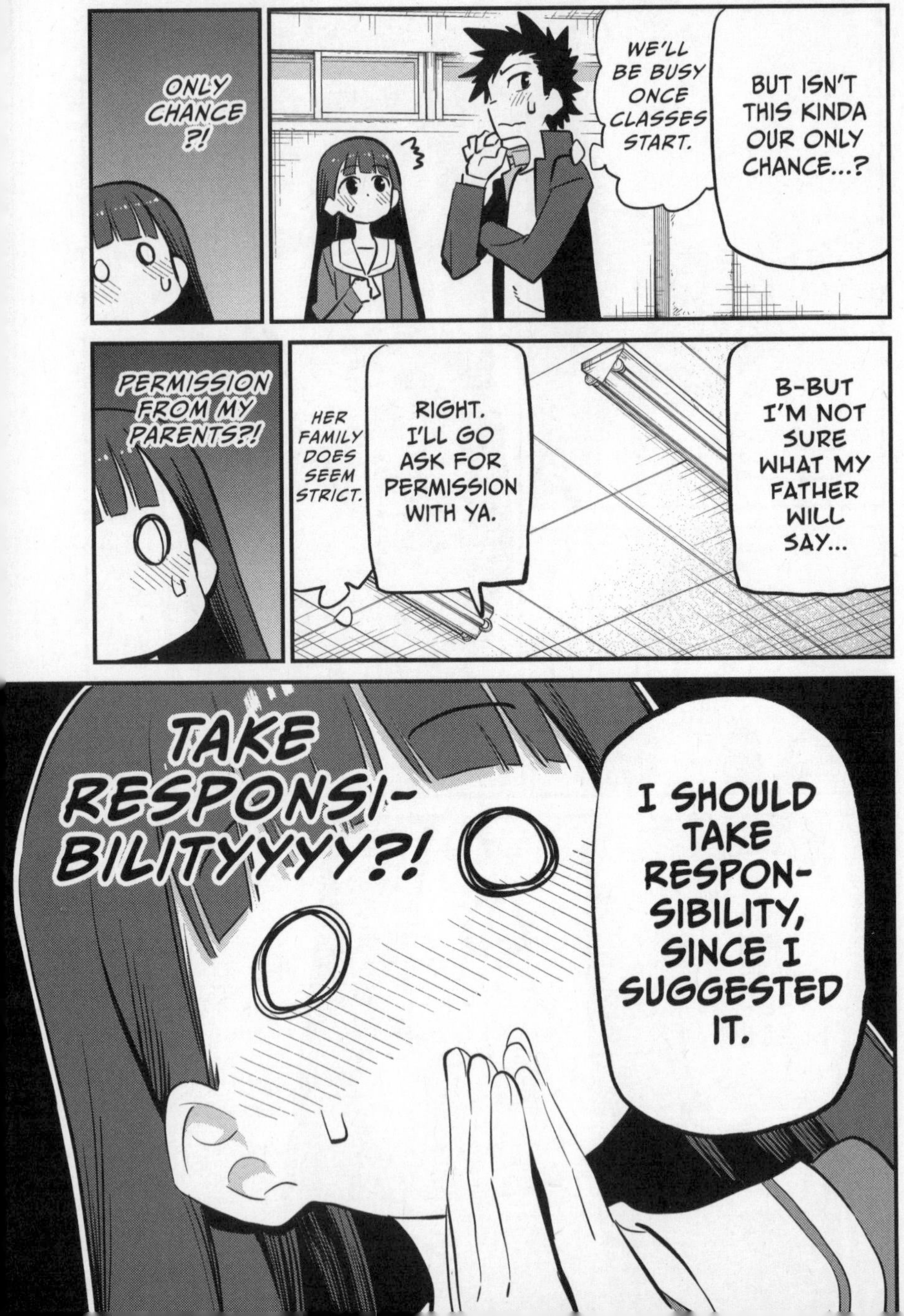
WE'LL BE BUSY ONCE CLASSES START.
BUT ISN'T THIS KINDA OUR ONLY CHANCE...?
ONLY CHANCE ?!
B-BUT I'M NOT SURE WHAT MY FATHER WILL SAY...
RIGHT. I'LL GO ASK FOR PERMISSION WITH YA.
HER FAMILY DOES SEEM STRICT.
PERMISSION FROM MY PARENTS?!
I SHOULD TAKE RESPON-SIBILITY, SINCE I SUGGESTED IT.
TAKE RESPONSI-BILITYYYY?!

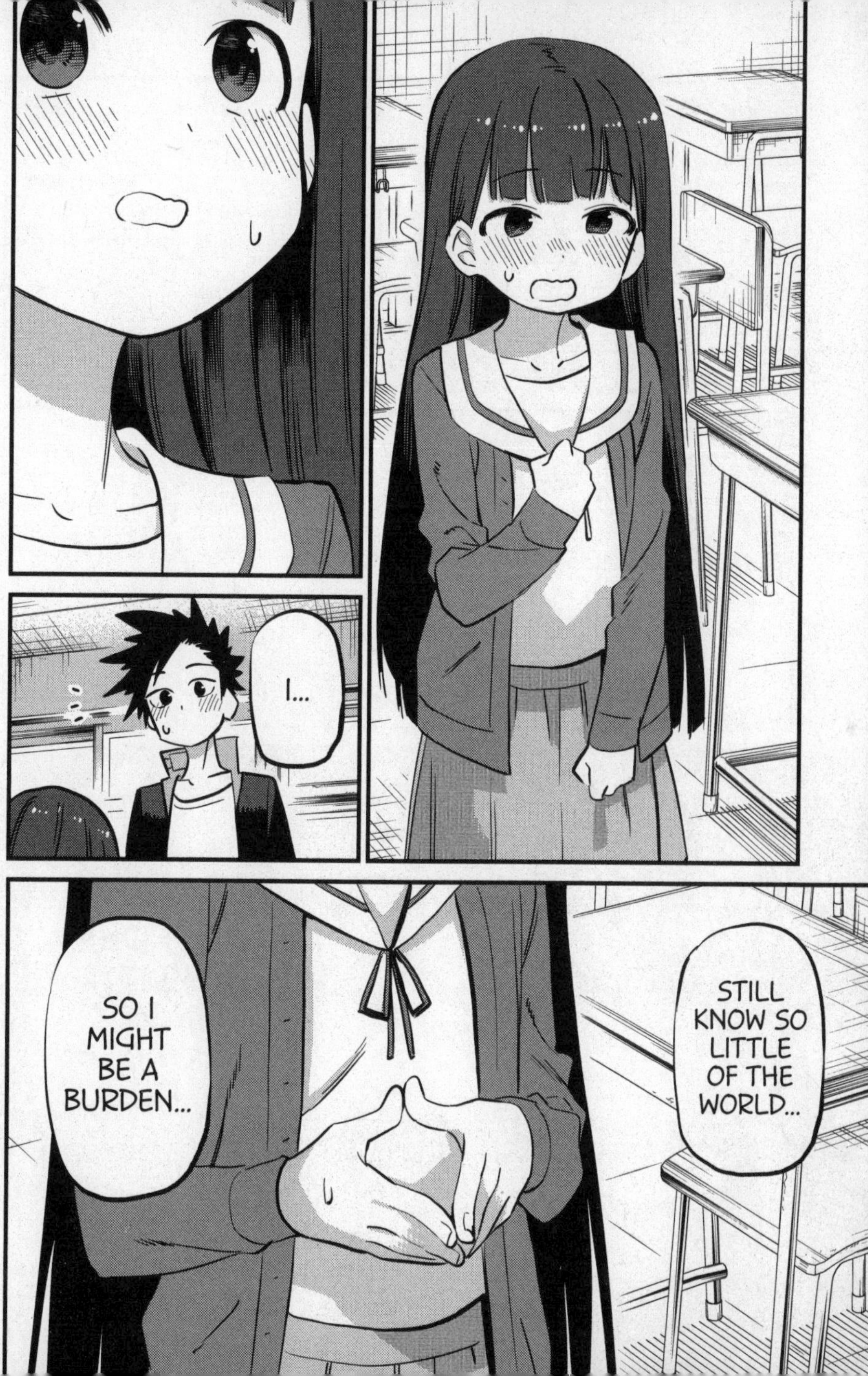
I...
STILL KNOW SO LITTLE OF THE WORLD...
SO I MIGHT BE A BURDEN...

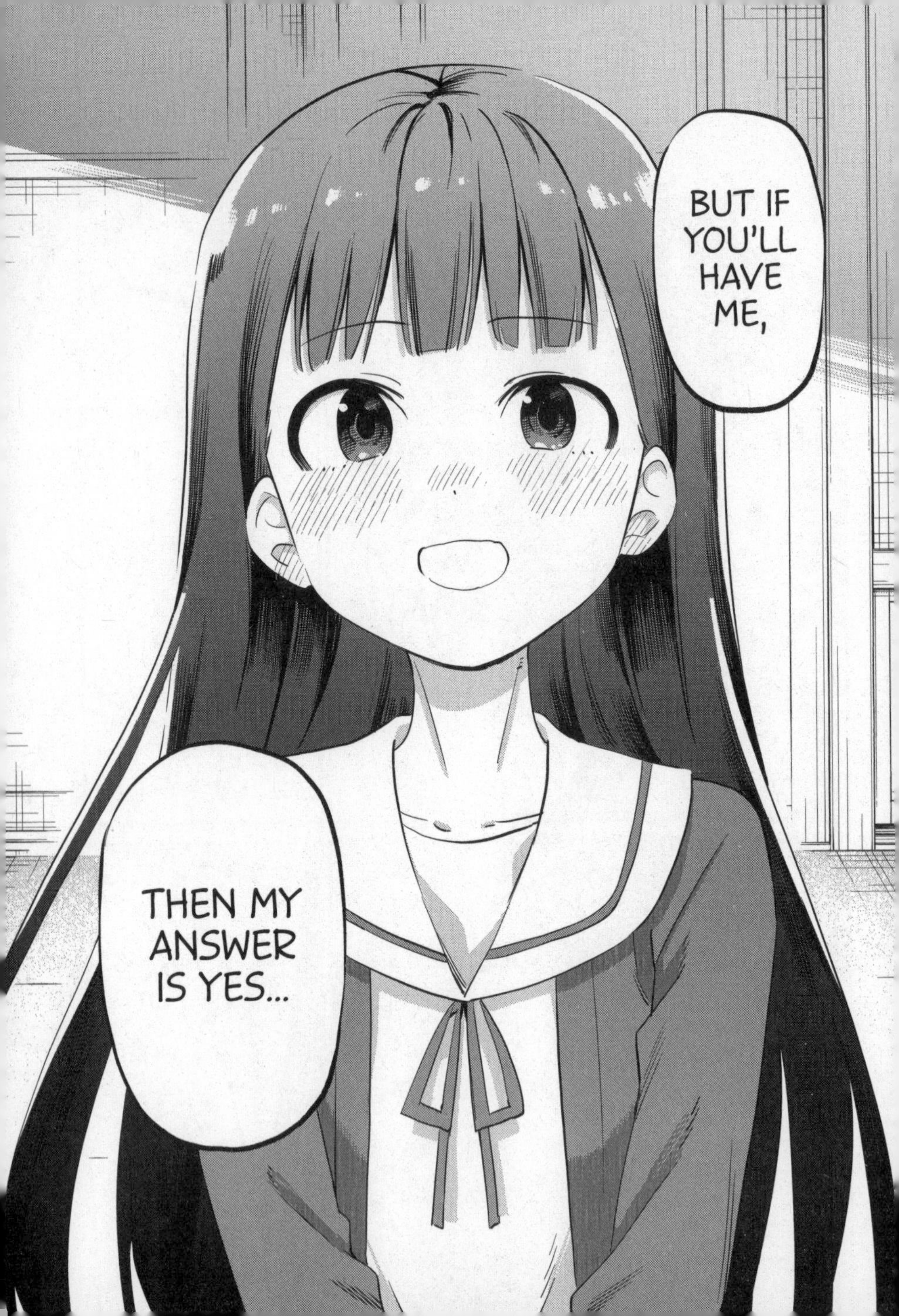
BUT IF YOU'LL HAVE ME,
THEN MY ANSWER IS YES...

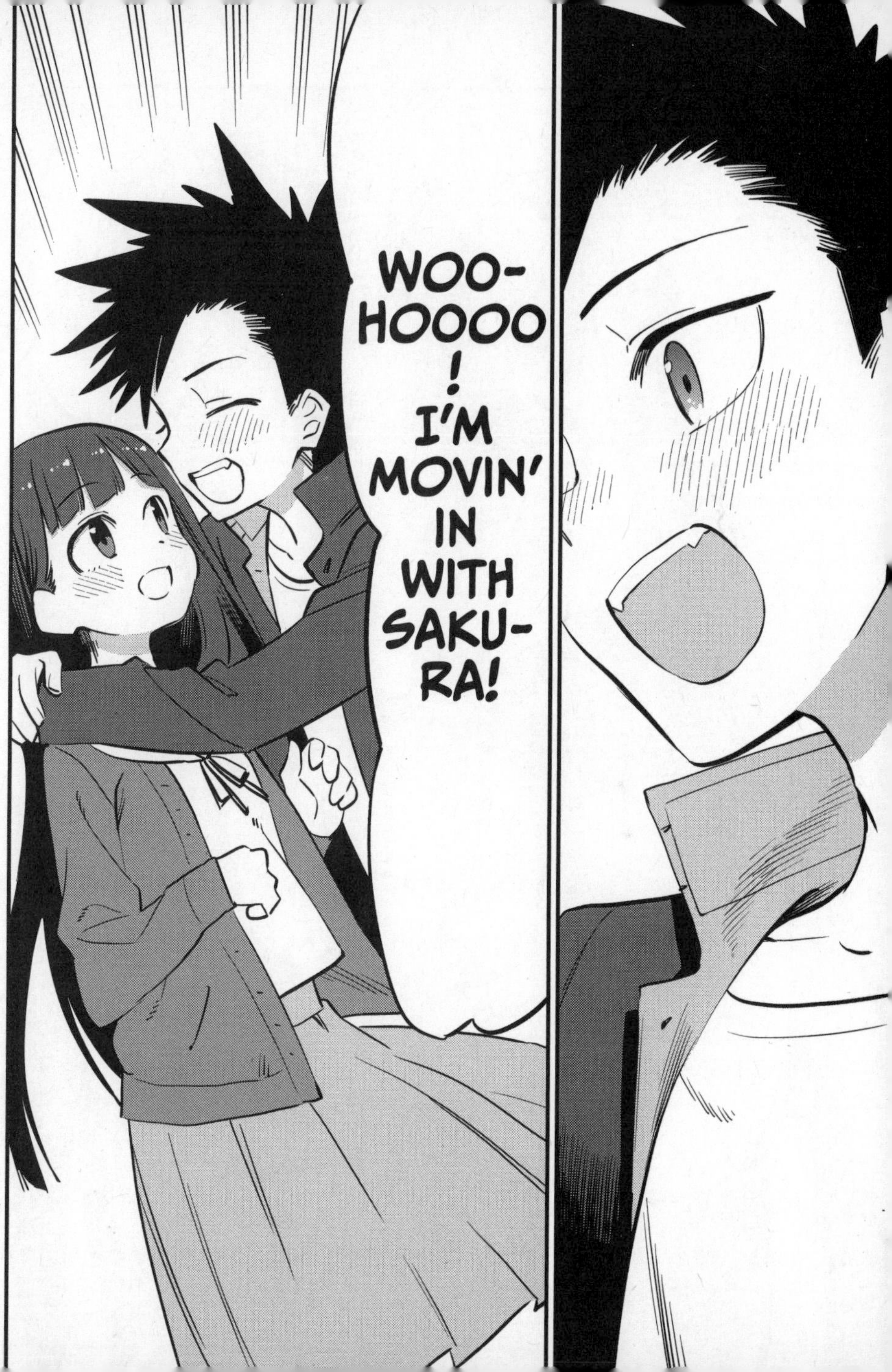
WOO-HOOOOO! I'M MOVIN' IN WITH SAKU-RA!

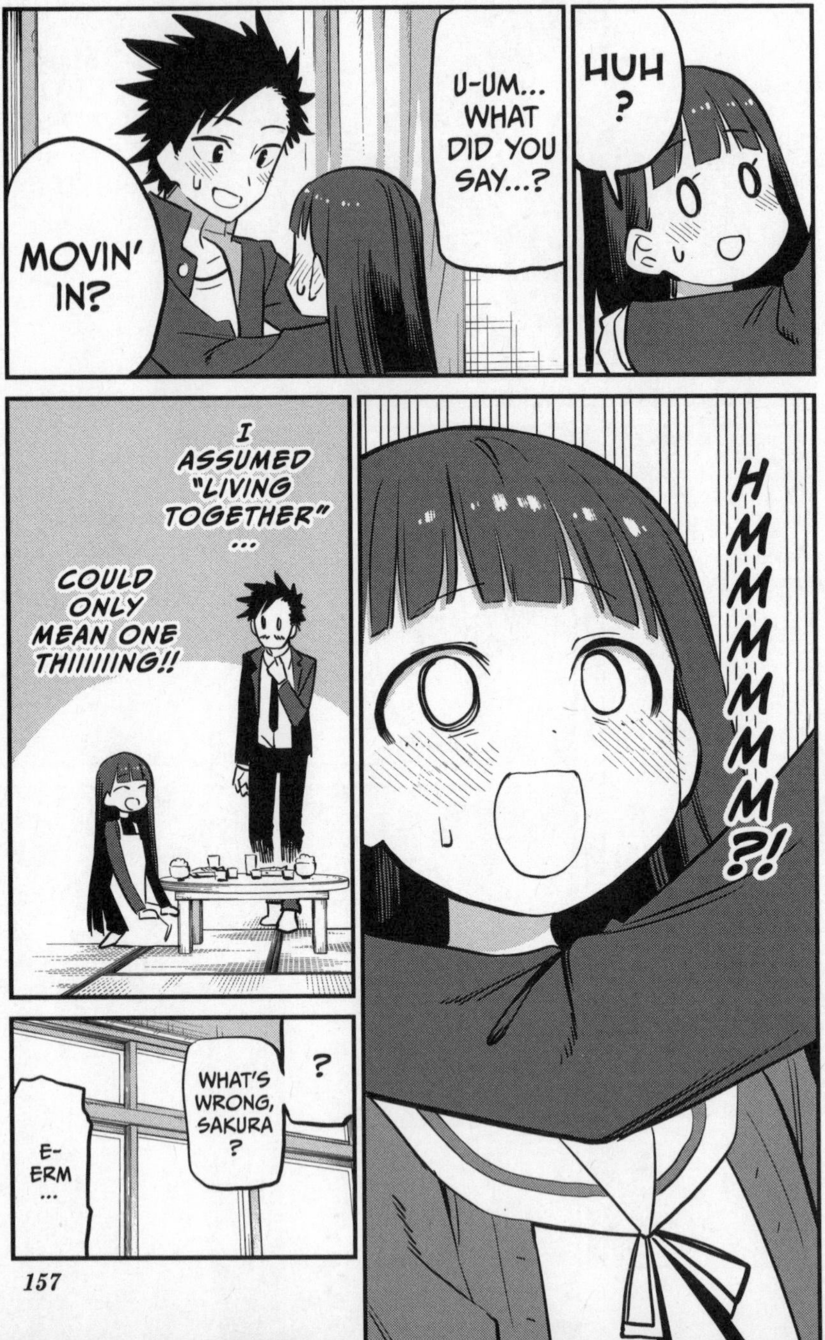
HUH?
U-UM... WHAT DID YOU SAY...?
MOVIN' IN?
HMMMMMMMMM?!
I ASSUMED "LIVING TOGETHER"...
COULD ONLY MEAN ONE THIIIIIING!!
?
WHAT'S WRONG, SAKURA?
E-ERM...

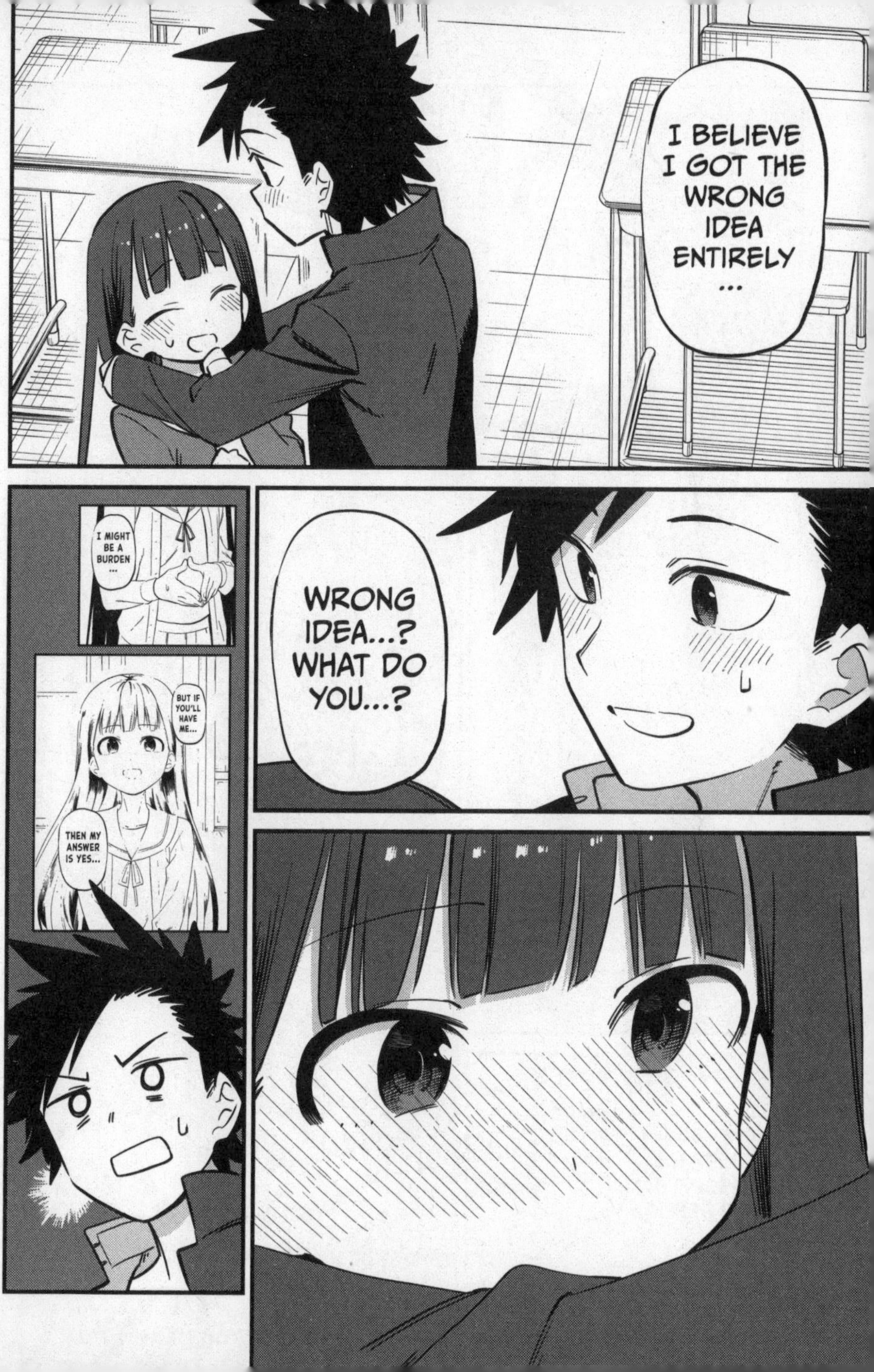
I BELIEVE I GOT THE WRONG IDEA ENTIRELY ...
WRONG IDEA...? WHAT DO YOU...?
I MIGHT BE A BURDEN ...
BUT IF YOU'LL HAVE ME...
THEN MY ANSWER IS YES...

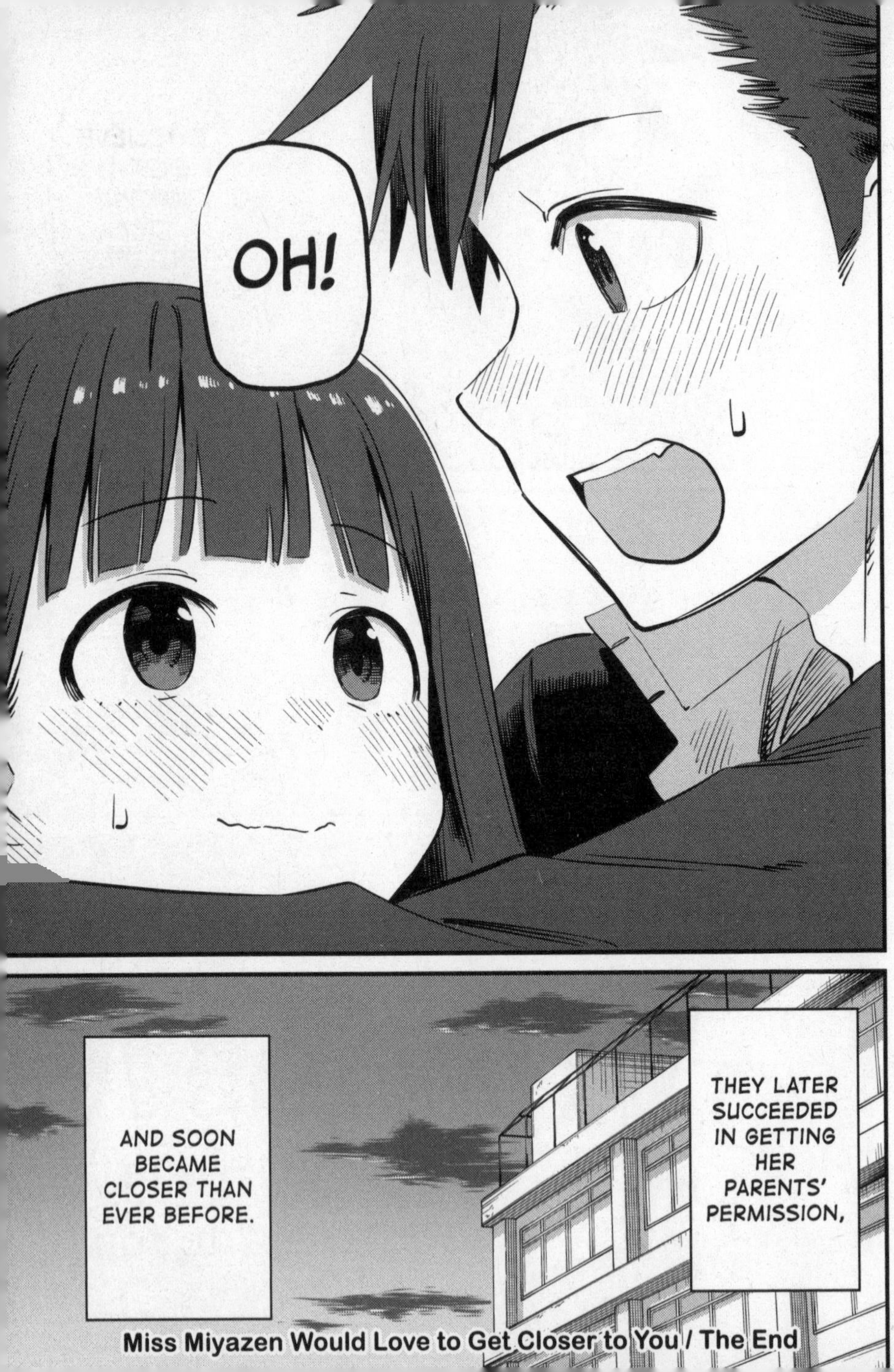
OH!
THEY LATER SUCCEEDED IN GETTING HER PARENTS' PERMISSION,
AND SOON BECAME CLOSER THAN EVER BEFORE.
Miss Miyazen Would Love to Get Closer to You / The End

Miss Miyazen
Would Love to
Get Closer to You

Miss Miyazen Would Love to Get Closer to You

4

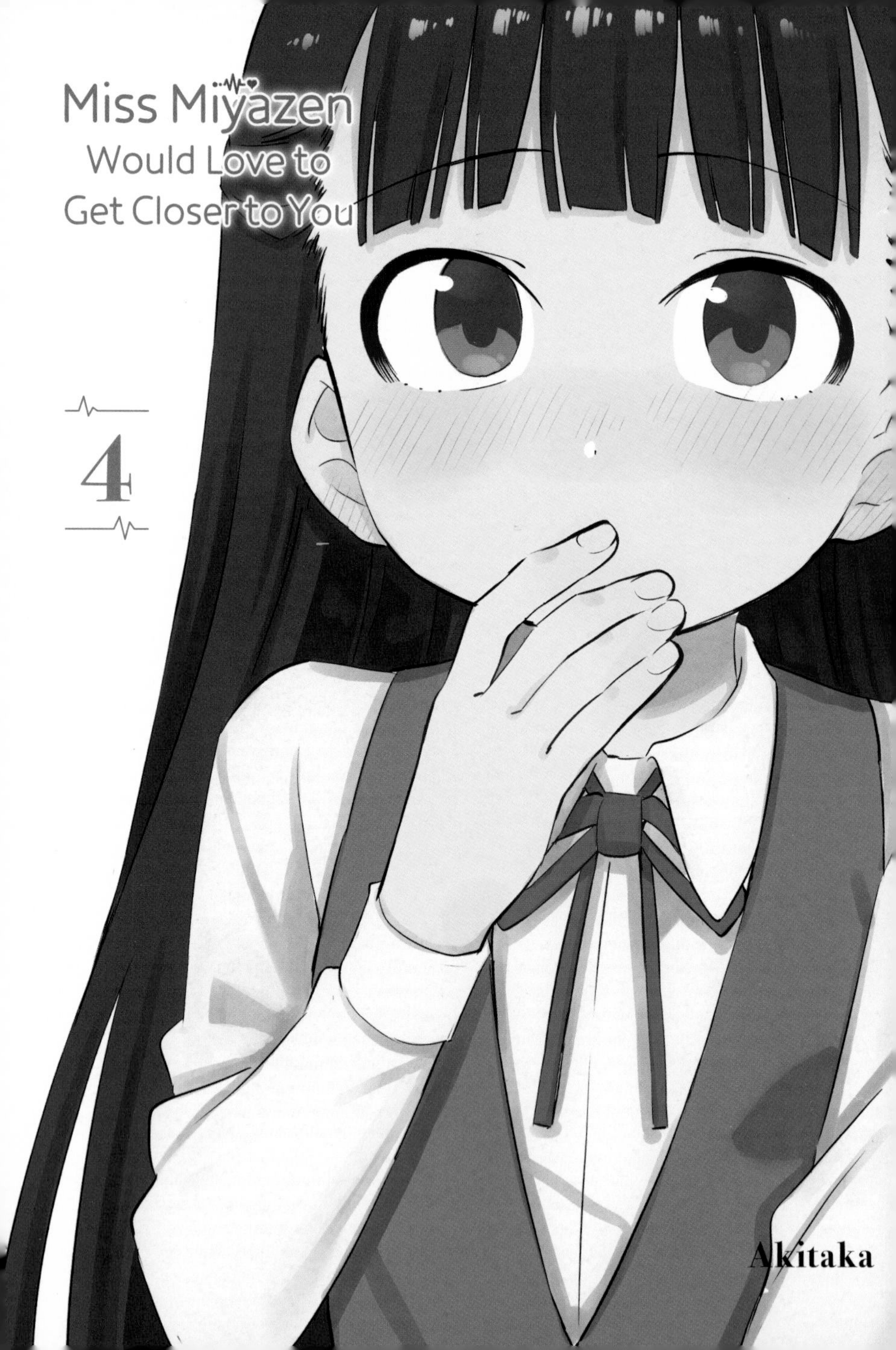

Akitaka

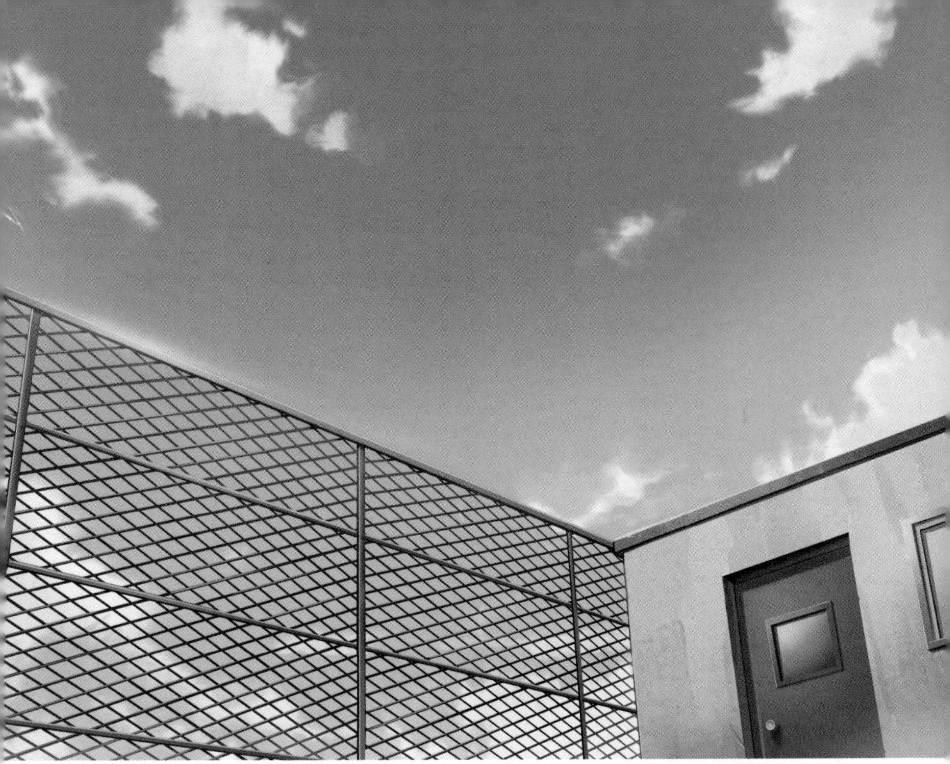

Miss Miyazen Would Love to Get Closer to You

contents

Miss Miyazen
Would Love to
Get Closer to You

Miss Miyazen
Would Love to
Get Closer to You

AFTERWORD

This concludes *Miss Miyazen Would Love to Get Closer to You.*

I'd like to leave how much closer they get after this to the reader's imagination. But knowing the two of them, I'm sure they'll eventually become as close as they can possibly be.

Thank you very much for reading this series!

Akitaka

SPECIAL THANKS

Yuki Tabei
Hiroki Misaki
Hatsumaru Ugebeso

Editor Y-moto
Daimaru
All of my
dear readers

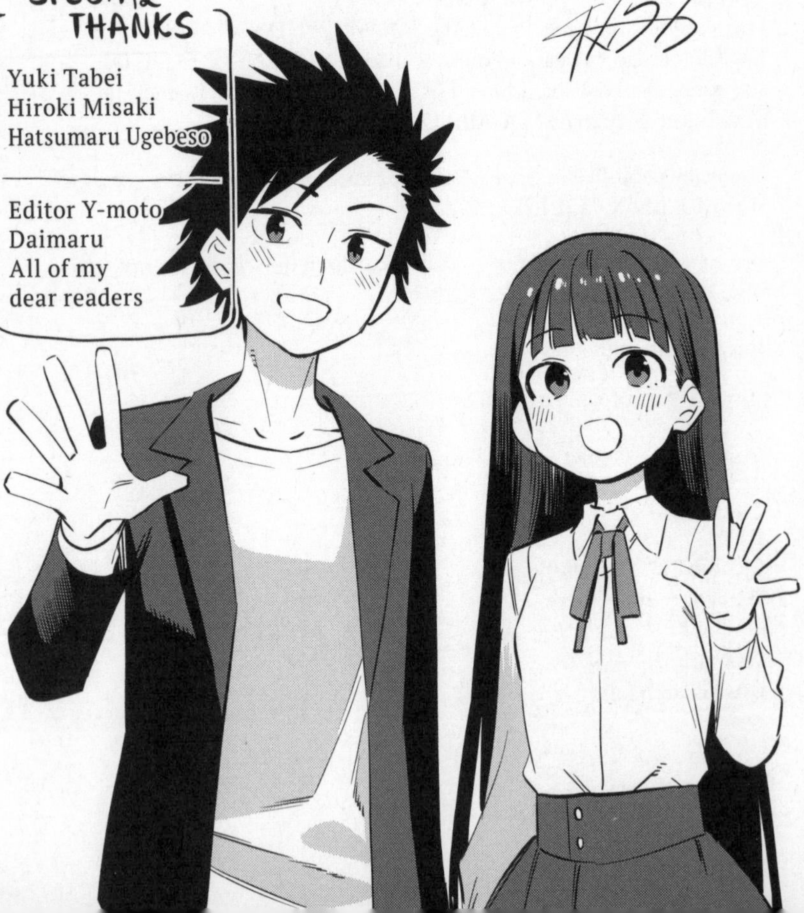

Miss Miyazen Would Love to Get Closer to You 4

A VERTICAL Book

Editor: Michelle Lin
Translation: Jenny McKeon
Production: Grace Lu
           Pei Ann Yeap
           Mercedes McGarry
Proofreading: Micah Q. Allen

Originally published in Japanese as *Ochikaduki ni Naritai Miyazen-san 4* by
SQUARE ENIX CO., LTD., 2022

Ochikaduki ni Naritai Miyazen-san first serialized in *Gekkan Gangan Joker*,
SQUARE ENIX CO., LTD., 2020-2021

This is a work of fiction.

ISBN: 978-1-64729-213-3

Printed in the United States of America

First Edition

Kodansha USA Publishing, LLC
451 Park Avenue South
7th Floor
New York, NY 10016
www.kodansha.us

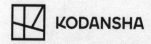

KODANSHA